# COLLINS COBUILD

COLLINS Birmingham University International Language Database

# ENGLISH GUIDES

## 2

# WORD FORMATION

**THE UNIVERSITY OF BIRMINGHAM**

**COLLINS COBUILD**

Harper

HarperCollins Publishers
77-85 Fulham Palace Road
London W6 8JB

COBUILD is a trademark of William Collins Sons & Co Ltd

ISBN 0 00 370521 8

Computer typeset by Promenade Graphics, Cheltenham

Printed and bound in Great Britain by HarperCollins Manufacturing,
Glasgow

輸入　日本総代理店
株式会社 秀文インターナショナル
東京都豊島区駒込 4 − 12− 7
◆原著作権者の背面による許諾なく、無断引用、転載、複製などは禁じます。

# Editorial Team

| | |
|---|---|
| *Editor in Chief* | John Sinclair |
| *Managing Editor* | Gwyneth Fox |
| *Senior Editor* | Stephen Bullon |
| *Editor* | Jane Bradbury |
| *Assistant Editors* | Helen Bruce<br>Deborah Kirby<br>Alyson McGee |
| *Computer Staff* | Zoe James<br>Tim Lane |
| *Secretarial Staff* | Sue Smith<br>Sue Crawley |

**Collins Publishers**
Annette Capel, Lorna Heaslip, Marina Maher,
Douglas Williamson

The project was originally designed by Rosamund Moon, and we
would like to thank her for her invaluable contribution. We would
also like to thank Janet Hilsdon, who read the whole text and
contributed to the exercises.

# COBUILD Publications

Collins COBUILD English Language Dictionary
Collins COBUILD Essential English Dictionary
Collins COBUILD Student's Dictionary
Collins COBUILD Dictionary of Phrasal Verbs
Collins COBUILD English Grammar
Collins COBUILD Student's Grammar
Collins COBUILD English Usage
Collins COBUILD English Guides: 1 Prepositions
Collins COBUILD English Guides: 2 Word Formation
Collins COBUILD English Guides: 3 Articles
Collins COBUILD English Guides: 4 Confusable Words
Collins COBUILD English Guides: 5 Reporting

Collins COBUILD English Course: levels 1, 2, and 3.
Collins COBUILD English Course: Tests
Collins COBUILD English Course: First Lessons

Looking Up
The Lexical Syllabus

# Foreword

The COBUILD GUIDES each deal with a key area of English. In addition to our general dictionaries and Grammar we have been planning for some time to add smaller but more detailed handbooks dealing with important aspects of grammar and usage.

Each book is specially designed for a specific job. Most have a reference-book style, and some include practice material as well. They are all based on real examples drawn from the 20 million words of the Birmingham Collection of English Text supplemented by a further 5 million words from the *Times* newspapers held on computer in Birmingham.

The advantages of a Guide which deals with one particular part of English are that there is room for more information than in a big general dictionary, and that this information is easier to find.

Making new words by adapting old ones is very popular at present, and many of the prefixes and suffixes described here are being used freely by writers and speakers of English. This book will give you a similar freedom.

This process of forming new words has been going on throughout the long history of English, and a number of words show by their structure that they were once formed from prefixes and suffixes; where they have become rather specialized in meaning they are listed to remind you to look them up in a dictionary. Many words formed from Greek and Latin prefixes and suffixes are included even though they are not productive in modern English. Showing the way they are formed will help you understand their meanings.

I hope that we have selected useful information and made it easy for you to find what you want, to understand it, and to use it with confidence. Please write to me with any comments or suggestions about how to improve COBUILD publications.

John Sinclair
Editor in Chief
Professor of Modern English Language
University of Birmingham

# Introduction

The vocabulary of the English Language is not a fixed list of words but a growing and developing store from which you can select words that are appropriate for your meaning and for the situation you are in. When you look at a large dictionary, you realize that there are an enormous number of words, and it is clearly not possible for one person to know them all. There are, of course, a certain number that you must know in order to be able to communicate in English: the basic verbs *take*, *have*, *give*, *put*, *set* and so on, and prepositions such as *at*, *in*, *of*, and *on*.

Once you have built up a basic vocabulary of English, you can begin to say what you want to. As you add more and more words to your vocabulary, you are able to express a greater range of ideas or talk about a wider range of topics.

This book is intended to help you increase your vocabulary by describing the patterns involved in building words. Some words are formed by putting a prefix at the beginning of an existing word, and some are formed by adding a suffix at the end. There are also words which have more than one prefix or suffix in them. Once you have learnt the main uses and meanings of a number of prefixes and suffixes, you will be able to recognize and understand a lot more words, even if you have never seen them before. By looking at how the word is used, and adding the meaning of the prefix or suffix to the meaning of the original word, you can work out the meaning of the whole word. Where the use of the prefix or suffix is productive, you will also be able to make up words which you have never seen before.

For example, if you read in a newspaper about a *pan-European agreement*, you might only know the sense of *pan* which refers to a pot that you use for cooking. But *pan-* is also a prefix that means *all of*, so here, a *pan-European* agreement is an agreement which involves all the countries in Europe. This is different from an *anti-European* movement, which would be a movement that worked against Europe. Both these prefixes, *pan-* and *anti-*, can occur in front of a large number of words. Once you have learnt the use of a number of prefixes, you will be able not only to recognize more words but also to make some up and use them yourself.

Other prefixes and suffixes are largely grammatical, and are used to change the word class of a word. For example, the suffix *-ion* is added to verbs to create nouns. So if you see a word that ends in *ion* you should check the first part of the word and see if it looks like a verb. If it does, then by combining the context with what you know about the meaning of the verb, you can often work out what the noun means.

This book contains a description of the use and meaning of about 300 prefixes and suffixes. At the end, there are a number of exercises which are designed to help you use the book productively and make use of the information that it contains. A key to the exercises is included.

We believe that using this book will help you to increase your confidence in dealing with words that you have never seen before, and hope that it will prove a useful aid in increasing your vocabulary of English quickly and efficiently.

# How to use the book

## The Headwords

The book contains an alphabetically ordered set of prefixes and suffixes. Each item has a hyphen either at the beginning or at the end. If the hyphen is at the beginning, then the item is a suffix, and comes at the end of the word. If the hyphen is at the end, then the item is a prefix and comes at the beginning of the word.

If the same form is both a prefix and a suffix, there will be two entries, with the prefix first, then the suffix.

So the order of items starting from **-first** is:
**-first**
**-fold**
**-folk**
**fore-**
**Franco-**
**free-**
**-free**
**fresh-**
**-ful**
**full-**

## The Entries

*The Explanations*

Each entry tells you what sort of word the prefix or suffix combines with, and what meaning the new words have. These words are illustrated by examples, taken from the 20 million words of the

Birmingham Collection of English Text. Each entry also contains lists of words which are formed in the way described.

Some prefixes and suffixes are very productive. That is to say, they can combine with a large number of words, and you can make up words yourself once you feel confident enough. These items are indicated by the heading PRODUCTIVE USE:

The entry tells you whether the word combines with verbs, nouns, or adjectives, and also tells you the word class of the new words. The entry for **under-** begins:

PRODUCTIVE USE: **under-** combines with verbs, nouns, and adjectives to form new verbs, nouns, and adjectives.

The entry then tells you the meaning that is shared by all the words.

Words formed in this way express the idea that there is not enough of something or that something has not been done as much or as well as is needed.

Then there are one or more examples whose meanings are explained:

If you describe something as 'underdeveloped', you think it has not been developed enough.

In some entries, there are spelling notes; these are explained below.

## The Examples

All the main entries have several examples which illustrate words that are formed in the way that has just been described. These examples are all taken from the Birmingham Collection of English Text, and show how the words have been used by speakers and writers of English. The examples are printed in *italic*.

## Spelling Notes

When there is anything difficult or unusual about how the words are spelled, a spelling note is given. This note tells you the rules for dropping letters or doubling consonants when adding a particular prefix or suffix. There are also notes telling you about whether you should write the words with a hyphen or not. If there is not a note about hyphenation, then you should consult the list of words in that paragraph for guidance.

## The Lists

After the examples, there is a list of words. When the use is productive, the list contains a selection of words that are formed in this way, but you can build further words for yourself. This type of list is headed

Here are some examples of words with this meaning:

Some prefixes combine freely with numbers or place names, and where this is the case, words formed in that way are not included in the lists.

If the use is not very productive, the list will again contain a selection of words, but you should be cautious about trying to form words like that yourself. This list will be headed

Here is a list of words with this meaning:

Sometimes there are words which begin with the same letters as a prefix, or end in the same letters as a suffix, but which are not actually examples of that particular prefix or suffix, or do not fit with the meanings that have been given. Important words like this are listed at the end of the entries, after the heading
**Words with other meanings**

Often, they will be words which you know, but if you do not know them, look them up in a dictionary, because their meaning cannot be derived from the prefix or suffix.

# Corpus Acknowledgements

We wish to thank the following, who have kindly given permission for the use of copyright material in the Birmingham Collection of English Texts.

Associated Business Programmes Ltd for: *The Next 200 Years* by Herman Kahn with William Brown and Leon Martel first published in Great Britain by Associated Business Programmes Ltd 1977 ' Hudson Institute 1976. David Attenborough and William Collins Sons & Co Ltd for: *Life on Earth* by David Attenborough first published by William Collins Sons & Co Ltd 1979 ' David Attenborough Productions Ltd 1979. James Baldwin for: *The Fire Next Time* by James Baldwin published in Great Britain by Michael Joseph Ltd 1963 ' James Baldwin 1963. B T Batsford Ltd for: *Witchcraft in England* by Christina Hole first published by B T Batsford Ltd 1945 ' Christina Hole 1945. Michael Billington for: 'Lust at First Sight' by Michael Billington in the *Illustrated London News* July 1981 and 'Truffaut's Tolerance' by Michael Billington in the *Illustrated London News* August 1981. Birmingham International Council For Overseas Students' Aid for: BICOSA Information Leaflets 1981. Basil Blackwell Publishers Ltd for: *Breaking the Mould? The Birth and Prospects of the Social Democratic Party* by Ian Bradley first published by Martin Robertson & Co Ltd 1981 ' Ian Bradley 1981. *Seeing Green (The Politics of Ecology Explained)* by Jonathon Porritt first published by Basil Blackwell Publisher Ltd 1984 ' Jonathon Porritt 1984. Blond & Briggs Ltd for: *Small is Beautiful* by E F Schumacher first published in Great Britain by Blond & Briggs Ltd 1973 ' E F Schumacher 1973. The Bodley Head Ltd for: *The Americans (Letters from America 1969-1979)* by Alistair Cooke first published by Bodley Head Ltd 1979 ' Alistair Cooke 1979. *Baby and Child Care* by Dr Benjamin Spock published in Great Britain by The Bodley Head Ltd 1955 ' Benjamin Spock MD 1945, 1946, 1957, 1968, 1976, 1979. *What's Wrong With The Modern World?* by Michael Shanks first published by The Bodley Head Ltd 1978 ' Michael Shanks 1978. *Future Shock* by Alvin Toffler first published in Great Britain by The Bodley Head Ltd 1970 ' Alvin Toffler 1970. *Zen and the Art of Motorcycle Maintenance* by Robert M Pirsig first published in Great Britain by The Bodley Head Ltd 1974 ' Robert M Pirsig 1974. *Marnie* by Winston Graham first published by the Bodley Head Ltd 1961 ' Winston Graham 1961. *You Can Get There From Here* by Shirley MacLaine first published in Great Britain by The Bodley Head Ltd 1975 ' Shirley MacLaine 1975. *It's An Odd Thing, But ...* by Paul Jennings first published by Max Reinhardt Ltd 1971 ' Paul Jennings 1971. *King of the Castle (Choice and Responsibility in the Modern World)* by Gai Eaton first published by the Bodley Head Ltd 1977 ' Gai Eaton 1977. *Revolutionaries in Modern Britain* by Peter Shipley first published by The Bodley Head Ltd 1976 ' Peter Shipley 1976. *The Prerogative of the Harlot (Press Barons and Power)* by Hugh Cudlipp first published by The Bodley Head Ltd 1980 ' Hugh Cudlipp 1980. *But What About The Children (A Working Parents' Guide to Child Care)* by Judith Hann first published by The Bodley Head Ltd 1976 ' Judith Hann 1976. *Learning to Read* by Margaret Meek first published by The Bodley Head Ltd 1982 ' Margaret Meek 1982. Bolt & Watson for: *Two is Lonely* by Lynne Reid Banks first published by Chatto & Windus 1974 ' Lynne Reid Banks 1974. The British and Foreign Bible Society with William Collins Sons & Co Ltd for: *Good News Bible (with Deuterocanonical Books/Apocrypha)* first published by The British and Foreign Bible Society with William Collins Sons & Co Ltd 1979 ' American Bible Society; Old Testament 1976, Deuterocanonical Books/Apocrypha 1979, New Testament 1966, 1971, 1976 ' Maps, British and Foreign Bible Society 1976, 1979. The British Council for: *How to Live in Britain (The British Council's Guide for Overseas Students and Visitors)* first published by The British Council 1952 ' The British Council 1984. Mrs R Bronowski for: *The Ascent of Man* by J Bronowski published by Book Club Associates by arrangement with The British Broadcasting Corporation 1977 ' J Bronowski 1973. Alison Busby for: *The Death of Trees* by Nigel Dudley first published by Pluto Press Ltd 1985 ' Nigel Dudley 1985. Tony Buzan for: *Make The Most of your Mind* by Tony Buzan first published by Colt Books Ltd 1977 ' Tony Buzan 1977. Campbell Thomson & McLaughlin Ltd for: *Ring of Bright Water* by Gavin Maxwell first published by Longmans Green & Co 1960, published in Penguin Books Ltd 1976 ' The Estate of Gavin Maxwell 1960. Jonathan Cape Ltd for: *Manwatching (A Field Guide to Human Behaviour)* by Desmond Morris first published in Great Britain by Jonathan Cape Ltd 1977 ' Text, Desmond Morris 1977 ' Compilation, Elsevier Publishing Projects SA, Lausanne, and Jonathan Cape Ltd, London 1977. *Tracks* by Robyn Davidson first published by Jonathan Cape Ltd 1980 ' Robyn Davidson 1980. *In the Name of Love* by Jill Tweedie first published by Jonathan Cape Ltd 1979 ' Jill Tweedie 1979. *The Use of Lateral Thinking* by Edward de Bono first published by Jonathan Cape 1967 ' Edward de Bono 1967. *Trout Fishing in America* by Richard Brautigan first published in Great Britain by Jonathan Cape Ltd 1970 ' Richard Brautigan 1967. *The Pendulum Years: Britain and the Sixties* by Bernard Levin first published by Jonathan Cape Ltd 1970 ' Bernard Levin 1970. *The Summer Before The Dark* by Doris Lessing first published in Great Britain by Jonathan Cape Ltd 1973 ' Doris Lessing 1973. *The Boston Strangler* by Gerold Frank first published in Great Britain by Jonathan Cape Ltd 1967 ' Gerold Frank 1966. *I'm OK - You're OK* by Thomas A Harris MD first published in Great Britain as The Book of Choice by Jonathan Cape Ltd 1970 ' Thomas A Harris MD, 1967, 1968, 1969. *The Vivisector* by Patrick White first published by Jonathan Cape Ltd 1970 ' Patrick White 1970. *The Future of Socialism* by Anthony Crosland first published by Jonathan Cape Ltd 1956 ' C A R Crosland 1963. *Funeral in Berlin* by Len Deighton first published by Jonathan Cape Ltd 1964 ' Len Deighton 1964. Chatto & Windus Ltd for: *A Postillion Struck by Lightning* by Dirk Bogarde first published by Chatto & Windus Ltd 1977 ' Dirk Bogarde 1977. *Nuns and Soldiers* by Iris Murdoch published by Chatto & Windus Ltd 1980 ' Iris Murdoch 1980. *Wounded Knee (An Indian History of the American West)* by Dee Brown published by Chatto & Windus Ltd 1978 ' Dee Brown 1970. *The Virgin in the Garden* by A S Byatt published by Chatto & Windus Ltd 1978 ' A S Byatt 1978. *A Story Like The Wind* by Laurens van der Post published by Clarke Irwin & Co Ltd in association with The Hogarth Press Ltd 1972 ' Laurens van der Post 1972. *Brave New World* by Aldous Huxley published by Chatto & Windus Ltd 1932 ' Aldous Huxley and Mrs Laura Huxley 1932, 1960. *The Reivers* By William Faulkner first published by Chatto & Windus Ltd 1962 ' William Faulkner 1962. *Cider With Rosie* by Laurie Lee published by The Hogarth Press 1959 ' Laurie Lee 1959 *The Tenants* by Bernard Malamud first published in Great Britain by Chatto & Windus Ltd 1972 ' Bernard Malamud 1971. *Kinflicks* by Lisa Alther first published in Great Britain by Chatto & Windus Ltd 1976 ' Lisa Alther 1975. William Collins Sons & Co Ltd for: *The Companion Guide to London* by David Piper published by William Collins Sons & Co Ltd 1964 ' David Piper 1964. *The Bedside Guardian 29* edited by

W L Webb published by William Collins & Sons Ltd 1980 ˙ Guardian Newspapers Ltd 1980. *Bear Island* by Alistair MacLean first published by William Collins Sons & Co Ltd 1971 ˙ Alistair MacLean 1971. *Inequality in Britain: Freedom, Welfare and the State* by Frank Field first published by Fontana Paperbacks 1981 ˙ Frank Field 1981. *Social Mobility* by Anthony Heath first published by Fontana Paperbacks 1981 ˙ Anthony Heath 1981. *Yours Faithfully* by Gerald Priestland first published by Fount Paperbacks 1979 ˙ British Broadcasting Corporation 1977, 1978. *Power Without Responsibility: The Press and Broadcasting in Britain* by James Curran and Jean Seaton first published by Fontana Paperbacks 1981 ˙ James Curran and Jean Seaton 1981. *The Times Cookery Book* by Katie Stewart first published by William Collins Sons & Co Ltd 1972 ˙ Times Newspapers Ltd. *Friends from the Forest* by Joy Adamson by Collins and Harvill Press 1981 ˙ Elsa Limited 1981. *The Media Mob* by Barry Fantoni and George Melly first published by William Collins Sons & Co Ltd 1980 ˙ Text, George Melly 1980 ˙ Illustrations, Barry Fantoni 1980. *Shalom (a collection of Australian and Jewish Stories)* compiled by Nancy Keesing first published by William Collins Publishers Pty Ltd 1978 ˙ William Collins Sons &Co Ltd 1978. *The Bedside Guardian 31* edited by W L Webb first published by William Collins Sons & Co Ltd 1982 ˙ Guardian Newspapers Ltd 1982. *The Bedside Guardian 32* edited by W L Webb first published by William Collins Sons & Co Ltd 1983 ˙ Guardian Newspapers Ltd 1983. *Design for the Real World* by Victor Papanek first published in Great Britain by Thames & Hudson Ltd 1972 ˙ Victor Papanek 1971. *Food For Free* by Richard Mabey first published by William Collins Sons & Co Ltd 1972 ˙ Richard Mabey 1972. *Unended Quest* by Karl Popper (first published as Autobiography of Karl Popper in The Philosophy of Karl Popper in The Library of Philosophers edited by Paul Arthur Schlipp by the Open Court Publishing Co 1974) published by Fontana Paperbacks 1976 ˙ The Library of Living Philosophers Inc 1974 ˙ Karl R Popper 1976. *My Mother My Self* by Nancy Friday first published in Great Britain by Fontana Paperbacks 1979 ˙ Nancy Friday 1977. *The Captain's Diary* by Bob Willis first published by Willow Books/William Collins Sons & Co Ltd 1984 ˙ Bob Willis and Alan Lee 1984 ˙ New Zealand Scorecards, Bill Frindall 1984. *The Bodywork Book* by Esme Newton-Dunn first published in Great Britain by Willow Books/William Collins Sons & Co Ltd 1982 ˙ TVS Ltd/Esme Newton-Dunn 1982. *Collins' Encyclopaedia of Fishing in the British Isles* edited by Michael Prichard first published by William Collins Sons & Co Ltd 1976 ˙ William Collins Sons & Co Ltd 1976. *The AAA Runner's Guide* edited by Heather Thomas first published by William Collins Sons & Co Ltd 1983 ˙ Sackville Design Group Ltd 1983. *Heroes and Contemporaries* by David Gower with Derek Hodgson first published by William Collins Sons & Co Ltd 1983 ˙ David Gower Promotions Ltd 1983. *The Berlin Memorandum* by Adam Hall first published by William Collins Sons & Co Ltd 1965 ˙ Jonquil Trevor 1965. *Arlott on Cricket: His Writings on the Game* edited by David Rayvern Allen first published by William Collins (Willow Books) 1984 ˙ John Arlott 1984. *A Woman in Custody* by Audrey Peckham first published by Fontana Paperbacks 1985 ˙ Audrey Peckham 1985. *Play Golf with Peter Alliss* by Peter Alliss published by the British Broadcasting Corporation 1977 ˙ Peter Alliss and Renton Laidlaw 1977. Curtis Brown Ltd for: *The Pearl* by John Steinbeck first published by William Heinemann Ltd 1948 ˙ John Steinbeck 1948. *An Unfinished History of the World* by Hugh Thomas first published in Great Britain by Hamish Hamilton Ltd 1979 ˙ Hugh Thomas 1979, 1981. *The Winter of our Discontent* by John Steinbeck first published in Great Britain by William Heinemann Ltd 1961 ˙ John Steinbeck 1961. *Burr* by Gore Vidal first published in Great Britain by William Heinemann Ltd 1974 ˙ Gore Vidal 1974. *Doctor on the Job* by Richard Gordon first published by William Heinemann Ltd 1976 ˙ Richard Gordon Ltd 1976. Andre Deutsch Ltd for: *How to be an Alien* by George Mikes first published by Andre Deutsch Ltd 1946 ˙ George Mikes and Nicholas Bentley 1946. *Jaws* by Peter Benchley first published in Great Britain by Andre Deutsch Ltd 1974 ˙ Peter Benchley 1974. *A Bend in the River* by V S Naipaul first published by Andre Deutsch Ltd 1979 ˙ V S Naipaul 1979. *Couples* by John Updike first published by Andre Deutsch Ltd 1968 ˙ John Updike 1968. *Games People Play* by Eric Berne published in Great Britain by Andre Deutsch Ltd 1966 ˙ Eric Berne 1964. *The Age of Uncertainty* by John Kenneth Galbraith first published by The British Broadcasting Corporation and Andre Deutsch Ltd 1977 ˙ John Kenneth Galbraith 1977. The Economist Newspaper Ltd for: *The Economist* (9-15 May 1981 and 22-28 August 1981) ˙ published by The Economist Newspaper Ltd 1981. Faber & Faber Ltd for: *Lord of the Flies* by William Golding first published by Faber & Faber Ltd 1954 ˙ William Golding 1954. *The Complete Book of Self-Sufficiency* by John Seymour first published in Great Britain by Faber & Faber Ltd 1976 ˙ Text, John Seymour 1976, 1977 ˙ Dorling Kindersley Ltd 1976, 1977. *Conversations with Igor Stravinsky* by Igor Stravinsky and Robert Craft first published by Faber & Faber Ltd 1959 ˙ Igor Stravinsky 1958,1959. John Farquharson Ltd for: *The Moon's A Balloon* by David Niven published in Great Britain by Hamish Hamilton Ltd 1971 ˙ David Niven 1971. John Gaselee for: 'Going it Alone' by John Gaselee in the *Illustrated London News* July 1981 and 'The Other Car's Fault' by John Gaselee in the *Illustrated London News* August 1981. Glidrose Publications Ltd for: *The Man with the Golden Gun* by Ian Fleming first published by Jonathan Cape Ltd ˙ Glidrose Productions Ltd 1965. Victor Gollancz Ltd for: *The Next Horizon* by Chris Bonnington published by Victor Gollancz Ltd 1976 ˙ Chris Bonnington 1973. *Summerhill: A Radical Approach to Education* by A S Neill first published by Victor Gollancz Ltd 1962 ˙ A S Neill 1926, 1932, 1937, 1953, 1961 (US permission by Hart Publishing Inc). *Lucky Jim* by Kingsley Amis first published by Victor Gollancz Ltd 1954 ˙ Kingsley Amis 1953. *The Mighty Micro (The Impact of the Computer Revolution)* by Christopher Evans first published by Victor Gollancz Ltd 1979 ˙ Christopher Evans 1979. *The Longest Day* by Cornelius Ryan published by Victor Gollancz Ltd 1960 ˙ Cornelius Ryan 1959. *Asking for Trouble (Autobiography of a Banned Journalist)* by Donald Woods published by Victor Gollancz Ltd 1980 ˙ Donald Woods 1980. *The Turin Shroud* by Ian Wilson first published in Great Britain by Victor Gollancz Ltd 1978 ˙ Ian Wilson 1978. *Murdo and Other Stories* by Iain Crichton Smith published by Victor Gollancz Ltd 1981 ˙ Iain Crichton Smith 1981. *The Class Struggle in Parliament* by Eric S Heffer published by Victor Gollancz Ltd 1973 ˙ Eric S Heffer 1973. *A Presumption of Innocence (The Amazing Case of Patrick Meehan)* by Ludovic Kennedy published by Victor Gollancz Ltd 1976 ˙ Ludovic Kennedy 1976. *The Treasure of Sainte Foy* by MacDonald Harris published by Victor Gollancz Ltd 1980 ˙ MacDonald Harris 1980. *A Long Way to Shiloh* by Lionel Davidson first published by Victor Gollancz Ltd 1966 ˙ Lionel Davidson 1966. *Education After School* by Tyrrell Burgess first published by Victor Gollancz Ltd 1977 ˙ Tyrrell Burgess 1977. *The View From Serendip* by Arthur C Clarke published by Victor Gollancz Ltd 1978 ˙ Arthur C Clarke 1967, 1968, 1970, 1972, 1974, 1976, 1977. *On Wings of Song* by Thomas M Disch published by Victor Gollancz Ltd 1979 ˙ Thomas M Disch 1979. *The World of Violence* by Colin Wilson published by Victor Gollancz Ltd 1963 ˙ Colin Wilson 1963. *The Lightning Tree* by Joan Aiken published by Victor Gollancz Ltd 1980 ˙ Joan Aiken

Enterprises 1980. *Russia's Political Hospitals* by Sidney Bloch and Peter Reddaway published by Victor Gollancz Ltd 1977 ' Sidney Bloch and Peter Reddaway 1977. *Unholy Loves* by Joyce Carol Oates first published in Great Britain by Victor Gollancz Ltd 1980 ' Joyce Carol Oates 1979. *Consenting Adults (or The Duchess will be Furious)* by Peter De Vries published by Victor Gollancz Ltd 1981 ' Peter De Vries 1980. *The Passion of New Eve* by Angela Carter published by Victor Gollancz Ltd 1977 ' Angela Carter 1977. Gower Publishing Co Ltd for: *Solar Prospects (The Potential for Renewable Energy)* by Michael Flood first published in Great Britain by Wildwood House Ltd in association with Friends of the Earth Ltd 1983 ' Michael Flood. *Voiceless Victims* by Rebecca Hall first published in Great Britain by Wildwood House Ltd 1984 ' Rebecca Hall 1984. Graham Greene and Laurence Pollinger Ltd for: *The Human Factor* by Graham Greene first published by The Bodley Head Ltd 1978 ' Graham Greene 1978. Syndication Manager, The Guardian, for: *The Guardian* (12 May 1981, 7 September 1981 and 15 September 1981) ' published by Guardian Newspapers Ltd 1981. Hamlyn for: *How to Play Rugby* by David Norrie published by The Hamlyn Publishing Group Ltd 1981 ' The Hamlyn Publishing Group Ltd 1981. *How to Play Badminton* by Pat Davies first published by The Hamlyn Publishing Group Ltd 1979 ' The Hamlyn Publishing Group Ltd 1979. *Margaret Hanbury for: Crisis and Conservation: Conflict in the British Countryside* by Charlie Pye-Smith and Chris Rose first published by Pelican/Penguin Books Ltd 1984 ' Charlie Pye-Smith and Chris Rose 1984. Paul Harrison for: *Inside the Third World* by Paul Harrison first published in Great Britain by The Harvester Press Ltd 1980 ' Paul Harrison 1979. A M Heath & Co Ltd for: *Rembrandt's Hat* by Bernard Malamud published by Chatto & Windus Ltd 1982 ' Bernard Malamud 1968, 1972, 1973. William Heinemann Ltd for: *It's an Old Country* by J B Priestley first published in Great Britain by William Heinemann Ltd 1967 ' J B Priestley 1967. Heinemann Educational Books Ltd and Gower Publishing Co Ltd for: *The Environmental Crisis (A Handbook for all Friends of the Earth)* edited by Des Wilson first published by Heinemann Educational Books Ltd 1984 ' Foreword, David Bellamy 1984 ' Individual Chapters, the Author of the Chapter 1984 ' In the selection and all other matters Des Wilson 1984. The Controller, Her Majesty's Stationery Office, for: Department of Health and Social Security leaflets published by Her Majesty's Stationery Office 1981 ' The Crown. David Higham Associates Ltd for: 'Two Peruvian Projects' by E R Chamberlain in the *Illustrated London News* September 1981. *Akenfield: Portrait of an English Village* by Ronald Blythe first published by Allen Lane, Penguin Books Ltd 1969 ' Ronald Blythe 1969. *The Far Pavillions* by M M Kaye first published by Allen Lane/Penguin Books Ltd 1978 ' M M Kaye 1978. *Staying On* by Paul Scott first published by William Heinemann Ltd 1977 ' Paul Scott 1977. *Let Sleeping Vets Lie* by James Herriot first published by Michael Joseph Ltd 1973 ' James Herriot 1973. *The Midwich Cuckoos* by John Wyndham first published in Great Britain by Michael Joseph Ltd 1957 ' The Estate of John Wyndham 1957. *The Girl in a Swing* by Richard Adams first published in Great Britain by Allen Lane in Penguin Books Ltd 1980 ' Richard Adams 1980. Dr K B Hindley for: 'Hot Spots of the Deep' by Dr K B Hindley in the *Illustrated London News July* 1981. Hodder and Stoughton Ltd for: *Supernature* by Lyall Watson first published by Hodder & Stoughton Ltd 1973 ' Lyall Watson 1973. *Tinker Tailor Soldier Spy* by John Le Carre first published by Hodder & Stoughton Ltd 1974 ' Le Carre Productions 1974. The Editor, Homes and Gardens, for: *Homes and Gardens* (October 1981) (Number 4 Volume 63) ' published by IPC Magazines Ltd 1981. Hughes Massie Ltd for: *Elephants Can Remember* by Agatha Christie first published by William Collins Sons & Co Ltd 1972 ' Agatha Christie Mallowan. Hutchinson Publishing Group Ltd for: *An Autobiography* by Angela Davis published in Great Britain by Hutchinson & Co Publishers Ltd by arrangement with Bantam Books Inc 1975 ' Angela Davis 1974. *The Day of the Jackal* by Frederick Forsyth published in Great Britian by Hutchinson & Co Publishers Ltd 1971 ' Frederick Forsyth 1971. *Roots* by Alex Haley first published in Great Britain by Hutchinson & Co Publishers Ltd 1977 ' Alex Haley 1976. *The Climate of Treason* by Andrew Boyle first published by Hutchinson & Co Publishers Ltd 1979 ' Andrew Boyle 1979. *The Collapsing Universe: The Story of Black Holes* by Isaac Asimov first published by Hutchinson & Co Publishers Ltd 1977 ' Isaac Asimov. *XPD* by Len Deighton published by Book Club Associates by arrangement with Hutchinson & Co Publishers Ltd 1981 ' Len Deighton 1981. *Show Jumping with Harvey Smith* by Harvey Smith first published by Stanley Paul & Co Ltd 1979 ' Tyne-Tees Television Ltd, A Member of the Trident Group 1979. *2001: A Space Odyssey* by Arthur C Clarke first published by Hutchinson & Co Publishers Ltd 1968 ' Arthur C Clarke and Polaris Productions Inc 1968 ' Epilogue material, Serendip BV 1982, 1983. The Illustrated London News and Sketch Ltd for: *The Illustrated London News* (July 1981, August 1981 and September 1981) ' published by the Illustrated London News and Sketch Ltd 1981. The Editor, International Herald Tribune, for: *International Herald Tribune* (25-26 July 1981) ' published by International Herald Tribune with The New York Times and The Washington Post 1981. Michael Joseph Ltd for: *Chronicles of Fairacre: Village School* by Miss Read first published in Great Britain by Michael Joseph Ltd 1964 ' Miss Read 1955, 1964. *Fire Fox* by Craig Thomas first published in Great Britain by Michael Joseph Ltd 1977 ' Craig Thomas 1977. William Kimber & Co Ltd for: *Exodus* by Leon Uris originally published in Great Britain by Alan Wingate Ltd 1959 ' Leon Uris 1958. Kogan Page Ltd for: *How to Save the World (Strategy for World Conservation)* by Robert Allen first published by Kogan Page Ltd 1980 ' IUCN-UNEP-WWF 1980. Marketing Department, Lloyds Bank PLC, for: *Lloyds Bank Leaflets* (1981) ' published by Lloyds Bank PLC 1981. Macmillan Publishers Ltd for: *Appropriate Technology: Technology with a Human Face* by P D Dunn first published by the Macmillan Press Ltd 1978 ' P D Dunn 1978. John Murray Publishers Ltd for: *A Backward Place* by Ruth Prawer Jhabvala first published by John Murray Publishers Ltd 1965 ' R Prawer Jhabvala 1965. *Food For All The Family* by Magnus Pyke first published by John Murray Publishers Ltd 1980 ' Magnus Pyke 1980. *Simple Movement* by Laura Mitchell and Barbara Dale first published by John Murray Publishers Ltd 1980 ' Laura Mitchell and Barbara Dale 1980. *Civilisation: A Personal View* by Kenneth Clark first published by the British Broadcasting Corporation and John Murray Publishers Ltd 1969 ' Kenneth Clark 1969. The Editor, National Geographic, for: *National Geographic* January, February and March (1980) ' published by The National Geographic Society 1979, 1980. The National Magazine Co Ltd for: *Cosmopolitan* (May 1981 and July 1981) ' published by the National Magazine Co Ltd 1981. Neilson Leisure Group Ltd for: NAT Holidays' '*Caravans and Tents in the Sun*' (Summer 1983) holiday brochure. Newsweek Inc for: *Newsweek* (11 May 1981, 27 July 1981 and August 1981) ' published by Newsweek Inc 1981. The Associate Editor, Now!, for: *Now!* (14-20 November 1980) ' published by Cavenham Communications Ltd 1980. Harold Ober Associates Inc for: *The Boys from Brazil* by Ira Levin first published by Michael Joseph Ltd 1976 ' Ira Levin 1976. Edna O'Brien and A M Heath & Co Ltd for: *August is a Wicked Month* by Edna O'Brien first published by Jonathan Cape Ltd 1965 ' Edna O'Brien

1965. Pan Books Ltd for: *Dispatches* by Michael Herr first published in Great Britain by Pan Books Ltd 1978 ' Michael Herr 1968, 1969, 1970, 1977. *Health and Safety at Work* by Dave Eva and Ron Oswald first published by Pan Books Ltd 1981 ' Dave Eva, Ron Oswald and the Workers' Educational Association 1981. *Democracy at Work* by Patrick Burns and Mel Doyle first published by Pan Books Ltd 1981 ' Patrick Burns,Mel Doyle and the Workers' Educational Association 1981. *Diet for Life (A Cookbook for Arthritics)* by Mary Laver and Margaret Smith first published by Pan Books Ltd 1981 ' Mary Laver and Margaret Smith 1981. Penguin Books Ltd for: *Inside the Company: CIA Diary* by Philip Agee first published in Allen Lane/Penguin Books Ltd 1975 ' Philip Agee 1975. Penguin Books Ltd and Spare Ribs Ltd for: *Spare Rib Reader* edited by Marsha Rowe first published in Penguin Books Ltd 1982 ' Spare Ribs Ltd 1982. A D Peters & Co Ltd for: 'The Dark Side of Israel' by Norman Moss in Illustrated London News July 1981, 'Aftermath of Osirak' by Norman Moss in the *Illustrated London News* August 1981 and 'Turning Point for Poland?' by Norman Moss in the *Illustrated London News* September 1981. 'Recent Fiction' by Sally Emerson in the *Illustrated London News* July 1981, August 1981 and September 1981. *The Complete Upmanship* by Stephen Potter first published in Great Britain by Rupert Hart-Davis Ltd 1970 ' Stephen Potter. Elaine Pollard for: Personal Letters 1981 donated by Elaine Pollard. Laurence Pollinger Ltd for: *A Glastonbury Romance* by John Cowper Powys first published by MacDonald & Co Ltd 1933. Murray Pollinger for: *Kiss Kiss* by Roald Dahl published in Great Britain by Michael Joseph Ltd 1960 ' Roald Dahl 1962. *Can You Avoid Cancer?* by Peter Goodwin first published by the British Broadcasting Corporation 1984 ' Peter Goodwin 1984. Preston Travel Ltd for: Preston Sunroutes 'Camping and Self-Catering' (April to October 1983) holiday brochure. Punch Publications Ltd for: *Punch* (6 May 1981, 29 July 1981, 12 August 1981, 26 August 1981 and 9 September 1981) ' published by Punch Publications Ltd 1981. Radala and associates for: *The Naked Civil Servant* by Quentin Crisp first published by Jonathan Cape Ltd 1968 ' Quentin Crisp 1968. The Rainbird Publishing Group Ltd for: *The Making of Mankind* by Richard E Leakey first published in Great Britain by Michael Joseph Ltd 1981 ' Sherma BV 1981. Robson Books Ltd for: *The Punch Book of Short Stories 3* selected by Alan Coren first published in Great Britain by Robson Books Ltd in association with Punch Publications Ltd 1981 ' Robson Books Ltd 1981.*The Best of Robert Morley* by Robert Morley first published in Great Britain by Robson Books Ltd 1981 ' Robert Morley 1981. Deborah Rogers Ltd for: 'Picasso's Late Works' by Edward Lucie-Smith in the *Illustrated London News* July 1981, 'David Jones at the Tate' by Edward Lucie-Smith in the *Illustrated London News* August 1981 and 'Further Light on Spanish Painting' by Edward Lucie-Smith in the *Illustrated London News* September 1981. *The Godfather* by Mario Puzo first published in Great Britain by William Heinemann Ltd 1969 ' Mario Puzo 1969. Routledge & Kegan Paul Ltd for: *How To Pass Examinations* by John Erasmus first published by Oriel Press Ltd 1967 ' Oriel Press Ltd 1980. *Daisy, Daisy* by Christian Miller first published by Routledge & Kegan Paul Ltd 1980 ' Christian Miller 1980. *The National Front* by Nigel Fielding first published by Routledge & Kegan Paul Ltd 1981 ' Nigel Fielding 1981. *The Myth of Home Ownership* by Jim Kemeny first published by Routledge & Kegan Paul Ltd 1980 ' J Kemeny 1981. *Absent With Cause (Lessons of Truancy)* by Roger White first published by Routledge & Kegan Paul Ltd 1980 ' Roger White 1980. *The Powers of Evil (in Western Religion, Magic and Folk Belief)* by Richard Cavendish first published by Routledge & Kegan Paul Ltd 1975 ' Richard Cavendish 1975. *Crime and Personality* by H J Eysenck first published by Routledge & Kegan Paul Ltd 1964 ' H J Eysenck 1964, 1977. Martin Secker & Warburg Ltd for: *Changing Places* by David Lodge first published in England by Martin Secker & Warburg Ltd 1975 ' David Lodge 1975. *The History Man* by Malcolm Bradbury first published by Martin Secker & Warburg 1975 ' Malcolm Bradbury 1975. *Humboldt's Gift* by Saul Bellow first published in England by The Alison Press/Martin Secker & Warburg Ltd 1975 ' Saul Bellow 1973, 1974, 1975. *Wilt* by Tom Sharpe first published in England by Martin Secker & Warburg Ltd 1976 ' Tom Sharpe 1976. *The Last Days of America* by Paul E Erdman first published in England by Martin Secker & Warburg Ltd 1981 ' Paul E Erdman 1981. *Autumn Manoeuvres* by Melvyn Bragg first published in England by Martin Secker & Warburg Ltd 1978 ' Melvyn Bragg 1978. *The Act of Being* by Charles Marowitz first published in England by Martin Secker & Warburg Ltd 1978 ' Charles Marowitz 1978. *As If By Magic* by Angus Wilson first published in England by Martin Secker & Warburg Ltd 1973 ' Angus Wilson 1973. *All the President's Men* by Carl Bernstein and Bob Woodward first published in England by Martin Secker & Warburg Ltd 1974 ' Carl Bernstein and Bob Woodward 1974. *The Myth of the Nation and the Vision of Revolution* by J L Talmon first published by Martin Secker & Warburg Ltd 1981 ' J L Talmon 1980. *Animal Farm* by George Orwell first published by Martin Secker & Warburg 1945 ' Eric Blair 1945. Anthony Sheil Associates Ltd for: *Daniel Martin* by John Fowles first published in Great Britain by Jonathan Cape Ltd 1977 ' J R Fowles Ltd 1977. *Love Story* by Erich Segal first published by Hodder & Stoughton Ltd 1970 ' Erich Segal 1970. Sidgwick & Jackson Ltd for: *The Third World War* by General Sir John Hackett and others first published in Great Britain by Sidgwick & Jackson Ltd 1978 ' General Sir John Hackett 1978. *Superwoman* by Shirley Conran first published by Sidgwick & Jackson Ltd 1975 ' Shirley Conran 1975, 1977. *An Actor and His Time* by John Gielgud first published in Great Britain by Sidgwick & Jackson Ltd 1979 ' John Gielgud, John Miller and John Powell 1979 ' Biographical Notes, John Miller 1979. Simon & Schuster for: *Our Bodies Ourselves (A Health Book by and for Women)* by the Boston Women's Health Book Collective (British Edition by Angela Phillips and Jill Rakusen) published in Allen Lane and Penguin Books Ltd 1978 ' The Boston Women's Health Collective Inc 1971, 1973, 1976 ' Material for British Edition, Angela Phillips and Jill Rakusen 1978. Souvenir Press Ltd for: *The Bermuda Triangle* by Charles Berlitz (An Incredible Saga of Unexplained Disappearances) first published in Great Britain by Souvenir Press Ltd 1975 ' Charles Berlitz 1974. Souvenir Press Ltd and Michael Joseph Ltd for: *Airport* by Arthur Hailey first published in Great Britain by Michael Joseph Ltd in association with Souvenir Press Ltd 1968 ' Arthur Hailey Ltd 1968. Sunmed Holidays Ltd for: 'Go Greek' (Summer 1983) holiday brochure. Maurice Temple Smith Ltd for: *Friends of the Earth Pollution Guide* by Brian Price published by Maurice Temple Smith Ltd 1983 ' Brian Price 1983. Maurice Temple Smith and Gower Publishing Co Ltd for: *Working the Land (A New Plan for a Healthy Agriculture)* by Charlie Pye-Smith and Richard North first published by Maurice Temple Smith Ltd 1984 ' Charlie Pye-Smith and Richard North 1984. Times Newspapers Ltd for: *The Sunday Times Magazine* (13 January 1980, 20 January 1980 and 11 May 1980) ' published by Times Newspapers Ltd 1981. *The Times* (7 September 1981) ' published by Times Newspapers Ltd 1981. Twenty's Holidays for: 'The Best 18-33 Holidays' (Winter 1982/83) holiday brochure. University of Birmingham for: Living in Birmingham (1984) ' published by The University of Birmingham 1984. Birmingham University Overseas Student Guide ' The University of Birmingham. Working with

Industry and Commerce ' published by The University of Birmingham 1984. University of Birmingham Prospectus (June 1985) ' published by The University of Birmingham 1985. University of Birmingham Library Guide ' published by The University of Birmingham. University of Birmingham Institute of Research and Development (1984) ' published by the University of Birmingham 1984. Biological Sciences at The University of Birmingham (1985) ' published by The University of Birmingham 1985. History at the University of Birmingham (1985) ' published by the University of Birmingham 1985. Faculty of Arts Handbook (1984-85) ' published by The University of Birmingham 1984. Virago Press Ltd for: Benefits by Zoe Fairbairns published by Virago Press Ltd 1979 ' Zoe Fairbairns 1979. Simple Steps to Public Life by Pamela Anderson, Mary Stott and Fay Weldon published in Great Britain by Virago Press Ltd 1980 ' Action Opportunities 1980. Tell Me A Riddle by Tillie Olsen published by Virago Press Ltd 1980 ' this edition Tillie Olsen 1980. A P Watt (& Sons) Ltd for: The Glittering Prizes by Frederic Raphael first published in Great Britain by Penguin Books Ltd 1976 ' Volatic Ltd 1976. Then and Now by W Somerset Maugham first published by William Heinemann Ltd 1946 ' W Somerset Maugham 1946. The Language of Clothes by Alison Lurie published by William Heinemann Ltd 1981 ' Alison Lurie 1981. 'Herschel Commemorative' by Patrick Moore in the Illustrated London News July 1981. 'The Outermost Giant' by Patrick Moore in the Illustrated London News August 1981. 'Cosmic Bombardment' by Patrick Moore in the Illustrated London News September 1981. Weidenfeld & Nicolson Ltd for: 'The Miraculous Toy' by Susan Briggs in the Illustrated London News August 1981. The Needle's Eye by Margaret Drabble first published by Weidenfeld & Nicolson Ltd 1972 ' Margaret Drabble 1972. Success Without Tears: A Woman's Guide to the Top by Rachel Nelson first published in Great Britain by Weidenfeld & Nicolson Ltd 1979 ' Rachel Nelson 1979. Education in the Modern World by John Vaizey published by Weidenfeld & Nicolson Ltd 1967 ' John Vaizey 1967. Rich Man, Poor Man by Irwin Shaw first published in Great Britain by Weidenfeld & Nicolson Ltd 1970 ' Irwin Shaw 1969, 1970. Lolita by Vladimir Nabokov first published in Great Britain by Weidenfeld & Nicolson Ltd 1959 ' Vladimir Nabokov 1955, 1959, 1968, ' G P Putnam's Sons 1963 ' McGraw-Hill International Inc 1971. The Third World by Peter Worsley first published by Weidenfeld & Nicolson Ltd 1964 ' Peter Worsley 1964, 1967. Portrait of a Marriage by Nigel Nicolson published by Weidenfeld & Nicolson Ltd 1973 ' Nigel Nicolson 1973. The Dogs Bark: Public People and Private Places by Truman Capote first published in Great Britain by Weidenfeld & Nicolson Ltd 1974 ' Truman Capote 1974. Great Planning Disasters by Peter Hall first published in Great Britain by George Weidenfeld & Nicolson Ltd 1980 ' Peter Hall 1980. The Writers and Readers Publishing Co-operative Ltd for: Working with Words, Literacy Beyond School by Jane Mace published by The Writers and Readers Publishing Co-operative Ltd 1979 ' Jane Mace 1979. The Alienated: Growing Old Today by Gladys Elder OAP published by The Writers and Readers Publishing Co-operative Ltd 1977 ' Text, The Estate of Gladys Elder 1977 ' Photographs, Mike Abrahams 1977. Beyond the Crisis in Art by Peter Fuller published by The Writers and Readers Publishing Co-operative Ltd 1980 ' Peter Fuller 1980. The War and Peace Book by Dave Noble published by The Writers and Readers Publishing Co-operative Ltd 1977 ' Dave Noble 1977. Tony Benn: A Political Biography by Robert Jenkins first published by The Writers and Readers Publishing Co-operative Ltd 1980 ' Robert Jenkins 1980. Nuclear Power for Beginners by Stephen Croall and Kaianders Sempler first published by The Writers and Readers Publishing Co-operative Ltd 1978 ' Text, Stephen Croall 1978, 1980 ' Illustrations Kaianders Sempler 1978, 1980. Yale University Press for: Life in the English Country House: A Social and Architectural History by Mark Girouard published by Yale University Press Ltd, London 1978 ' Yale University 1978. The British Broadcasting Corporation for transcripts of radio transmissions of 'Kaleidoscope', 'Any Questions', 'Money Box' and 'Arts and Africa' 1981 and 1982. The British Broadcasting Corporation and Mrs Shirley Williams for transcripts of television interviews with Mrs Shirley Williams 1979. Dr B L Smith, School of Mathematics and Physical Sciences, University of Sussex for programmes on Current Affairs, Science and The Arts originally broadcast on Radio Sussex 1979 and 1980 ' B L Smith. The following people in the University of Birmingham: Professor J McH Sinclair, Department of English, for his tapes of informal conversation (personal collection). Mr R Wallace, formerly Department of Accounting and Finance, and Ms D Houghton, Department of English, for transcripts of his accountancy lectures. Dr B K Gazey, Department of Electrical Engineering and Dr M Montgomery, University of Strathclyde, Department of English, for a transcript of Dr Gazey's lecture. Dr L W Poel, Department of Plant Biology, and Dr M Montgomery, University of Strathclyde, Department of English, for a transcript of Dr Poel's lecture. Professor J G Hawkes, formerly Department of Plant Biology, for recordings of his lectures. Dr M S Snaith, Department of Transportation for recordings of his lectures. Dr M P Hoey, Department of English, and Dr M Cooper, The British Council, for a recording of their discussion on discourse analysis. Ms A Renouf, Department of English, for recordings of job and academic interviews 1977. Mr R H Hubbard, formerly a B Phil (Ed) student, Faculty of Education, for his research recordings of expressions of uncertainty 1978-79. Mr A E Hare, formerly a B Phil (Ed) student, Faculty of Education, for his transcripts of telephone conversations 1978. Dr A Tsui, formerly Department of English, for her recordings of informal conversation. Mr J Couperthwaite, formerly Department of English, for a recording of informal conversation 1981. Ms C Emmott, M Litt student, Department of English, for a recording of informal conversation 1981. Mrs B T Atkins for the transcript of an account of a dream 1981. The British Council for 'Authentic Materials Numbers 1-28' 1981. Professor M Hammerton and Mr K Coghill, Department of Psychology, University of Newcastle-upon-Tyne, for tape recordings of their lectures 1981. Mr G P Graveson, formerly research student, University of Newcastle, for his recordings of teacher discussion 1977. Mr W R Jones, formerly research student, University of Southampton, for his recordings of classroom talk. Mr Ian Fisher, formerly BA student, Newcastle Polytechnic, for his transcripts of interviews on local history 1981. Dr N Coupland, formerly PhD student, Department of English, UWIST, for his transcripts of travel agency talk 1981. Professor D B Bromley, Department of Psychology, University of Liverpool, for his transcript of a research recording. Mr Brian Lawrence, formerly of Saffron Walden County High School, for a tape of his talk on 'The British Education System' 1979.

Thanks are also due to Times Newspapers Ltd for providing machine-readable copies of The Times and The Sunday Times for linguistic analysis.

Every effort has been made to trace the copyright holders, but if any have been inadvertently overlooked the publishers will be pleased to make the necessary acknowledgments at the first opportunity.

# a-

**a-** occurs in words which have 'not', 'without', or 'opposite to' as part of their meaning. For example, someone who is 'apolitical' has no opinions about political matters and takes no interest in them; someone who is 'amoral' has no moral standards or principles.

Here is a list of words with this meaning:

| | | | |
|---|---|---|---|
| aformal | apolitical | asexual | atypical |
| amoral | asensual | asocial | |
| aphasic | aseptic | atonal | |

# -ability

**-ability** replaces '-able' at the end of adjectives ending in '-able' to form nouns. Nouns formed in this way refer to the state or quality described by the adjective.

Note that the nouns formed from 'unable' and 'unstable' are 'inability' and 'instability'.

*...the ready availability of fresh fish from the sea.*
*Acrylic blankets have the best combination of warmth and washability.*
*...the likeability of George Brown.*

For more information see **-able.**

# -able

## 1 Possibility

PRODUCTIVE USE: **-able** combines with verbs to form adjectives. Adjectives formed in this way describe someone or something that is affected by the action or process described by the verb. For example, if someone has 'admirable' qualities, they have qualities that other people admire; if something is 'avoidable', it can be avoided.

**Spelling:** A final 'e' is removed before adding **-able,** except when it occurs after a 'c' or a 'g'. A final 'y' after a consonant is replaced by 'i' before adding **-able.** A final 'ate' is replaced by **-able.**

*Her progress was slow in spite of her admirable determination.*
*Deaths caused by reckless driving are avoidable.*
*Edward was a mischievous but lovable child.*

# -able

*Acrylic blankets and shawls are both warm and washable.*

Here are some examples of words with this meaning:

| | | | |
|---|---|---|---|
| acceptable | desirable | manageable | recognizable |
| admirable | disposable | noticeable | remarkable |
| adorable | enjoyable | peelable | tolerable |
| advisable | identifiable | predictable | understandable |
| comparable | imaginable | preferable | variable |
| dependable | irritable | profitable | washable |

Note that a number of adjectives formed from verbs and with this meaning end in '-ible' rather than **-able**.

For more information see **-ible**.

## 2 Having certain qualities

**-able** combines with nouns to form adjectives that describe someone or something as having the qualities or characteristics referred to by the original noun. For example, if something is 'comfortable', it gives comfort; if a particular style of clothing is 'fashionable', it is in fashion.

*...the comfortable feeling of security and ease that his company gave her.*
*...one of his habitual striped shirts that were fashionable in 1963.*
*Critics argued that the only honourable course of action open to him was resignation.*

Here is a list of words with this meaning:

| | | |
|---|---|---|
| comfortable | honourable | pleasurable |
| fashionable | knowledgeable | valuable |

### Words with other meanings

| | | | |
|---|---|---|---|
| agreeable | companionable | miserable | sizeable |
| amiable | considerable | parable | sociable |
| arable | damnable | personable | suitable |
| available | habitable | practicable | tenable |
| capable | hospitable | reasonable | veritable |
| charitable | memorable | reputable | |

# aero-

**aero-** occurs in words which have 'air' or 'air travel' as part of their meaning. For example, an 'aeroplane' is a vehicle that flies through the air; an 'aerodrome' is a place where small aircraft can land and take off.

Here is a list of words with this meaning:

| | | |
|---|---|---|
| aerodrome | aerofoil | aeronautics |
| aerodynamic | aerograph | aeroplane |
| aeroengines | aeronaut | aerospace |

**Words with other meanings**

| | | |
|---|---|---|
| aerobic | aerobics | aerosol |

# after-

## 1 Timing of activities

PRODUCTIVE USE: **after-** combines with nouns that refer to an activity or event in order to form adjectives. Adjectives formed in this way describe something that happens after a particular activity or event, which is specified in the adjective formed. For example, 'after-school' activities take place when lessons have finished for the day; you drink an 'after-dinner' drink after eating your dinner.

*After-school play centres are valuable for all children.*
*We had an after-dinner drink in the bar.*
*...the inadequate provision of after-sales service.*

Here are some examples of words with this meaning:

| | | |
|---|---|---|
| after-dinner | after-lunch | after-school |
| after-hours | after-sales | after-work |

## 2 Results

PRODUCTIVE USE: **after-** combines with nouns to form new nouns. Nouns formed in this way refer to one thing that happens as a result of another. For example, an 'aftertaste' is a taste that remains after you have eaten something; the 'after-effects' of an activity or an event are the feelings, illness, or condition that result from it, and that usually remain for a long time afterwards.

**Spelling:** Words formed in this way can be written with a hyphen or as one word.

*...the bitter aftertaste sometimes caused by saccharine.*
*There was a faint afterglow from the sunset.*

# after-

*Alas, in practice, the after-care of elderly patients leaves a great deal to be desired.*

Here are some examples of words with this meaning:

| | | | |
|---|---|---|---|
| after-care | afterglow | afterpain | after-smell |
| after-effects | after-image | aftershock | aftertaste |

## Words with other meanings

| | | |
|---|---|---|
| afterbirth | afternoon | afterward |
| afterlife | aftershave | afterwards |
| aftermath | afterthought | afterworld |

# -age

## 1 A process or state

**-age** combines with verbs, nouns, and adjectives to form new nouns. Words formed in this way refer to a process, the result of a process, or a state. For example, 'leakage' can refer to the process of leaking, or to the liquid or gas which escapes from a container when it leaks; a 'shortage' is a situation when there is not enough of something, or when the supply of something begins to decrease.

*Our fuel was almost gone due to a mysterious leakage from the containers.*
*The South-east has already been hit by a shortage of skilled labour.*
*All breakages must be paid for.*
*When buying material allow 10 per cent extra for shrinkage.*

Here is a list of words with this meaning:

| | | | | |
|---|---|---|---|---|
| assemblage | drainage | marriage | slippage | storage |
| blockage | leakage | seepage | spillage | wastage |
| breakage | leverage | shortage | spoilage | wreckage |
| coverage | linkage | shrinkage | stoppage | |

## 2 Measurement

**-age** combines with nouns which refer to units of measurement to form new nouns which refer to a measurement made in the units indicated by the noun. For example, 'mileage' is the distance that a person or vehicle has travelled, measured in miles; 'voltage' is an electrical force measured in volts.

*...the approximate mileage for the complete journey.*
*Colour monitors run at a higher voltage than monochrome ones.*

*The connecting pipelines would require little acreage and could be buried if necessary.*

Here is a list of words with this meaning:

| | | |
|---|---|---|
| acreage | mileage | tonnage |
| footage | percentage | voltage |
| litreage | poundage | yardage |

## Words with other meanings

| | | | |
|---|---|---|---|
| advantage | cottage | luggage | patronage |
| anchorage | damage | manage | peerage |
| average | disadvantage | massage | pilgrimage |
| baggage | dosage | message | postage |
| bandage | garage | orphanage | sewage |
| barrage | garbage | outrage | sewerage |
| carriage | hostage | package | vicarage |
| coinage | language | passage | village |

# agro-

**agro-** occurs in words which have 'soil' or 'agriculture' as part of their meaning. For example, 'agrochemicals' are chemicals such as pesticides that are used in agriculture; 'agrology' is the study of soils and their productivity.

Here is a list of words with this meaning:

| | | | |
|---|---|---|---|
| agrochemical | agrology | agronomist | agronomy |

# -aholic, -oholic

**-aholic** or **-oholic** is derived from the word 'alcoholic', which describes someone who is addicted to alcohol.

**-aholic** combines with nouns and verbs to form new nouns. Nouns formed in this way refer to a person who needs, wants, or likes a particular thing so much that they appear to be addicted to it. For example, a 'chocoholic' is someone who cannot stop eating chocolate; a 'workaholic' is someone who is obsessed with their work and spends most of their time working.

**Spelling:** The noun formed from 'chocolate' is 'chocoholic'.

Note that it is possible to form new words with this meaning by adding **-aholic** to nouns. However, words formed in this way are very informal and are usually intended to be humorous. Few of them occur frequently.

*We've become a nation of chocoholics.*

# -aholic, -oholic

*A cashaholic is someone who's hopeless with money.*
*The author describes himself as a writaholic.*

Here are some examples of words with this meaning:

| | | | |
|---|---|---|---|
| bookaholic | chocoholic | shopaholic | writaholic |
| cashaholic | newsaholic | workaholic | |

# -al

## 1 Connection

PRODUCTIVE USE: **-al** combines with nouns to form adjectives.
Adjectives formed in this way describe something that is connected
with the thing referred to by the original noun. For example,
'environmental' problems are related to the environment;
something that is 'accidental' happens by accident.

**Spelling:** A final 'y' is replaced by 'ical' rather than **-al**. 'ial' is
sometimes used instead of **-al,** especially with nouns ending in 'er',
'or', and 'ent'.

*...environmental pollution and the erosion of natural resources.*
*...a treaty to reduce the risk of accidental nuclear war.*
*Some of the clothes worn were national costume.*
*...the performance of his presidential duties.*

Here are some examples of words with this meaning:

| | | | |
|---|---|---|---|
| accidental | environmental | musical | professional |
| additional | experimental | national | regional |
| classical | fanatical | occasional | residential |
| continental | geographical | oriental | sceptical |
| conventional | global | original | sensational |
| conversational | governmental | ornamental | sentimental |
| cynical | historical | parental | statistical |
| departmental | institutional | philosophical | traditional |
| educational | logical | political | transitional |
| emotional | mechanical | presidential | vocational |

Note that **-al** sometimes combines with adjectives ending in '-ic' to
form new adjectives with the same meaning. For example, 'comical'
means the same as comic; 'electrical' means the same as electric.

*He filled the frequent silences with comical anecdotes.*
*...two small electrical screwdrivers.*
*He smiled a friendly, slightly ironical smile.*

## 2 Actions

**-al** combines with verbs to form nouns. Nouns formed in this way
refer to the action or process described by the verb. For example, a

6

'denial' is a statement that denies something such as an accusation;
the 'withdrawal' of something is the process or action of
withdrawing it.

*The New York Evening Post reported Sherman's denial of the
accusation.
...the Cuban withdrawal from Angola.
Twelve employees made a complaint of unfair dismissal.
...a gradual renewal of links with the mainland.*

Here is a list of words with this meaning:

| | | | |
|---|---|---|---|
| avowal | burial | disavowal | renewal |
| bestowal | committal | dismissal | rental |
| betrayal | denial | portrayal | withdrawal |

## Words with other meanings

| | | | | |
|---|---|---|---|---|
| banal | incidental | mineral | provisional | special |
| canal | internal | minimal | sandal | verbal |
| editorial | marshal | normal | several | |
| impartial | medical | personal | signal | |

# all-

## 1 One thing or quality

PRODUCTIVE USE: **all-** combines with nouns and adjectives to form
new adjectives. Adjectives formed in this way describe something
that consists entirely of the thing referred to by the noun, or that
only has those qualities described by the original adjective. For
example, if a piece of clothing is 'all-wool', it is made entirely out of
wool; if a group of people is 'all-male', it consists only of men.

*That sweater was all-wool.
...the all-electric, automatic kitchen.
...the creation of an all-volunteer army.
...an all-steel umpire's chair.*

Here are some examples of words with this meaning:

| | | | |
|---|---|---|---|
| all-acrylic | all-electric | all-rubber | all-white |
| all-action | all-female | all-star | all-woman |
| all-aluminium | all-grey | all-steel | all-wood |
| all-black | all-male | all-union | all-wool |
| all-cash | all-new | all-volunteer | |

## 2 Every type

PRODUCTIVE USE: **all-** combines with nouns to form adjectives.
Adjectives formed in this way describe something that is suitable

## all-

for or includes every type of a particular thing. For example, an 'all-weather' football pitch can be used in every kind of weather condition; an 'all-purpose' glue can be used for any type of repairs.

*It has an all-weather pitch which will be used for the cricket event.*
*The campaign commanded all-party support.*
*...an all-sports channel, with live broadcasts.*

Here are some examples of words with this meaning:

| | | | |
|---|---|---|---|
| all-age | all-party | all-season | all-weather |
| all-function | all-purpose | all-sports | |

## 3 Affecting everyone or everything

**all-** combines with present participles to form adjectives which describe something that includes or affects everyone or everything. For example, if someone is 'all-loving', they love everyone; if something is 'all-pervading', it is present or is felt everywhere in a particular place.

Note that words formed in this way are often literary or very formal, and very few of them occur frequently.

*Mother presents herself as all-loving.*
*An all-pervading dishonesty hung over our enterprise.*
*Her all-consuming passions were kangaroos and rabbits.*
*...the camera's all-seeing eye.*

Here is a list of words with this meaning:

| | | |
|---|---|---|
| all-absorbing | all-engulfing | all-loving |
| all-conquering | all-enveloping | all-pervading |
| all-consuming | all-giving | all-prevailing |
| all-demanding | all-inclusive | all-seeing |
| all-embracing | all-invading | |
| all-encompassing | all-knowing | |

### Words with other meanings

| | | | |
|---|---|---|---|
| all-clear | all-fours | all-night | all-round |
| all-comers | all-important | all-out | |
| all-day | all-in | all-powerful | |

## -an

**-an** combines with the names of places to form words which describe someone or something that comes from the place mentioned. For example, an 'American' is a person who comes from the United States of America; 'Australian' wine is produced in Australia.

**Spelling:** A final 'a' is replaced by **-an.** A final 'y' is replaced by 'ian'. When the place name ends in a consonant, 'ian' is added to the end.

*...an American airline pilot.*
*Among the journalists were two Russians.*
*Many people these days prefer Italian clothes.*

Here is a list of words with this meaning:

| | | | |
|---|---|---|---|
| African | Brazilian | Hungarian | Nigerian |
| Algerian | Bulgarian | Indian | Persian |
| American | Californian | Indonesian | Russian |
| Angolan | Cambodian | Iranian | Scandinavian |
| Arabian | Chilean | Italian | Sicilian |
| Armenian | Cuban | Jamaican | Syrian |
| Asian | Egyptian | Jordanian | |
| Australian | Ethiopian | Korean | |
| Austrian | European | Libyan | |

There are some exceptions to the general rules. Here is a list of words formed in an irregular way:

| | | | |
|---|---|---|---|
| Argentinian | Canadian | Norwegian | Ukrainian |
| Belgian | Moroccan | Palestinian | |

# -ance

## 1 With verbs

**-ance** combines with some verbs to form nouns which refer to the action, process, or state indicated by the verb. For example, 'admittance' is the act of entering a place or being allowed to enter it; 'observance' is the process of observing something.

**Spelling:** A final 'ate' is replaced by **-ance.**

*A dozen officers stood at the front porch, waiting for admittance.*
*...Rothermere's observance of the comet.*
*Through the war America confirmed her position of global dominance.*
*...his meek acceptance of the insult.*

Here is a list of words with this meaning:

| | | | |
|---|---|---|---|
| acceptance | attendance | endurance | performance |
| admittance | clearance | entrance | radiance |
| alliance | defiance | guidance | reliance |
| appearance | disappearance | insurance | resemblance |
| assistance | disturbance | maintenance | resistance |
| assurance | dominance | observance | tolerance |

## -ance

### 2 With adjectives

PRODUCTIVE USE: **-ance** replaces 'ant' at the end of adjectives to form nouns that refer to the state or quality described by the adjective. For example, 'arrogance' is the quality of being arrogant; 'elegance' is the quality of being elegant.

*'I ought to be chief,' said Jack with simple arrogance.*
*The table was laid with more elegance than usual.*
*She accepted his gifts with some reluctance.*
*A matter of overwhelming importance occurred to him.*

Here are some examples of words with this meaning:

| | | | |
|---|---|---|---|
| abundance | fragrance | invariance | repugnance |
| arrogance | ignorance | irrelevance | significance |
| brilliance | importance | petulance | vigilance |
| elegance | insignificance | predominance | |
| extravagance | intemperance | preponderance | |
| exuberance | intolerance | reluctance | |

### Words with other meanings

| | | | |
|---|---|---|---|
| accordance | allowance | inheritance | surveillance |
| acquaintance | appliance | instance | vengeance |
| allegiance | grievance | renaissance | |

# Anglo-

**Anglo-** occurs in words which have 'England' or 'Britain' as part of their meaning. For example, 'Anglo-American' relations are the relations between Britain and America.

# -ant

### 1 Occupations and participation

**-ant** combines with verbs to form nouns which refer to somebody who does a particular thing. For example, an 'assistant' is somebody who helps or assists another person; a 'contestant' is somebody who competes for a prize in a contest or competition.

**Spelling:** A final 'ate', 'y', or 'e' is replaced by **-ant**.

*She was now the assistant cook in the house.*
*The first prize will be awarded to the contestant who correctly identifies the famous personalities.*
*...a participant in a radio programme about writing.*

*The officer gave the attendant a hearty slap on the back.*

Here is a list of words with this meaning:

| | | | | |
|---|---|---|---|---|
| accountant | attendant | contestant | emigrant | occupant |
| applicant | claimant | defendant | immigrant | participant |
| assailant | combatant | dependant | informant | servant |
| assistant | consultant | descendant | inhabitant | |

Note that a 'confidant' is not someone who confides, but the person who is confided in.

## 2 Things which have an effect

-ant combines with verbs to form nouns which refer to an object or substance which has a particular effect. For example, a 'coolant' is a liquid used to keep a machine cool while it is operating; a 'pollutant' is a substance which pollutes the environment.

*...a refrigerator using a new 'ozone friendly' compound as its coolant.*
*Is there some additive or pollutant in your water?*
*He wiped the table with disinfectant.*
*Economic issues are the main determinant of political attitudes.*

Here is a list of words with this meaning:

| | | | |
|---|---|---|---|
| accelerant | decongestant | determinant | pollutant |
| contaminant | defoliant | disinfectant | sealant |
| coolant | depressant | lubricant | |

## 3 Adjectives

-ant also occurs in adjectives, many of which are formed from stems which are not current words in English.

Here is a list of words with this meaning:

| | | | | |
|---|---|---|---|---|
| abundant | constant | ignorant | pleasant | significant |
| adamant | distant | important | pregnant | tolerant |
| arrogant | dominant | indignant | redundant | triumphant |
| brilliant | elegant | instant | relevant | vacant |
| buoyant | extravagant | militant | reluctant | |

# ante-

ante- occurs in some words which have 'before' as part of their meaning. For example, if one thing 'antedates' another, it happened or existed before the other; an 'anteroom' is a small room where people can wait before going into a larger room.

# ante-

For more information on words that have 'before' as part of their meaning, see **pre-**.

Here is a list of words with this meaning:

| | | |
|---|---|---|
| antecedent | antedate | ante-natal |
| antechamber | antediluvian | anteroom |

# anthrop-

**anthrop-** occurs in words which have 'people' as part of their meaning. For example, 'anthropology' is the study of people, society, and culture; a 'philanthropic' organization gives money and help to people who need it.

Note that **anthrop-** sometimes occurs in the middle of words.

Here is a list of words with this meaning:

| | | |
|---|---|---|
| anthropocentric | anthropomorphic | philanthropist |
| anthropoid | anthropomorphism | philanthropy |
| anthropologist | misanthropy | |
| anthropology | philanthropic | |

# anti-

## 1 Opposition

PRODUCTIVE USE: **anti-** combines with nouns and adjectives to form words which describe someone or something that is opposed to the thing referred to or described by the original noun or adjective. For example, if somebody is 'anti-war', they are opposed to war; 'anti-colonialism' is the belief that colonialism is wrong.

*She had become involved, as a student, in anti-racist movements.*
*...a big demonstration in town during the height of the anti-war movement.*
*An anti-EEC resolution was passed.*
*...an intensification of the international anti-apartheid campaign.*
*...the group which ran the anti-census campaign in 1985.*

Here are some examples of words with this meaning:

| | | |
|---|---|---|
| anti-abortion | anti-colonial | anti-marriage |
| anti-aggression | anti-communist | anti-Marxist |
| anti-apartheid | anti-democratic | anti-nuclear |
| anti-authority | anti-discrimination | anti-racist |
| anti-British | anti-EEC | anti-religious |
| anti-capitalist | anti-establishment | anti-vivisection |
| anti-catholic | anti-fascist | anti-war |
| anti-census | anti-government | |

Note that **anti-** is often used in this way with names.

*The anti-Dukakis campaign has worked most effectively in Texas.*
*...calls for an anti-Thatcher coalition.*
*Revolutionaries were trying to start an anti-Wilson movement in the party.*

## 2 Prevention

PRODUCTIVE USE: **anti-** combines with nouns and adjectives to form words which describe one thing as being intended to prevent or destroy another. For example, an 'anti-depressant' is a drug which prevents people from being depressed; an 'anti-tank' weapon is designed to destroy military tanks.

*He no longer takes anti-depressants or tranquillizers.*
*Mike's brother, an inventor, was in trouble with the police because his anti-car-thief device was dangerous.*
*...an anti-cholesterol drug.*
*...anti-submarine torpedos.*
*The anti-fraud unit had now been set up.*

Here are some examples of words with this meaning:

| | | | |
|---|---|---|---|
| anti-aircraft | anti-cholesterol | anti-fungal | anti-pollution |
| anti-bacterial | anti-coagulant | anti-infection | anti-rust |
| anti-burglar | anti-depressant | anti-inflation | anti-seasickness |
| anti-cancer | anti-fraud | anti-invasion | anti-submarine |
| anti-car-thief | anti-freeze | anti-missile | anti-tank |

### Words with other meanings

| | | |
|---|---|---|
| antibody | anti-clockwise | antimatter |
| Antichrist | anti-cyclone | antiseptic |
| anti-climax | antihero | antithesis |

# aqua-

**aqua-** occurs in words which have 'water' as part of their meaning. For example, an 'aqualung' is a piece of equipment which provides divers with air when they are underwater; an 'aquarium' is a glass tank filled with water which is used to keep fish in.

Here is a list of words with this meaning:

| | | |
|---|---|---|
| aqualung | aquarium | aquatic |

# arch-

## 1 Higher rank

**arch-** combines with nouns that refer to someone's position in the aristocracy or in the Church in order to form new nouns. Nouns

# arch-

formed in this way refer to people who have reached the highest
position possible. For example, an 'archdeacon' is a deacon of the
highest rank; an 'archduke' is a member of the aristocracy who has
a higher rank than a duke.

*The archdeacon said that cruelty to animals was worse than ever
before.*
*...the assassination of the Archduke Ferdinand.*

Here is a list of words with this meaning:

| | | |
|---|---|---|
| archangel | archdeacon | archduke |
| archbishop | archduchess | |

Note that the 'ch' is pronounced as in 'change' in all these words
except in 'archangel' where it is pronounced as a 'k'.

## 2 More extreme

PRODUCTIVE USE: **arch-** combines with nouns that refer to people
who are opposed to something or who are considered to be bad in
order to form new nouns. Nouns formed in this way refer to people
who are extreme representatives of whatever the original noun
refers to. For example, your 'arch-rival' in a competition is the
competitor whom you most want to beat; someone's 'arch-enemy' is
their most hated enemy.

*Mr Boris Yeltsin called yesterday for the removal of his arch-rival,
Mr Yegor Ligachev and two other members of the Politburo.*
*The arch-sinner, deserving the most horrible punishment in
Christian theory, was Judas Iscariot.*

Here are some examples of words with this meaning:

| | | |
|---|---|---|
| arch-capitalist | arch-fiend | arch-rival |
| arch-communist | arch-manipulator | arch-sinner |
| arch-enemy | arch-opponent | arch-traitor |
| arch-exploiter | arch-rebel | arch-villain |

# -archy

**-archy** occurs in words which have 'rule' or 'government' as part of
their meaning. For example, the political 'hierarchy' is the group of
people in politics who have the power; an 'oligarchy' is a small
group of people who control and run a particular country or
organization.

Here is a list of words with this meaning:

| | | |
|---|---|---|
| anarchy | matriarchy | oligarchy | squirearchy |
| hierarchy | monarchy | patriarchy | |

# -arian

**-arian** occurs in nouns which indicate that someone or something is associated with a particular thing. For example, a 'librarian' is someone who works in a library; a 'vegetarian' is someone who eats mainly vegetables because they do not eat meat or fish.

Here is a list of words with this meaning:

| | | | |
|---|---|---|---|
| agrarian | egalitarian | parliamentarian | unitarian |
| authoritarian | humanitarian | sabbatarian | vegetarian |
| communitarian | libertarian | sectarian | veterinarian |
| disciplinarian | librarian | totalitarian | |

# -ary

## 1 Forming adjectives

**-ary** combines with nouns and occasionally verbs to form adjectives. Adjectives formed in this way describe someone or something that is connected to, involves, or shares some of the characteristics of the things referred to by the original nouns or verbs. For example, if you say something 'complimentary' to someone, you pay them a compliment; if something is 'imaginary', someone has imagined it.

*His action is not insulting; it is meant to be complimentary.*
*...an ineffable joy sometimes so momentary it almost goes unnoticed.*
*He admired the troops rather as though they were legendary figures in a history book.*
*...tantalizingly fragmentary snatches of news.*

Here is a list of words with this meaning:

| | | | |
|---|---|---|---|
| cautionary | discretionary | momentary | residuary |
| complementary | fragmentary | monetary | rudimentary |
| complimentary | honorary | parliamentary | salutary |
| customary | imaginary | planetary | secondary |
| dietary | inflationary | precautionary | supplementary |
| disciplinary | legendary | probationary | voluntary |

Note that there are a number of adjectives ending in **-ary** that are formed from stems which are not current words in English.

*She had invented and imposed routine, but it seemed arbitrary and superficial.*

# -ary

*We cooked spinach pies and other culinary delights.*

Here is a list of words formed in this way:

| | | | |
|---|---|---|---|
| ancillary | culinary | military | sanitary |
| arbitrary | extraordinary | necessary | sedentary |
| auxiliary | hereditary | ordinary | solitary |
| binary | incendiary | preliminary | subsidiary |
| contemporary | literary | primary | temporary |
| contrary | mercenary | proprietary | veterinary |

## 2 Forming nouns

**-ary** also occurs in nouns. Some of these nouns refer to people. For example, a 'missionary' is a person who is a member of a religious mission; your 'adversary' is a person who is opposing you or who holds an adverse point of view.

*The missionary schools sought to produce converts to Christianity.*
*Wells was a great visionary, but not visionary enough to foresee computers.*
*... his secretary, typist, clerk and book-keeper.*
*Neither would launch an attack upon the homeland of its adversary.*

Here is a list of words with this meaning:

| | | | |
|---|---|---|---|
| actuary | beneficiary | luminary | secretary |
| adversary | dignitary | missionary | visionary |
| antiquary | emissary | notary | voluptuary |
| apothecary | intermediary | prebendary | |

Some of these nouns refer to places where something is kept or done. For example, a 'mortuary' is a building or room where dead bodies are kept before they are buried or cremated; a 'dispensary' is a place where medicines are prepared and dispensed.

*Before the funeral the body was in a mortuary in King William's Town.*
*It will be an aviary; the grounds, the park, will be a bird sanctuary.*
*It will be possible to store large books on a microchip and a whole library in a space about the size of a paperback.*
*...a nurse in the infirmary.*

Here is a list of words with this meaning:

| | | | |
|---|---|---|---|
| apiary | granary | mortuary | seminary |
| aviary | infirmary | penitentiary | |
| dispensary | library | sanctuary | |

## Words with other meanings

| | | | |
|---|---|---|---|
| anniversary | centenary | glossary | summary |
| boundary | commentary | itinerary | tributary |
| burglary | constabulary | obituary | vocabulary |
| bursary | dictionary | ovary | |
| canary | documentary | quandary | |
| capillary | estuary | salary | |

# astr-

**astr-** occurs in words which have 'star' or 'space' as part of their meaning. For example, an 'astronomer' is a scientist who studies the stars; an 'astronaut' is trained to fly in a spacecraft.

Here is a list of words with this meaning:

| | | |
|---|---|---|
| astral | astrology | astronomy |
| astrolabe | astronaut | astrophysicist |
| astrologer | astronomer | astrophysics |

# -ation

See **-ion**.

# audio-

**audio-** occurs in words which have 'sound' or 'hearing' as part of their meaning. For example, an 'audio-typist' is someone who types letters and reports that have been dictated into a tape-recorder.

Here is a list of words with this meaning:

| | | | |
|---|---|---|---|
| audio-cassette | audio-tape | audio-typist | audio-visual |

# auto-

## 1 Automatic

**auto-** combines with nouns and verbs to form new nouns and verbs. Words formed in this way describe a device or mechanism that works automatically, without having to be operated by a person. For example, an 'auto-timer' turns something such as a cooker on and off at times which have been set in advance; if a machine such as a video-recorder 'auto-records' a programme, it records it automatically at a time which has been set in advance.

Note that this use of **auto-** is an abbreviation of 'automatic'.

## auto-

**Spelling:** Words formed in this way are usually written with a hyphen, but some of the more common ones are written as one word.

*Auto-timers on cookers will have to be reset after a power cut.*
*...a fifty-watt six speaker stereo with an auto-reverse cassette player.*
*...microwave ovens with an auto-cook device.*

Here is a list of words with this meaning:

| | | | |
|---|---|---|---|
| auto-cook | autodial | autoredial | auto-timer |
| autocue | auto-play | auto-reverse | |
| auto-defrost | auto-record | auto-rotate | |

## 2 Oneself

**auto-** occurs in words which express the idea that someone does something to, for, or about themselves. For example, your 'autobiography' is an account of your life which you have written yourself; a country or group of people that is 'autonomous' is governed or controlled by itself rather than by others.

*In his own autobiography, Attlee makes no mention of the report.*
*The paper's editorial department was totally autonomous.*
*He signed an autograph for her grandson.*

Here is a list of words with this meaning:

| | | |
|---|---|---|
| autobiography | autonomous | auto-suggestion |
| autograph | autonomy | |

## 3 Cars

**auto-** combines with nouns to form new nouns which refer to something that is connected with cars. For example, the 'auto-industry' is the car manufacturing industry; 'autosport' is another name for motor racing.

Note that this use of **auto-** is an abbreviation of 'automobile' or 'automotive'.

*Auto-industry experts say General Motors and Ford will have to work even harder than usual next year.*
*...the RAC autosport rally championship in Hampshire.*

Here is a list of words with this meaning:

| | | |
|---|---|---|
| auto-industry | autosport | autoworker |

# -based

## 1 The major part of something

PRODUCTIVE USE: **-based** combines with nouns to form adjectives. Adjectives formed in this way express the idea that the thing referred to by the original noun is the most important part or feature of something. For example, an 'acid-based' powder has acid as its main ingredient; 'computer-based' teaching relies heavily on the use of computers.

*...an acid-based powder supplied to police forces all over the world to trace fingerprints on paper.*
*Traditional class-based loyalties were breaking down.*
*...the nineteenth-century coal-based industrial economy.*
*...petroleum-based detergents.*

Here are some examples of words with this meaning:

| | | | |
|---|---|---|---|
| acid-based | export-based | mercury-based | project-based |
| cash-based | fuel-based | money-based | property-based |
| class-based | hydrogen-based | nitrogen-based | protein-based |
| coal-based | lead-based | nuclear-based | science-based |
| computer-based | leisure-based | oil-based | service-based |
| education-based | market-based | petroleum-based | water-based |

Note that **-based** sometimes combines in this way with adjectives.

*Many are religious-based schools.*

## 2 The basis of something

**-based** combines with adjectives and adverbs such as 'broad', 'broadly', 'widely', and 'solidly' to form adjectives. Adjectives formed in this way describe the qualities of the basis of something, rather than telling you what it is composed of. The adjectives formed typically describe such things as governments, beliefs, and movements.

*We want to develop it into a broadly-based industrial group.*
*The anti-war movement had become more broad-based and less radical.*
*We should build up a firmly-based, democratic administration in Hong Kong.*
*...a widely-based dialogue.*

Here is a list of words with this meaning:

| | | |
|---|---|---|
| broad-based | firmly-based | soundly-based |
| broadly-based | solidly-based | widely-based |

# -based

## 3 Places

PRODUCTIVE USE: **-based** combines with nouns and adjectives that refer to places, or with adjectives of nationality, to form new adjectives. Adjectives formed in this way describe something as being positioned or existing mainly in a particular place, or as being organized from that place. For example, if an industry is 'British-based', most of its operations take place in Britain.

*...a British-based engineering group.*
*...smaller, community-based hospitals.*
*Home-based industry may be severely shaken by higher interest rates.*
*...Reuters, the London-based news agency.*
*...ground-based telescopes.*
*...Mr Tito Tettamanti, a Swiss-based Italian lawyer.*

Here are some examples of words with this meaning:

| | | |
|---|---|---|
| American-based | foreign-based | overseas-based |
| Belfast-based | ground-based | Paris-based |
| British-based | home-based | school-based |
| campus-based | hospital-based | Shanghai-based |
| city-based | land-based | shore-based |
| community-based | London-based | Swiss-based |
| country-based | marine-based | town-based |
| European-based | ocean-based | US-based |

# be-

## 1 Wearing something or covered with something

**be-** occurs in adjectives that describe someone or something as wearing something or being covered in a substance. For example, someone who is 'bespectacled' is wearing spectacles; someone who is 'bejewelled' is wearing jewels or is covered in jewels.

*...a short, bespectacled man with thinning hair.*
*...the dignified death of the bewigged Queen of Scots.*

Here is a list of words with this meaning:

| | | |
|---|---|---|
| bejewelled | bespectacled | bewigged |

## 2 To cause to become

**be-** occurs in adjectives and transitive verbs which describe someone or something as being in a particular state or going into that state. For example, someone who is 'beloved' is loved by someone else; if you 'belittle' someone or their achievements, you cause them to be thought of as less important than they really are.

*Claude Lebel emerged from the conference room dazed and bewildered.*
*He was pleased still to be in Austria and close to his beloved wife.*
*I won't let you belittle yourself, it is the most important work anyone can do.*
*...a soaked, bedraggled figure by the side of the road.*

Here is a list of words with this meaning:

| | | | |
|---|---|---|---|
| becalmed | belie | bereaved | betrothed |
| bedraggled | belittle | besotted | bewildered |
| befuddled | beloved | betray | bewitched |
| beguile | bemused | betrothal | bewitching |

## 3 Transitive verbs

**be-** occurs in a number of other transitive verbs. For example, if you 'befriend' someone, you help them and look after them as if they were your friend; to 'behold' something means to see or notice it; if soldiers 'besiege' a place, they surround it in an attempt to capture it.

*For the first time he realized how much he owed to this man who had befriended him.*
*The city of Toulouse was besieged by the Crusaders.*
*The women were wringing their hands, weeping and bemoaning their fate.*
*I didn't begrudge him the food, since he was obviously starving.*

Here is a list of words with this meaning:

| | | | |
|---|---|---|---|
| befriend | beleaguered | berate | besiege |
| begrudge | bemoan | beseech | bestow |
| behold | bequeath | beset | bewail |

### Words with other meanings:

| | | | |
|---|---|---|---|
| become | begone | belay | beware |
| befall | behave | believe | |
| begin | beheaded | belong | |

# bi-

## 1 Two

**bi-** occurs in words which have 'two' as part of their meaning. For example, a 'bicycle' is a vehicle with two wheels; someone who is 'bilingual' can speak two languages fluently.

*Mr Sutton came home from work on his bicycle.*

## bi-

*Mina peered at Lewis through her bifocals.*

Here is a list of words with this meaning:

| | | | |
|---|---|---|---|
| bicarbonate | bifocals | bilingual | biplane |
| bicentenary | bigamy | binary | bisect |
| bicycle | bilateral | binoculars | |

## 2 Twice

**bi-** can also be used to indicate that something happens twice during a particular period of time or once every two periods of time. For example, a 'biennial' event happens every two years.

*Every Union has its own annual or biennial conference.*
*...a bi-weekly magazine for teenage girls.*

Here is a list of words with this meaning:

| | | | | |
|---|---|---|---|---|
| bi-annual | bi-annually | biennial | bi-monthly | bi-weekly |

# bio-

**bio-** occurs in words which have 'life' or 'living things' as part of their meaning. For example, a 'biography' is a written account of someone's life; 'biology' is a science which describes and classifies living things.

Note that **bio-** sometimes occurs in the middle of words.

Here is a list of words with this meaning:

| | | | |
|---|---|---|---|
| antibiotics | biochemistry | biologist | biosphere |
| autobiography | biodegradable | biology | biosystem |
| biochemical | biography | biopsy | symbiotic |

# -bound

## 1 Restrictions

**-bound** combines with nouns to form adjectives. Adjectives formed in this way describe someone or something as being restricted or limited by the thing referred to by the original noun. For example, someone who is 'housebound' cannot leave their home, perhaps because they are ill or very old; something that is 'culture-bound' is restricted by the culture in which it occurs.

*...the housebound housewife who never, ever goes out.*
*...home-bound women, desperate for extra cash or self-fulfilment.*
*...desk-bound Yale graduates who usually hadn't visited Europe.*

*Young village men are beginning to doubt whether they are duty-bound to work on the land.*

Here is a list of words with this meaning:

| | | |
|---|---|---|
| class-bound | earthbound | housebound |
| culture-bound | fog-bound | snowbound |
| desk-bound | home-bound | tradition-bound |
| duty-bound | honour-bound | wheelchair-bound |

Note that 'home-bound' also has another meaning. This is explained in paragraph 2 of this entry.

Some adjectives formed in this way describe something as being surrounded by a particular thing. Words formed in this way are fairly literary, and few of them occur frequently.

*...the cold, shattered, mist-bound hills.*

## 2 Direction

**-bound** combines with nouns that refer to places, or with adverbs and adjectives that express direction, to form new adjectives. Adjectives formed in this way describe someone or something as travelling to that place or in that direction. For example, a 'southbound' train is heading towards the south; 'London-bound' passengers are travelling to London.

*...the westbound passenger express.*
*...London-bound passengers.*
*...homeward-bound ships.*
*...treating city-bound migrants with contempt.*

Here is a list of words with this meaning:

| | | |
|---|---|---|
| earthbound | inbound | southbound |
| eastbound | London-bound | westbound |
| home-bound | northbound | |
| homeward-bound | outbound | |

## 3 Coverings and books

**-bound** combines with some nouns to form adjectives which indicate the sort of covering that something has: these adjectives are mainly used to describe books. For example, a 'leather-bound' book has a leather cover.

Note that this use of **-bound** is related to the verb 'bind' and the noun 'binding'.

*On the bedside table lay a red leather-bound copy of the Bible.*
*He went over to his bookshelf and picked out a small, blue, cardboard-bound book.*

## -bound

*Esther came in unsteadily, carrying four thick blue-bound volumes.*

Here is a list of words with this meaning:

| | | |
|---|---|---|
| brass-bound | cloth-bound | metal-bound |
| cardboard-bound | leather-bound | paper-bound |

### Words with other meanings

| | | |
|---|---|---|
| hidebound | muscle-bound | spellbound |

# cardi-

**cardi-** occurs in words which have 'heart' as part of their meaning. For example, a 'cardiac' arrest is a heart attack; a 'cardiologist' is a doctor who deals with heart disease.

Note that **cardi-** sometimes occurs in the middle of words.

Here is a list of words with this meaning:

| | |
|---|---|
| cardiac | cardiologist |
| cardiograph | electrocardiogram |

# cent-

**cent-** occurs in words which indicate that something has a hundred parts. For example, a 'century' is a period of a hundred years; a 'percentage' is a fraction of a hundred.

Note that **cent-** sometimes occurs in the middle of words.

Here is a list of words with this meaning:

| | | | |
|---|---|---|---|
| bicentenary | centenary | centimetre | percent |
| bicentennial | centennial | centipede | percentage |
| centenarian | centigrade | century | |

# -centric

**-centric** occurs in adjectives which describe something as being centred on a particular thing or involving a particular thing. For example, if someone has an 'anthropocentric' outlook, they regard people as the most important thing in the universe; if something is 'heliocentric', it has the sun at its centre.

Here is a list of words with this meaning:

| | | | |
|---|---|---|---|
| anthropocentric | egocentric | Eurocentric | heliocentric |

# chron-

**chron-** occurs in words which have 'time' as part of their meaning. For example, the 'chronology' of a number of past events is the order in which they occurred; if two events are 'synchronized', they occur at the same time.

Note that **chron-** sometimes occurs in the middle of words.

Here is a list of words with this meaning:

| | | | |
|---|---|---|---|
| anachronism | chronicle | chronometer | synchronized |
| anachronistic | chronological | synchronic | |
| chronic | chronology | synchronize | |

Note that 'chronic' has another meaning, and is used to describe a very bad or unpleasant situation.

# -cide

**-cide** occurs in words which have 'killing' as part of their meaning. For example, an 'insecticide' is a chemical that kills insects; if someone commits 'suicide', they kill themselves.

Here is a list of words with this meaning:

| | | | | |
|---|---|---|---|---|
| fratricide | herbicide | insecticide | pesticide | suicide |
| fungicide | homicide | parricide | regicide | |
| genocide | infanticide | patricide | spermicide | |

# cine-

**cine-** occurs in words which have 'motion pictures' or 'films' as part of their meaning. For example, a 'cinema' is a place where you go to watch films; a 'cine-camera' is a camera which takes moving pictures rather than still photographs.

Here is a list of words with this meaning:

| | | |
|---|---|---|
| cine-camera | cinema | cinematography |
| cine-film | cinematic | |

# circum-

**circum-** occurs in words which have 'around' as part of their meaning. For example, the 'circumference' of a circle, place, or round object is its edge or the line around it.

Here is a list of words with this meaning:

| | | |
|---|---|---|
| circumcise | circumlocution | circumspect |
| circumference | circumnavigate | circumstantial |
| circumflex | circumscribe | circumvent |

# co-

PRODUCTIVE USE: **co-** combines with nouns to form new nouns which refer to people doing things together. **co-** can be used in this way

## co-

with almost any noun which refers to a job, task, or status which two or more people can share. For example, the 'co-authors' of a book are the people who write it together; if you talk about the 'co-ownership' of a house, you are referring to the fact that it is owned by more than one person.

*...Dr John Baldwin, co-author of a detailed research project.*
*The Captain is responsible for flying the aircraft, while the co-pilot has to operate the radio.*
*...Mr Alastair Morton, the British co-chairman of Eurotunnel.*
*...her co-star, John Lithgoe, who played George.*

Here are some examples of words with this meaning:

| | | | |
|---|---|---|---|
| co-author | co-driver | co-membership | co-producer |
| co-chairman | co-founder | co-ownership | co-selector |
| co-defendant | co-leader | co-pilot | co-star |
| co-director | co-manager | co-presenter | |

**co-** also combines with this meaning with verbs. For example, if two people 'co-direct' a film, they direct it together.

*Maurice Brown co-directed the production of Othello.*
*In Scotland and Wales red and grey squirrels coexist without problems.*
*Britain and the Soviet Union already co-operate in the fight against drugs.*

Here is a list of words with this meaning:

| | | | | |
|---|---|---|---|---|
| co-direct | co-edit | coexist | co-operate | co-star |

### Words with other meanings

| | | |
|---|---|---|
| co-educational | coincidence | co-ordinate |
| cohabit | co-opt | |

## col-, com-, con-

**col-**, **com-**, and **con-** occur in words which have 'together' or 'with' as part of their meaning. For example, your 'colleagues' are the people you work with, especially in professional jobs; if you 'combine' two or more things, you put them together to make one thing; if you 'connect' two things such as pipes or wires, you join them together.

*I talked to colleagues of yours recently.*
*The plants converge under the trees.*

*She was a somewhat gruff companion on our expeditions.*

Here is a list of words with this meaning:

| | | | |
|---|---|---|---|
| collaborate | commerce | comrade | consortium |
| collate | communal | concur | conspiracy |
| colleague | communication | condolences | contact |
| collect | community | confederation | contemporary |
| collide | companion | conference | converge |
| collocation | company | conjunction | |
| collude | compatible | connect | |
| combine | compound | consensus | |

# -conscious

PRODUCTIVE USE: **-conscious** combines with nouns to form adjectives. Adjectives formed in this way describe someone who considers a particular aspect of their life or situation to be important, often when other people do not seem to notice it or to be interested in it. **-conscious** can be used in this way with almost any noun which describes something you might be interested in. For example, if someone is 'image-conscious', they are very interested in the way they appear to other people and are keen to create a particular impression; if someone is 'health-conscious', they are very concerned about their health and try to have a healthy lifestyle.

*...an image-conscious Hollywood actor.*
*The country had long since had its hedgerows ripped away by cost-conscious farmers.*
*Ian was the most safety-conscious member of the team.*
*She is self-conscious about the weight she has put on since we last saw her.*
*The company plans to market the low-calorie sweetener in diet-conscious America.*

Here are some examples of words with this meaning:

| | | |
|---|---|---|
| age-conscious | design-conscious | profit-conscious |
| budget-conscious | diet-conscious | race-conscious |
| camera-conscious | ecology-conscious | risk-conscious |
| cash-conscious | energy-conscious | safety-conscious |
| class-conscious | future-conscious | self-conscious |
| clock-conscious | health-conscious | status-conscious |
| colour-conscious | image-conscious | time-conscious |
| cost-conscious | media-conscious | trend-conscious |

# contra-

**Contra-** occurs in words which indicate that one thing opposes or has the opposite effect to another. For example, if you 'contradict'

## contra-

someone, you say the opposite of what they have just said; a 'contraceptive' is a drug or device which prevents a woman from becoming pregnant.

Here is a list of words with this meaning:

| | | | |
|---|---|---|---|
| contraception | contradict | contraflow | contrary |
| contraceptive | contradiction | contraindication | contravene |

# counter-

PRODUCTIVE USE: **counter-** combines with nouns and verbs to form new nouns and verbs. Words formed in this way refer to or describe actions or activities that oppose another action or activity. For example, a 'counter-measure' is an action you take in order to weaken the effect of another action or situation; if one thing 'counteracts' another, it reduces its effect by doing something that produces the opposite effect.

**Spelling:** Words formed in this way are usually written with a hyphen, but some of the more common ones are written as one word.

*Unless specific counter-measures are taken, unemployment will continue to rise.*
*...political power counterbalances the other influences in society.*
*Rumours and counter-rumours will fly in all directions.*
*This could lead to a series of strikes and counterstrikes.*
*We hadn't expected them to counter-attack so soon.*

Here are some examples of words with this meaning:

| | | |
|---|---|---|
| counter-accusation | counter-claim | counterplan |
| counteract | counter-espionage | counter-plot |
| counter-appeal | counterexample | counter-proposal |
| counterargument | counterfire | counterreaction |
| counterattack | counterforce | counter-reform |
| counterattraction | counter-irritant | counter-revolution |
| counterbalance | counter-measure | counter-strategy |
| counter-bid | counter-move | counterstrike |
| counterblow | counter-offensive | counter-thrust |
| countercharge | counter-offer | counterweight |

## Words with other meanings

| | |
|---|---|
| counterfoil | counterpoint |
| counterpart | countersign |

# -craft

## 1 Vehicles

**-craft** combines with nouns and present participles to form new nouns. Nouns formed in this way refer to vehicles which move in a particular way or have a particular purpose. For example, an 'aircraft' is a vehicle that flies through the air, such as an aeroplane or glider; a 'landing-craft' is a small boat which is used to land troops on beaches.

*Union members refused to handle baggage from the diverted aircraft.*
*The Voyager spacecraft will fly past Saturn in November.*
*...climbing down slippery ladders into the heaving beaching-craft.*

Here is a list of words with this meaning:

| | | | |
|---|---|---|---|
| aircraft | hovercraft | passengercraft | watercraft |
| beaching-craft | landing-craft | spacecraft | |

## 2 Abilities and skills

**-craft** combines with nouns to form new nouns which refer to an activity or job that involves making or doing something skilfully. For example, 'handicrafts' are activities such as embroidery or pottery which involve creating things with your hands; 'stagecraft' is skill in the art of writing and staging plays.

Note that 'handicrafts' always occurs in the plural form.

*...traditional Indian handicrafts industries.*
*...the American market leader in the supply of needlecraft kits.*
*Her father, who was skilled in woodcraft, had made the table for her.*

Here is a list of words with this meaning:

| | | |
|---|---|---|
| bushcraft | housecraft | statecraft |
| filmcraft | needlecraft | witchcraft |
| handicrafts | stagecraft | woodcraft |

# cross-

## 1 Movement

PRODUCTIVE USE: **cross-** combines with nouns that refer to a place or area to form adjectives. Adjectives formed in this way describe something that moves across the place or area mentioned. For example, a 'cross-country' race takes place across fields and the open countryside instead of along roads or a running track; a 'cross-channel' ferry sails across the English Channel.

## cross-

*He was in training for a cross-country run.*
*The cross-channel ferry problems should soon sort themselves out.*
*They exchanged cross-table chat with other diners.*

Here are some examples of words with this meaning:

| | | | |
|---|---|---|---|
| cross-border | cross-channel | cross-court | cross-harbour |
| cross-campus | cross-country | cross-frontier | cross-town |

Note that **cross-** occasionally combines in this way with adjectives.

*...a large cross-national survey.*

## 2 Position or direction

**cross-** combines with nouns and adjectives to form new nouns and adjectives. Words formed in this way refer to or describe something that is positioned at, or that moves at, an angle to something else. For example, a 'crosswind' is a strong wind that blows across the direction that vehicles are travelling in; if someone is sitting 'cross-legged', they are sitting on the floor with their legs in the shape of a cross.

**Spelling:** Words formed in this way are written with a hyphen with the exception of 'crossroads' and 'crosswind', which are written as one word.

*These cars have poor stability on motorways in crosswinds.*
*The bird settled on a cross-beam near the top of the thatch.*
*A sudden cross-gust of cold air came heavy with the smell of pines.*

Here is a list of words with this meaning:

| | | | |
|---|---|---|---|
| cross-bar | cross-draught | cross-gust | crossroads |
| cross-beam | cross-flow | cross-legged | crosswind |
| cross-current | cross-grained | cross-piece | |

## 3 More than one person or thing

**cross-** combines with nouns and adjectives to form new nouns and adjectives. Words formed in this way refer to or describe something that takes place between, or is relevant to, two or more people or things. For example, a 'cross-reference' is a note in one part of a book which tells the reader that there is relevant or more detailed information in another part of it; a 'cross-cultural' organization involves or deals with more than one culture.

*It contains many added entries and cross-references to help you find what you want.*
*...an influential cross-cultural study of housing policy.*

*The Government is dependent on cross-party support.*

Here is a list of words with this meaning:

| | | |
|---|---|---|
| cross-breed | cross-indexed | cross-reference |
| cross-cultural | cross-party | cross-training |

## Words with other meanings

| | | | |
|---|---|---|---|
| cross-bow | cross-eyed | cross-question | crossword |
| cross-check | crossfire | cross-section | |
| cross-examine | cross-purposes | cross-shape | |

# crypto-

**crypto-** combines with nouns to form words which describe the thing referred to by the original noun as being secret or concealed. It is often used to show that somebody is not being honest about their true beliefs or aims. For example, a 'crypto-fascist' is somebody who secretly believes in the principles of fascism but does not admit that they do; a 'crypto-coalition' is a coalition made in secret.

PRODUCTIVE USE: It is possible to form new words with this meaning by adding **crypto-** to nouns. However, words formed in this way are fairly formal and do not occur frequently.

*The President fulfils a dual role—as a political leader and as crypto-monarch.*
*They thought that I was the sort of crypto-democrat who would try to overturn the government!*

Here are some examples of words with this meaning:

| | | |
|---|---|---|
| crypto-coalition | crypto-fascist | crypto-Trotskyist |
| crypto-communist | crypto-monarch | |
| crypto-democrat | crypto-republican | |

Note that **crypto-** also occurs with this meaning in words formed form stems that are not current words in English. For example, 'cryptography' is the science of analysing and deciphering codes; a 'cryptogenic' disease is a disease whose origin is unknown or obscure.

*...the science of code-making and code-breaking—cryptography.*
*CIA cryptonyms are used in place of true names.*

Here is a list of words with this meaning:

| | | |
|---|---|---|
| cryptogenic | cryptography | cryptonym |
| cryptograph | cryptology | |

# -cy

## 1 A state or quality

-cy combines with adjectives, and occasionally nouns, to form new nouns. Nouns formed in this way refer to the state, quality, or experience described by the adjective. For example, 'pregnancy' is the state of being pregnant; 'accuracy' is the ability to perform a task accurately without making a mistake.

**Spelling:** A final 't' or 'te' is replaced by -cy.

*She lay on the bed, sick from her first pregnancy.*
*The President restored dignity and decency.*
*Cramped homes prevent privacy.*
*There was no hesitancy in his words.*

Here is a list of words with this meaning:

| | | | |
|---|---|---|---|
| accuracy | despondency | inadequacy | obstinacy |
| ascendancy | diplomacy | inconsistency | poignancy |
| buoyancy | discrepancy | inefficiency | potency |
| complacency | efficiency | infancy | pregnancy |
| consistency | expectancy | insufficiency | privacy |
| decency | fluency | intimacy | proficiency |
| deficiency | frequency | irrelevancy | redundancy |
| delicacy | hesitancy | legitimacy | secrecy |
| delinquency | illiteracy | literacy | transparency |
| dependency | immediacy | militancy | urgency |

## 2 Rank, position or occupation

-cy combines with nouns that refer to people with a particular rank, position, or occupation in order to form new nouns. Nouns formed in this way refer directly to that rank, position, or occupation. For example, a 'baronetcy' is the rank or position of a baronet; 'accountancy' is the theory and practice of being an accountant.

**Spelling:** A final 't' or 'te' is replaced by -cy with the exception of 'baronetcy' and 'viscountcy', where the 't' is retained.

*He succeeded to the baronetcy on the death of his father.*
*France takes over the EC presidency from Spain in the second half of this year.*
*David Gower took on the England cricket captaincy again.*
*He had not rejected the idea of candidacy in the coming elections.*

Here is a list of words with this meaning:

| | | | |
|---|---|---|---|
| accountancy | candidacy | consultancy | presidency |
| advocacy | captaincy | magistracy | regency |
| baronetcy | chaplaincy | occupancy | tenancy |
| bureaucracy | chieftaincy | piracy | viscountcy |

## Words with other meanings

| | | | |
|---|---|---|---|
| agency | contingency | fancy | primacy |
| confederacy | currency | legacy | procuracy |
| conservancy | efficacy | mercy | prophecy |
| conspiracy | emergency | pharmacy | tendency |
| constituency | fallacy | policy | |

# de-

## 1 The opposite action

PRODUCTIVE USE: **de-** combines with verbs to form new verbs. Verbs formed in this way describe an action which has the opposite effect of, or reverses, the process described by the original verb. For example, if an organization is 'deregulated', the rules and regulations which control how it operates are removed; if something 'dehumanizes' people, it takes away from them the qualities that make them human.

**Spelling:** Words formed in this way can be written with a hyphen or as one word.

*...measures to deregulate the television industry.*
*Word processors are likely to depersonalize working relationships.*
*Accommodation would have to be decontaminated after exposure to radiation.*

Here are some examples of words with this meaning:

| | | | |
|---|---|---|---|
| deactivate | decompression | dehumanize | demystify |
| decentralize | decongestion | dehydrate | denaturalize |
| decertify | decontaminate | deindustrialize | depersonalize |
| declassify | decouple | dematerialize | depoliticize |
| decolonize | de-emphasize | demilitarize | deregulate |
| decommission | de-escalate | demobilize | destabilize |

Note that a number of verbs combine with 'dis-' rather than **de-** to describe an action which reverses a process.

For more information on prefixes with a negative meaning, see **dis-, il-, non-,** and **un-.**

## 2 The removal of something

PRODUCTIVE USE: **de-** combines with nouns to form verbs which indicate that the thing referred to by the noun is removed. For example, if you 'de-ice' the windows of your car, you remove all the ice from them.

**Spelling:** Words formed in this way can be written with a hyphen or as one word.

# de-

*De-icing the aircraft delayed departures.*
*You should defrost your fridge once a fortnight.*
*...the de-inking of waste paper for recycling.*
*Descale your kettle for faster boiling.*

Here are some examples of words with this meaning:

| | | | | |
|---|---|---|---|---|
| debristle | de-curtain | de-gut | de-ink | descale |
| debug | de-feather | dehouse | delouse | de-skill |
| decoke | defrost | de-ice | de-mist | |

## Words with other meanings

| | | | | |
|---|---|---|---|---|
| debase | deface | degenerate | demoralize | deserve |
| decease | defile | degrade | denote | design |
| decipher | deform | delay | depart | despite |
| declaim | defraud | delegate | depress | detest |
| decrease | defray | delight | derail | devalue |
| decry | defuse | delimit | derange | devote |

# deca-

**deca-** occurs in words which have 'ten' as part of their meaning. For example, a 'decade' is a period of ten years; a 'decathlon' is a sporting competition in which each athlete takes part in ten different events.

Here is a list of words with this meaning:

| | | |
|---|---|---|
| decade | decahedron | decametre |
| decagon | decalitre | decathlon |

# deci-

**deci-** occurs in words which have 'tenth' as part of their meaning. For example, the 'decimal' system involves counting in units of ten.

Here is a list of words with this meaning:

| | | | |
|---|---|---|---|
| decibel | decilitre | decimal | decimetre |

# demi-

**demi-** occurs in words which have 'half' as part of their meaning. For example, a 'demi-god' is a mythological being which is part mortal and part god.

Here is a list of words with this meaning:

| | | |
|---|---|---|
| demi-devil | demi-god | demi-world |

For more information on prefixes which mean 'half', see **half-** and **semi-**.

# derm-

**derm-** occurs in words which have 'skin' as part of their meaning. For example, 'dermatitis' is an inflammation of the skin.

Note that **derm-** sometimes also occurs in the middle of words. For example, your 'epidermis' is the thin protective outer layer of your skin.

Here is a list of words with this meaning:

| | | |
|---|---|---|
| dermal | dermatologist | dermis |
| dermatitis | dermatology | epidermis |

# dia-

**dia-** occurs in words which have 'through', 'across', or 'between' as part of their meaning. For example, a 'diachronic' study shows the development of something through time; a 'dialogue' is a conversation between two or more people.

Here is a list of words with this meaning:

| | | |
|---|---|---|
| diagonal | dialogue | diaphanous |
| dialectic | diameter | diaphragm |

# dis-

## 1 The opposite action

**dis-** combines with verbs to form new verbs. Verbs formed in this way describe an action that has the opposite effect of, or reverses, the process described by the original verb. For example, if you 'disobey' someone, you do not do what they tell you to; if you 'disapprove' of something, you do not like or approve of it.

*In all these years I've never known you to disobey an order.*
*The boy disappeared from the hotel during the night.*
*Mr Binford disapproves of kids using beach houses for holidays.*
*The farmer was riding a mule and was about to dismount.*

Here is a list of words with this meaning:

| | | | |
|---|---|---|---|
| disagree | discontinue | disinherit | displace |
| disallow | discredit | disintegrate | displease |
| disappear | disembark | disinvest | dispossess |
| disapprove | disenfranchise | dislike | disprove |
| disarm | disengage | dislodge | disqualify |
| disassociate | disentangle | dismount | dissatisfy |
| disband | dishearten | disobey | distrust |
| disbelieve | disincline | disorganize | disunite |
| disconnect | disinfect | disown | disuse |

# dis-

Note that **dis-** also combines with this meaning with nouns formed from the verbs listed above.

*There was little disagreement over what needed to be done.*
*Thomas had been feeling a little dissatisfaction with his daughters.*

Note that a number of verbs combine with 'de-' rather than **dis-** to describe an action which reverses a process. See the entry for **de-**.

## 2 Opposite states, attitudes, or qualities

**dis-** combines with adjectives and nouns to form new adjectives and nouns. Words formed in this way describe a state, characteristic, or quality which is the opposite of the one referred to or described by the original noun or adjective. For example, a 'dishonest' person is someone who is not truthful, honest, or able to be trusted; a 'disadvantage' is something in someone's character or situation which causes them problems or difficulties.

*The hard-working carpenter had never done a dishonest thing in his life.*
*...vast and disorderly assemblies of soldiers.*
*Her letter caused him some discomfort.*
*I stared at Judith in disbelief, but I could see she meant what she said.*

Here is a list of words with this meaning:

| | | | |
|---|---|---|---|
| disadvantage | disfavour | disinterested | disproportionate |
| disbelief | disharmony | disloyal | disreputable |
| discomfort | dishonest | disobedience | disrepute |
| discontent | dishonour | disobliging | disrespect |
| discourteous | disincentive | disorder | disservice |
| discourtesy | disingenuous | disorderly | dissimilar |

For more information on prefixes with a negative meaning, see **de-**, **il-**, **non-**, and **un-**.

## Words with other meanings

| | | | |
|---|---|---|---|
| disappoint | discourage | disillusion | display |
| disarray | discourse | disintegrate | disquiet |
| discharge | discover | disjointed | disregard |
| disclaim | disease | dislocate | disrepair |
| disclose | disembodied | dislodge | dissolve |
| discolour | disfigure | dismiss | distaste |
| disconcert | disgrace | disparity | |
| discount | dishearten | displace | |

# -dom

## 1 A state or condition

PRODUCTIVE USE: **-dom** combines with nouns and adjectives to form new nouns. Nouns formed in this way refer to the experience of whatever is indicated by the original nouns and adjectives. For example, 'freedom' is the state of being free; 'stardom' is the state or experience of being a star or celebrity.

**Spelling:** The noun formed from 'wise' is 'wisdom'.

*In the world of today political freedom is still rare.*
*...the accumulated wisdom and knowledge of society.*
*He had had long experience of outwitting officialdom.*

Here are some examples of words with this meaning:

| | | | |
|---|---|---|---|
| boredom | earldom | hippiedom | princedom |
| chiefdom | freedom | martyrdom | stardom |
| dukedom | gangsterdom | officialdom | wisdom |

Note that 'dukedom', 'earldom' and 'princedom' all have two meanings and are included in both sections of this entry.

## 2 A realm or territory

**-dom** also combines with titles or names to refer to the land that someone controls. For example, a 'kingdom' is the land or country that a king rules over; 'Christendom' is an old-fashioned word that refers to the countries and peoples that are Christian and follow Christ's teachings.

*The kingdom had shrunk, it had been reduced to a handful of villages.*
*...a princedom by the sea.*

Here is a list of words with this meaning:

| | | |
|---|---|---|
| Christendom | earldom | princedom |
| dukedom | kingdom | |

# double-

## 1 Two

PRODUCTIVE USE: **double-** combines with nouns, adjectives, and verbs to form words which indicate that there are two of something or that something happens twice. For example, a 'double-decker' bus has two decks or levels; if you 'double-check' something, you check it for a second time to make sure it is correct or safe.

# double-

*He was the best double-decker driver in Stroud.*
*...a double-edged rake of heavy gauge metal.*
*The first issue had a double-page spread.*
*...a double-barrelled shotgun.*

Here are some examples of words with this meaning:

| | | | |
|---|---|---|---|
| double-action | double-doors | double-locked | double-sided |
| double-barrelled | double-edged | double-page | double-strength |
| double-breasted | double-glazed | double-parked | |
| double-check | double-handed | double-pronged | |
| double-decker | double-length | double-seamed | |

## 2 Deception

**Double-** combines with a small number of verbs and nouns to form
new verbs and nouns which express the idea that one person is
deceiving another. For example, if someone 'double-crosses' you,
they cheat you by pretending that they are doing what you had
planned or agreed together, when in fact they are doing something
else; 'double-talk' is speech or writing which has two possible
meanings and which is meant to be confusing.

*You want me to double-cross the man I work for?*
*...double-dealing, innuendo and character assassination.*
*...bureaucratic double-talk.*

Here is a list of words with this meaning:

| | | | |
|---|---|---|---|
| double-cross | double-deal | double-dealing | double-talk |

### Words with other meanings

| | | | |
|---|---|---|---|
| double-act | double-bill | double-jointed | double-time |
| double-bed | double-dutch | double-take | |

# down-

## 1 Direction or position

**down-** combines with nouns and verbs to form words which
describe someone or something as moving towards, or being
situated in, a lower place or position. For example, if you go
'downhill', you move down a slope or hill towards a lower place; if
your eyes are 'downcast', they are looking towards the ground.

*The car lurched forward and began to speed downhill.*
*They were steering downriver towards the open water of the Broads.*

*I am paralysed from the armpits downwards.*

Here is a list of words with this meaning:

| | | | |
|---|---|---|---|
| down-draught | downstage | downswing | downwind |
| downhill | downstairs | downward | |
| downriver | downstream | downwards | |

## 2 Becoming worse

**down-** combines with nouns and verbs to form new nouns and verbs. Words formed in this way indicate that something has become worse than it was previously. For example, when the economy of a country suffers a 'downturn', it becomes less efficient; someone's 'downfall' is their failure or ruin.

*The company blamed its downturn on interest rates.*
*These strikes brought about the downfall of the country's leader.*
*We are downgrading the quality of our lives.*

Here is a list of words with this meaning:

| | | | | |
|---|---|---|---|---|
| downfall | downgrade | downplay | downtrend | downturn |

### Words with other meanings

| | | | |
|---|---|---|---|
| downbeat | downmarket | downpour | downside |
| downcast | down-payment | downright | downtown |

# -down

PRODUCTIVE USE: **-down** combines with nouns which refer to parts of the body in order to form adverbs which describe the position in which something is done. For example, if somebody walks 'head-down', they have their head lowered; if you place your hand on something 'palm-down', you touch it with the palm of your hand.

*The pussmoth caterpillar browses head-down on leaves.*
*I brought my right hand flattened and palm-down against the side of my neck.*
*I watched while a plane flew nose-down and released its load against the base of a hill.*
*A hundred little boats lie belly-down on the shore.*

Here are some examples of words with this meaning:

| | | |
|---|---|---|
| belly-down | head-down | palm-down |
| face-down | nose-down | top-down |

### Words with other meanings

| | | | |
|---|---|---|---|
| breakdown | eiderdown | sundown | tumbledown |
| crackdown | showdown | thumbs-down | |
| dressing-down | splashdown | touchdown | |

# dys-

**dys-** occurs in words which have 'abnormal', 'diseased', or 'unpleasant' as part of their meaning. For example, if someone has 'dysentery' they have an infection in their intestines; 'dyslexia' is an abnormal brain condition which causes difficulty in reading.

Note that these words are formal and usually medical.

Here is a list of words with this meaning:

| | | | | |
|---|---|---|---|---|
| dysentery | dysfunction | dyslexia | dyspepsia | dystrophy |

# eco-

**eco-** occurs in words which refer to or describe things that are connected with the environment in which plants, animals, and people live. For example, 'ecology' is the study of the relationships between plants, animals, people, and their environment; the 'ecosystem' of a place is the relationship between plants, animals, and their environment.

*The clearing of the jungle is threatening the delicate ecology of the rainforests.*
*Forest fires are an additional danger where the ecosystem is particularly fragile.*

Here is a list of words with this meaning:

| | | | |
|---|---|---|---|
| ecologist | ecology | ecosphere | ecosystem |

PRODUCTIVE USE: **eco-** combines with nouns and adjectives to form new nouns and adjectives. Words formed in this way indicate that the person or thing mentioned by the original noun or adjective is connected with the environment.

Note that words formed in this way are fairly uncommon and usually occur in newspapers or magazines.

*Man is moving into a totally new stage of eco-technological development.*
*When natural controls are removed, population explosions and eco-disasters can occur.*

Here are some examples of words with this meaning:

| | | |
|---|---|---|
| eco-catastrophe | eco-doom | eco-philosopher |
| eco-disaster | eco-freak | eco-technological |

### Words with other meanings:

| | | | | |
|---|---|---|---|---|
| economic | economical | economics | economize | economy |

# -ectomy

**-ectomy** occurs in medical words which refer to the surgical removal of a part of the body. For example, a 'tonsillectomy' is a surgical operation to have your tonsils removed; a 'hysterectomy' is a surgical operation to remove a woman's womb.

Here is a list of words with this meaning:

| | | |
|---|---|---|
| appendectomy | mastectomy | tonsillectomy |
| hysterectomy | splenectomy | vasectomy |

# -ed

## 1 Past tense and past participles

**-ed** combines with the base forms of verbs to form the past tense and past participles.

*One of the men talked about getting married.*
*We have waited too long for our freedom.*

## 2 Past participles used as adjectives

The past participles of transitive verbs are often used as adjectives indicating that something has been affected in some way.

*...strips of cooked meat.*
*...hordes of excited children.*
*I got bored at the farm in Devon.*

The past participles of a few intransitive verbs are used as adjectives indicating that a person or thing has done something. For example, a 'retired' person is someone who has retired.

*The escaped convict was hiding in the loft.*
*...a retired police officer.*
*Electrical fittings should be removed by a qualified electrician.*

**-ed** also combines with nouns to form adjectives which describe someone or something as having a particular feature.

*...a bearded old man.*
*...intricately patterned bead necklaces.*
*...a three-mile stretch of heavily wooded, hilly countryside.*

## 3 Forming compound adjectives

Some past participles ending in **-ed** combine with other words to form compound adjectives.

*...his face was pear-shaped.*

# -ed

*...a maroon-coloured car.*
*She is blonde, blue-eyed, and just under six feet tall.*

Note that there are a number of adjectives ending in **-ed** that are formed from stems which are not current words in English.

*...the clatter of the antiquated air-conditioning machine.*
*We are, most of us, doomed to unhappiness.*
*The parched soil soaked up the rain.*

Here is a list of words with this meaning:

| | | | |
|---|---|---|---|
| antiquated | beloved | doomed | sophisticated |
| ashamed | concerted | indebted | tinned |
| assorted | crazed | parched | |
| belated | deceased | rugged | |

For more information about the past participle of verbs, see the Collins Cobuild English Grammar.

# -ee

## 1 Someone who is affected by an action

**-ee** combines with transitive verbs which describe actions to form nouns. Nouns formed in this way refer to the person that the action is being done to. For example, an 'employee' is someone who is employed by a firm; a 'trainee' is someone who is being trained to do a particular job.

*Conflict arose between employer and employee.*
*...the year's nominee for the exchange scheme.*
*...various appointees to lesser posts.*

Here is a list of words with this meaning:

| | | | | |
|---|---|---|---|---|
| addressee | deportee | examinee | licensee | trainee |
| amputee | detainee | franchisee | mortgagee | transferee |
| appointee | employee | internee | nominee | trustee |
| assignee | evacuee | interviewee | payee | |

## 2 Someone who performs an action

**-ee** combines with some verbs to form nouns which refer to someone who has performed a particular action. For example, an 'escapee' is someone who has escaped from captivity; a 'devotee' of a subject or an activity is someone who is very enthusiastic about it.

*Road blocks by police and prison staff ensured that no escapee would get through.*
*...absentees from school.*

*...a Church of England measure which would allow divorcees to be ordained.*

Here is a list of words with this meaning:

| | | | |
|---|---|---|---|
| absentee | devotee | escapee | returnee |
| cohabitee | divorcee | retiree | |

## Words with other meanings

| | | | |
|---|---|---|---|
| matinee | puree | refugee | soiree |
| negligee | referee | repartee | toupee |

# electro-

**electro-** occurs in words which have 'electric' as part of their meaning. For example, if you are 'electrocuted' you are accidentally killed or badly injured by touching something that is connected to a source of electricity; 'electromagnetic' effects are caused by electrical and magnetic forces.

Here is a list of words with this meaning:

| | | |
|---|---|---|
| electrocardiograph | electrode | electromagnetic |
| electrochemistry | electrolysis | electronic |
| electrocute | electrolyte | electro-nuclear |
| electrocution | electromagnet | electroplating |

# em-, en-

**em-** and **en-** occur in verbs that describe the process of moving into or being placed into a different state or condition, or being placed in a different position. For example, if something 'enables' you to do something, it gives you an opportunity so that you become able to do it; if you 'enrich' something, you improve its quality or value by adding something else to it; if someone is 'entombed', they are buried underground.

**Spelling:** em- combines with words beginning with 'b', 'm', or 'p'; en- combines with words beginning with other letters.

*She moved her head to enable her to speak more clearly.*
*He nodded his head and smiled to encourage her.*

## em-, en-

*He was emboldened by his success.*
*The security of the country was not endangered.*
*We embarked on the MacLeods' boat.*
*She imagined herself enfolding him in her arms.*

Here is a list of words with this meaning:

| | | | | |
|---|---|---|---|---|
| embark | encase | enfeeble | ennoble | entangle |
| embed | encircle | enfold | enrage | enthrone |
| embitter | enclose | enforce | enrapture | entomb |
| embody | encode | enfranchise | enrich | entrance |
| embolden | encourage | engulf | enshrine | entrap |
| empower | encrust | enlarge | enshroud | entrench |
| enable | endanger | enliven | enslave | entwine |
| encamp | endear | enmesh | ensnare | |

### Words with other meanings

| | | | | |
|---|---|---|---|---|
| embalm | enchant | engrain | enlighten | entitle |
| embark | encompass | engrave | enlist | entreat |
| embattled | encounter | engross | ensue | entrust |
| embrace | engender | enjoin | ensure | |
| enact | engorge | enjoy | entail | |

## -en

### 1 Changing the quality or state of something

**-en** combines with nouns and adjectives that refer to or describe a quality or state in order to form verbs. Verbs formed in this way describe the process of causing something to have a particular quality or to be in a particular state. For example, if a fire 'blackens' a wall, the flames make the wall turn black; if rain 'moistens' the ground, it makes it moist.

*...a small patch of ground, blackened by the ashes of old camp fires.*
*The lacquer dries very quickly and hardens in an hour.*
*...fruit juice sweetened with sugar.*

Verbs formed in this way can also be used to express the idea that someone or something has more of a quality than it had previously. For example, if a river 'deepens', it becomes deeper than it was before; if your hair is 'lightened' by the sun, it becomes lighter than it usually is.

*She laughed, and that seemed to deepen her voice.*

*She was trying on a blue suede jacket and wondering if she could have the sleeves shortened.*

Here is a list of words with this meaning:

| | | | | |
|---|---|---|---|---|
| blacken | fatten | loosen | slacken | weaken |
| brighten | flatten | moisten | stiffen | whiten |
| broaden | freshen | quicken | straighten | widen |
| cheapen | harden | quieten | strengthen | worsen |
| dampen | heighten | redden | sweeten | |
| darken | lengthen | sharpen | thicken | |
| deafen | lessen | shorten | tighten | |
| deepen | lighten | sicken | toughen | |

## 2 Indicating what something is made of or resembles

**-en** combines with nouns to form adjectives which describe something that is made from or resembles the substance referred to by the original noun. For example, a 'woollen' jumper is made of wool; if something is 'silken', it is smooth, soft and luxurious, like silk.

*People here wear woollen clothing even on hot days.*
*The traditional breakfast of porridge was cooked in earthen pots over a fire built among three rocks.*
*...a rosy, frail girl with bright golden hair.*

Here is a list of words with this meaning:

| | | | |
|---|---|---|---|
| ashen | golden | silken | woollen |
| earthen | leaden | waxen | |
| flaxen | oaken | wooden | |

### Words with other meanings

| | | | |
|---|---|---|---|
| deaden | enlighten | enliven | hasten | hearten |

# -ence

**-ence** combines with verbs to form nouns. Nouns formed in this way refer to the action, process, or state described by the original verbs. For example, 'insistence' is the act of insisting on something.

*...her insistence on staying in the best hotel.*
*Brian fought off alcoholism and dependence on painkilling drugs.*
*...the scientist revealed the existence of a 'hole' in the ozone layer.*

# -ence

*There was growing concern about the increasing occurrence of food poisoning.*

Here is a list of words with this meaning:

| | | | |
|---|---|---|---|
| adherence | existence | pretence | subsidence |
| coherence | indulgence | recurrence | subsistence |
| correspondence | insistence | reference | transcendence |
| defence | interference | reminiscence | transference |
| dependence | occurrence | residence | |
| divergence | persistence | resurgence | |
| emergence | preference | reverence | |

PRODUCTIVE USE: **-ence** also combines with adjectives ending in 'ent' in order to form nouns. Nouns formed in this way refer to the state or quality described by the original adjectives. For example, 'obedience' is the state of being obedient.

**Spelling:** A final 'ent' is replaced by **-ence**.

*With dreary obedience the choir raised their hands.*
*Working in a group gives you a bit more confidence, because everyone is in the same position.*
*The accident was cause solely by the negligence of another motorist.*

Here are some examples of words with this meaning:

| | | | |
|---|---|---|---|
| absence | convenience | eminence | obedience |
| adolescence | decadence | impotence | patience |
| affluence | diffidence | indifference | presence |
| benevolence | diligence | innocence | prominence |
| competence | disobedience | insolence | reticence |
| confidence | eloquence | intelligence | violence |

## Words with other meanings

| | | | |
|---|---|---|---|
| ambience | continence | influence | quintessence |
| audience | credence | jurisprudence | science |
| cadence | essence | licence | sentence |
| circumference | evidence | offence | sequence |
| coincidence | experience | pestilence | silence |
| conference | incidence | prescience | valence |
| conscience | inexperience | providence | |

# -ent

**-ent** combines with verbs to form adjectives and nouns. Words formed in this way describe or refer to a person or thing that performs the action or that experiences the process described by the original verb. For example, if one thing is 'different' from another, it differs from it; a 'student' is someone who studies something.

*The new house was not much different from the old one.*

*Gradually the children became less dependent on their parents.*
*A woman holds out her hand for money, importunate, insistent,*
*desperate.*
*...a farm-worker and day-release student at the Agricultural*
*Training Centre.*

Here is a list of words with this meaning:

| | | | |
|---|---|---|---|
| absorbent | dependent | insistent | student |
| ascendent | different | persistent | superintendent |
| correspondent | existent | respondent | transcendent |

**Words with other meanings**

| | | | |
|---|---|---|---|
| accent | consistent | intent | patent |
| assent | content | lament | potent |
| cogent | extent | moment | stringent |
| consent | fluent | parent | tangent |

# equi-

**equi-** occurs in words which have 'equal' or 'equally' as part of their
meaning. For example, a place that is 'equidistant' from two other
places is exactly the same distance from both of them; two things
that are 'equivalent' have the same use, size, or value as each other.

Here is a list of words with this meaning:

| | | |
|---|---|---|
| equidistant | equilibrium | equivocal |
| equilateral | equivalent | equivocate |

# -er

## 1 Forming comparative adjectives

**-er** combines with qualitative adjectives to form comparative
adjectives. Comparative adjectives describe someone or something
as having more of a particular characteristic or quality than
someone or something else. For example, if you are 'older' than
someone else, you have been alive longer than they have; if one
person is 'sillier' than another, their behaviour is more foolish.

PRODUCTIVE USE: **-er** combines with this meaning with adjectives of
one syllable.

**Spelling:** A final 'd', 'b', 'g', 't', or 'n' preceded by a single vowel is
doubled before adding **-er**. A final 'e' is replaced by **-er**.

*Andrea was two years older than me.*
*Does she look bigger and fatter to you?*

# -er

*I have cousins only just ten years younger than myself.*

Here are some examples of words with this meaning formed from adjectives of one syllable:

| | | | | |
|---|---|---|---|---|
| bigger | fatter | longer | safer | thinner |
| brighter | fuller | louder | slower | tougher |
| colder | larger | newer | smaller | wetter |
| darker | later | older | softer | younger |
| deeper | lighter | sadder | thicker | |

Note that the comparative form of 'good' is 'better', and the comparative form of 'bad' is 'worse'.

**-er** also combines with this meaning with some adjectives of two syllables.

**Spelling:** A final 'y' is replaced by 'i' before adding **-er**. A final 'e' is replaced by **-er**.

*Two hours earlier I had made the acquaintance of the hall porter.*
*I'm definitely happier than I was years ago.*
*You're much cleverer than she is.*

Here is a list of words with this meaning formed from adjectives of two syllables:

| | | | | |
|---|---|---|---|---|
| angrier | funnier | lovelier | politer | steadier |
| busier | gentler | luckier | prettier | stupider |
| cleverer | handsomer | maturer | remoter | tinier |
| dirtier | happier | narrower | shallower | |
| earlier | heavier | obscurer | sillier | |
| friendlier | likelier | pleasanter | simpler | |

**-er** sometimes combines with this meaning with colour adjectives.

*His face was redder than usual and he seemed embarrassed.*
*The clouds were whiter yesterday than they are today.*

## 2 Occupation or pastime

**-er** combines with verbs to form nouns. Nouns formed in this way refer to people who do the action described by the original verb, usually because it is their job. For example, a 'baker' is someone who bakes and sells bread and cakes; the 'leader' of a group of people or organization is the person who leads it or who is in charge of it.

*He sometimes helped Mr Mueller in the kitchen as a cook and baker.*
*The driver went back and started the bus.*
*I went to London and tried to earn my living as a portrait painter.*

*She was a student teacher, spending a year in a school in Cambridge.*

Here is a list of words with this meaning:

| | | | |
|---|---|---|---|
| baker | lecturer | producer | teacher |
| commander | manager | reader | waiter |
| driver | observer | reporter | walker |
| employer | painter | rider | winner |
| farmer | photographer | runner | worker |
| leader | player | speaker | writer |

**-er** also combines with verbs to form nouns that refer to things rather than people. For example, a 'computer' is an electronic machine that can perform computations and that stores and retrieves information.

*The entire operation is done by computer.*
*Have you seen my electric food mixer?*

Here is a list of words with this meaning:

| | | | | |
|---|---|---|---|---|
| blender | digger | holder | recorder | slicer |
| computer | duster | mixer | roller | strainer |
| cooker | grinder | mower | sander | strainer |
| cutter | hanger | printer | scraper | wiper |

Note that a number of nouns formed from verbs and with this meaning end in **-or** rather than **-er**.

For more information see **-or**.

# -ery

## 1 Actions

**-ery** combines with some verbs to form nouns which refer to an action. For example, when someone makes a 'discovery,' they find out or discover something that they did not previously know; if someone makes a 'delivery', they deliver something.

**Spelling:** A final 'e' or 'er' is replaced by **-ery**.

*Two British researchers have made a discovery about 'computer viruses'.*
*...everyone there was arrested on charges of armed robbery.*
*...a persistent campaign of mockery by the satirical fortnightly magazine Private Eye.*

# -ery

*The cheque might have been a forgery.*

Here is a list of words with this meaning:

| | | | |
|---|---|---|---|
| bribery | debauchery | embroidery | mockery |
| butchery | delivery | flattery | recovery |
| cajolery | discovery | forgery | robbery |
| cookery | drudgery | lechery | trickery |

## 2 Behaviour

PRODUCTIVE USE: **-ery** combines with adjectives which describe a type of behaviour, or with nouns which refer to a person who behaves in that way, in order to form new nouns. Nouns formed in this way refer to that type of behaviour. For example, 'savagery' is the violent cruelty associated with savages; 'foolery' is foolish behaviour.

Note that many of these words are old-fashioned and are not used very often.

*Dan went for him with sudden savagery.*
*'What is the purpose of this foolery?'*
*...the prudery of the Victorians.*
*...an incident of unpardonable brutality and thuggery.*

Here are some examples of words with this meaning:

| | | | |
|---|---|---|---|
| bravery | knavery | savagery | tomfoolery |
| buffoonery | prudery | snobbery | |
| foolery | roguery | thuggery | |

## 3 Places

**-ery** combines with verbs or nouns to form new nouns. Nouns formed in this way refer to a place where something is done or kept. For example, a 'bakery' is a place where bread and cakes are baked; a 'piggery' is a building where pigs are kept.

*I met her at the bakery where we were both buying brownies.*
*...a shrubbery of lilac bushes and evergreens.*
*Five gallons of milk a day went to the Stowmarket Creamery.*
*...a fish hatchery in Idaho.*
*...a two- hundred acre vineyard and a well established winery.*

Here is a list of words with this meaning:

| | | | |
|---|---|---|---|
| bakery | creamery | nunnery | refinery |
| brewery | distillery | nursery | shrubbery |
| cannery | fishery | orangery | tannery |
| colliery | gunnery | piggery | winery |

## 4 Groups

A number of words ending in **-ery** refer to a group or collection of objects of a particular kind. For example, 'jewellery' refers to ornaments you wear on your body, such as rings and bracelets; 'pottery' refers to pots, dishes, and other articles made of clay.

*They were all fond of jewellery, and some wore rings and some fine gold chains.*
*There was no electricity, the machinery had failed again.*
*...the brilliance of two huge crimson flower vases spilling with blossoms and greenery.*

Here is a list of words with this meaning:

| | | | |
|---|---|---|---|
| artillery | finery | ironmongery | pottery |
| crockery | greenery | jewellery | scenery |
| drapery | imagery | machinery | |

### Words with other meanings

| | | | | |
|---|---|---|---|---|
| adultery | cemetery | hosiery | misery | stationery |
| archery | cutlery | joinery | monastery | surgery |
| artery | effrontery | livery | mystery | treachery |
| battery | gallery | lottery | slavery | upholstery |
| celery | grocery | mastery | sorcery | |

# -ese

## 1 Origin

**-ese** combines with the names of places to form words which describe someone or something as being from the place mentioned. For example, a 'Chinese' person comes from China; the 'Viennese' Opera is based in Vienna; the 'Maltese' refers to all the people who come from Malta.

*He was a Chinese businessman.*
*...classical Balinese dance movements.*
*Her father was Portuguese.*
*She arranged to deliver a petition to the Japanese.*

Here is a list of words with this meaning:

| | | | | |
|---|---|---|---|---|
| Balinese | Japanese | Maltese | Portuguese | Taiwanese |
| Burmese | Javanese | Milanese | Senegalese | Viennese |
| Chinese | Lebanese | Nepalese | Sudanese | Vietnamese |

## 2 Languages

**-ese** combines with nouns which refer to countries in order to form new nouns. Nouns formed in this way refer to the language spoken in that country. For example, 'Japanese' is the language spoken in Japan; 'Portuguese' is the language spoken in Portugal.

*Mr Takahashi was speaking in animated Japanese.*
*When they saw us they rushed forward, chanting in Chinese.*

Here is a list of words with this meaning:

| | | | |
|---|---|---|---|
| Burmese | Japanese | Maltese | Vietnamese |
| Chinese | Javanese | Portuguese | |

PRODUCTIVE USE: **-ese** combines in this way with nouns to form new nouns. Nouns formed in this way refer to an unattractive or confusing way of speaking or writing that is typical of the person or place mentioned. For example 'journalese' refers to the way in which journalists speak and write; 'Brooklynese' is the accent and dialect spoken by people from Brooklyn.

*'Torturous' is now common journalese.*
*...a classic phrase of diplomatic officialese.*
*He was already speaking Americanese.*

Here are some examples of words with this meaning:

| | | | |
|---|---|---|---|
| Americanese | Brooklynese | journalese | officialese |

# -esque

PRODUCTIVE USE: **-esque** combines with names of famous people, for example writers, composers, or painters, in order to form adjectives. Adjectives formed in this way describe someone or something that is similar in style to something made or done by the person mentioned. For example, if a piece of music is 'Haydnesque', it is similar in style to music by the composer Haydn; if a play is 'Pinteresque', it is similar in style to plays written by Harold Pinter.

*The orchestra's performance was perfectly Haydnesque.*
*He loved being the centre of attraction and dropped easily into Tarzanesque poses.*
*...this Chaplinesque incident roused the household.*
*...an extraordinary Rembrandtesque painting by Murillo.*

Here are some examples of words with this meaning:

| | | |
|---|---|---|
| Beethovenesque | Haydnesque | Rembrandtesque |
| Chaplinesque | Hoffmanesque | Tarzanesque |
| Dantesque | Pinteresque | |

# -ess

**-ess** combines with nouns that refer to a person or animal in order to form new nouns. Nouns formed in this way refer to a woman or a female animal. For example, a 'princess' is a woman who has a rank equal to a prince, or who is married to a prince; a 'lioness' is a female lion.

*...the king's younger daughter, the Princess Elizabeth.*
*A lion and lioness leapt over the walls of a cattle pen.*
*Thynne's bride was the richest heiress in England.*

Here is a list of words with this meaning:

| | | | | |
|---|---|---|---|---|
| actress | empress | lioness | priestess | viscountess |
| authoress | goddess | manageress | princess | waitress |
| countess | heiress | mistress | stewardess | |
| duchess | hostess | pantheress | tigress | |

Note that many people do not like to use words ending in **-ess** to refer to women, and prefer to use a noun which can refer to both men and women. For example, a female writer is more likely to be referred to as an 'author' than as an 'authoress'.

For more information on nouns that refer specifically to women, see **-woman.**

# -est

**-est** combines with qualitative adjectives to form superlative adjectives. Superlative adjectives describe someone or something as having more of the quality mentioned than anything else of its kind. For example, if a building is the 'tallest' in the world, there is no other building as tall as that one; if a boy is described as the 'cleverest' in his class, there is no one in his class as clever as him.

Note that superlative adjectives are nearly always preceded by 'the'.

PRODUCTIVE USE: **-est** combines with this meaning with adjectives of one syllable.

**Spelling:** A final 'g', 't', or 'n' preceded by a single vowel is doubled before adding **-est**. A final 'e' is replaced by **-est**.

*The Maharajah was the tallest man she knew.*
*The loudest applause went to John Faddis.*
*When we got inside the cemetery we stopped. It was the biggest one we had ever seen.*
*There are three types of ant-eater. The smallest lives entirely in trees.*

# -est

Here are some examples of words with this meaning formed from adjectives of one syllable:

| | | | | |
|---|---|---|---|---|
| biggest | fattest | longest | slowest | thinnest |
| brightest | fullest | loudest | smallest | toughest |
| coldest | largest | newest | softest | wettest |
| darkest | latest | oldest | tallest | youngest |
| deepest | lightest | saddest | thickest | |

Note that the superlative form of 'good' is 'best', and the superlative form of 'bad' is 'worst'.

**-est** also combines with this meaning with some adjectives of two syllables.

**Spelling:** A final 'y' is replaced by 'i' before adding **-est**. A final 'e' is replaced by **-est**.

Here is a list of words with this meaning formed from adjectives of two syllables:

| | | | | |
|---|---|---|---|---|
| angriest | funniest | likeliest | pleasantest | simplest |
| busiest | gentlest | loveliest | politest | steadiest |
| commonest | handsomest | luckiest | prettiest | stupidest |
| dirtiest | happiest | maturest | remotest | tiniest |
| easiest | heaviest | narrowest | shallowest | |
| friendliest | likeliest | obscurest | silliest | |

**-est** sometimes combines with this meaning with colour adjectives.

*...driving a shining new car through some of the greenest scenery in America.*
*...the reddest shooting star they had ever seen.*

# Euro-

PRODUCTIVE USE: **Euro-** combines with nouns to form new nouns. Nouns formed in this way refer to something that is connected with Europe or the European Community (EC) in some way. For example, a 'Euro-election' is held to elect the members of the European Parliament; a 'Eurocheque' is a cheque you can use in any country in Europe.

Note that words formed in this way usually occur in newspapers or in broadcast reports of news.

**Spelling: Euro-** is always written with a capital letter. Words formed in this way are usually written with a hyphen, but some of the more common ones are written as one word.

*...a bitterly contested Euro-election campaign.*
*Euro-MPs have been banned from flying first class on foreign trips.*
*...burgundy-coloured Euro-passports.*

*...a London-based Euro-bank.*

Here are some examples of words with this meaning:

| | | |
|---|---|---|
| Euro-bank | Euro-constituency | Euro-passport |
| Eurobond | Euro-currency | Euro-policy |
| Euro-campaign | Euro-election | Euro-socialism |
| Euro-candidate | Euromoney | Euro-summit |
| Eurocheque | Euro-MP | |
| Euro-communism | Europarliament | |

**Euro-** occasionally combines with adjectives such as 'African' or 'Chinese' to form new adjectives. Adjectives formed in this way describe an organization or activity that involves Europe and the continent or nation mentioned.

*...Euro-American political domination.*
*...a Euro-African tennis match.*

# ever-

## 1 Always

PRODUCTIVE USE: **ever-** combines with present participles and adjectives to form new adjectives. Adjectives formed in this way describe something that continually performs the action mentioned, or that always has the characteristics or qualities mentioned. For example, when the amount of something is 'ever-increasing', it is always increasing; if something such as food is 'ever-available', it is always available and therefore easy to obtain.

**Spelling:** Words formed in this way are written with a hyphen with the exception of 'everlasting', which is written as one word.

*...the ever-increasing demand for energy.*
*...ever-available supplies of consumer goods.*
*...the everlasting snows of the mighty Himalayas.*
*...the ever-present threat of physical danger.*
*I could hear nothing but the sound of ever-moving water.*

Here are some examples of words with this meaning:

| | | |
|---|---|---|
| ever-available | ever-helpful | ever-present |
| ever-changing | ever-increasing | ever-rising |
| ever-decreasing | everlasting | ever-shrinking |
| ever-diminishing | ever-lengthening | ever-smiling |
| ever-efficient | ever-moving | ever-watchful |
| ever-expanding | ever-narrowing | ever-widening |
| ever-faithful | ever-open | ever-willing |
| ever-growing | ever-popular | ever-worsening |

# ever-

## 2 Increasingly

PRODUCTIVE USE: **ever-** combines with the comparative form of adjectives to form new adjectives. Adjectives formed in this way describe someone or something that has an increasing amount of the characteristic or quality described by the original adjective. For example, if you describe someone as 'ever-bolder', you mean that you think that they are becoming more and more bold; if something is becoming 'ever-smaller', it is continually getting smaller.

*Thelma encouraged me to ask ever-bolder questions.*
*I focused in on an ever-smaller segment of the slide.*
*Men will build homes in ever-stranger places.*
*...the ever-colder nights.*
*The sides closed in, towering above us with an ever-closer proximity.*

Here are some examples of words with this meaning:

| | | | |
|---|---|---|---|
| ever-bolder | ever-faster | ever-larger | ever-smaller |
| ever-briefer | ever-fiercer | ever-narrower | ever-stranger |
| ever-closer | ever-greater | ever-scarcer | ever-stronger |
| ever-colder | ever-higher | ever-shorter | ever-wider |

### Words with other meanings

evergreen      evermore

# ex-

PRODUCTIVE USE: **ex-** combines with nouns that refer to people in order to form new nouns. Nouns formed in this way refer to someone who used to be the thing referred to by the original noun. For example, the 'ex-president' of a country used to be its president; an 'ex-policeman' is someone who used to work as a policeman.

*...Jose Luis Bustamante, ex-president of Peru.*
*...Gaylord Koffritz, Renata's ex-husband.*
*...first-hand accounts of ex-inmates of mental hospitals.*
*Ex-lovers rarely meet again or even write.*

Here are some examples of words with this meaning:

| | | | |
|---|---|---|---|
| ex-accountant | ex-employer | ex-minister | ex-secretary |
| ex-boxer | ex-friend | ex-policeman | ex-soldier |
| ex-chairman | ex-husband | ex-president | ex-tenant |
| ex-communist | ex-inmate | ex-prisoner | ex-wife |
| ex-convict | ex-journalist | ex-professor | |
| ex-dictator | ex-lover | ex-pupil | |

# extra-

## 1 Very

PRODUCTIVE USE: **extra-** combines with adjectives to form new adjectives. Adjectives formed in this way describe something as having a large amount of the quality or characteristic described by the original adjective. For example, if you describe something as 'extra-special', you mean that you think that it is very special; if something is 'extra-large', it is very large.

*'A spectacular goal, extra-special,' the West Ham manager enthused.*
*...an extra-strong rope for towing vehicles.*
*...the extra-bright child.*
*...a special edition of the book on extra-thin paper.*

Here are some examples of words with this meaning:

| | | | |
|---|---|---|---|
| extra-bright | extra-large | extra-small | extra-strong |
| extra-fine | extra-long | extra-smooth | extra-thin |
| extra-firm | extra-low | extra-soft | |
| extra-hard | extra-short | extra-solid | |
| extra-hot | extra-slow | extra-special | |

## 2 Outside

**extra-** also combines with adjectives to form new adjectives that describe something as being outside, beyond, or different from what was described by the original adjective. For example, 'extra-curricular' activities are those you do outside the normal curriculum or timetable in schools or colleges; anything described as 'extra-terrestrial' comes from beyond the planet.

*Many students benefit greatly from involvement in extra-curricular activities.*
*I have an open mind on the subject of so-called telepathy and extra-sensory perception.*
*Before the nineteenth century, the extra-European world supplied Europe with luxuries.*

Here is a list of words with this meaning:

| | | |
|---|---|---|
| extra-curricular | extra-mural | extra-terrestrial |
| extra-European | extra-parliamentary | extra-territorial |
| extra-marital | extra-sensory | |

# -first

PRODUCTIVE USE: **-first** combines with nouns which refer to parts of the body in order to form adverbs. Adverbs formed in this way

# -first

indicate that a person or animal moves with the part of their body that is mentioned pointing in the direction in which they are moving. For example, if you move somewhere 'head-first', your head is the part of your body that is furthest forward as you are moving.

*Douglas had fallen head-first into the snow.*
*When gorillas descend, they do so feet-first, lowering themselves with their arms.*
*The foot is placed on the ground heel-first.*

Here are some examples of words with this meaning:

| | | |
|---|---|---|
| chin-first | feet-first | heel-first |
| face-first | head-first | nose-first |

# -fold

PRODUCTIVE USE: **-fold** combines with numbers to form adjectives. Adjectives formed in this way describe something as having a particular number of parts. For example, if you say that something is 'twofold', you mean that it has two equally important parts or reasons.

**Spelling:** Words formed in this way can be written with a hyphen or as one word.

*My interests were twofold; the first to make money, and the second to sell the public reliable goods.*
*Criticisms of the old system were threefold.*
*The aims of the new organization are eight-fold.*

Words formed in this way are occasionally used as adverbs to indicate that something is multiplied a particular number of times.

*Juvenile crimes of violence multiplied seventeenfold in twenty-five years.*

# -folk

**-folk** combines with nouns to form new nouns which refer to groups of people. For example, the 'womenfolk' of a community are the women who live in it; the 'townsfolk' of a town are the people who live there.

Note that nouns formed in this way are old-fashioned and occur infrequently.

*The womenfolk could not use the cricket pavilion.*
*Where did the menfolk of the community work?*

*Pasta and noodles have for years been the staple dishes of economical Italian countryfolk.*

Here is a list of words with this meaning:

countryfolk    kinsfolk    menfolk    townsfolk    womenfolk

For more information on words that refer to people, see **-kind, -man, -people, -person,** and **-woman.**

# fore-

## 1 The front

**fore-** combines with nouns to form new nouns. Nouns formed in this way refer to the front part of something, or to one thing that is at the front of another. For example, a 'foredeck' is the front part of a ship's deck; the 'forelegs' of an animal are its two front legs.

*The wave crashed down on the foredeck of the trawler.*
*...a tall, thin man with a deeply lined forehead.*
*...wiping the sweat from his face with a dirty forearm.*

Here is a list of words with this meaning:

| | | | |
|---|---|---|---|
| forearm | forefoot | foreleg | forepart |
| foredeck | forehead | forelimb | foreshore |

## 2 Before

**fore-** combines with nouns, verbs, and adjectives to form new nouns, verbs, and adjectives. Words formed in this way describe or refer to one thing that comes before and is relevant to another. For example, if you 'forewarn' someone about something, you tell them in advance that you think something unpleasant or dangerous is going to happen; your 'forefathers' are the people from whom you are descended, and whose ways and traditions you have adopted.

*We were forewarned that the food would be terrible.*
*The critics foresaw a long and profitable future for the play.*
*A bee, bumbling lazily up and down the window-pane, gave a foretaste of summer joys.*
*An intelligent film is not necessarily foredoomed to failure.*

Here is a list of words with this meaning:

| | | | |
|---|---|---|---|
| forebears | foreknowledge | foresight | forewarn |
| foreboding | foreordained | forestall | foreword |
| forecast | forerunner | foretaste | |
| foredoomed | foresee | foretell | |
| forefathers | foreshadow | forethought | |

## fore-

### Words with other meanings

| | | | |
|---|---|---|---|
| forearmed | forefront | forego | foremost |
| forefinger | foregather | foreman | forename |

# Franco-

**Franco-** occurs in words which have 'French' or 'France' as part of their meaning. For example, a 'Franco-Italian' agreement is an agreement made between France and Italy.

## free-

**free-** combines with present participles to form adjectives. Adjectives formed in this way describe someone or something as moving or behaving without the restrictions or controls that you might normally expect. For example, traffic that is 'free-flowing' is moving freely, without any obstructions; if someone has a 'free-ranging' mind, their way of thinking is not restricted by one particular set of ideas.

*Freedom from congestion could be achieved only by a new system of free-flowing roads.*
*...free-floating chemicals.*
*...an amazing man with a free-ranging intelligence.*
*Light free-draining land was a prerequisite to success.*
*Kimonos are very popular with men and women and they are both modest and free-moving.*

Here is a list of words with this meaning:

| | | | |
|---|---|---|---|
| free-draining | free-flowing | free-running | free-thinking |
| free-falling | free-moving | free-standing | |
| free-floating | free-ranging | free-swimming | |

## -free

PRODUCTIVE USE: **-free** combines with nouns which refer to something considered to be undesirable in order to form adjectives. Adjectives formed in this way describe something which does not have the thing mentioned. For example, if a source of income is 'tax-free', you do not have to pay tax on it; if someone is 'carefree', they have no troubles, problems, or responsibilities.

**Spelling:** Words formed in this way are written with a hyphen with the exception of 'carefree', which is written as one word.

*...retirement benefits including tax-free cash and a regular income.*

*Not until mid-July do the lakes become ice-free and the snow begins to melt.*
*...to keep our fields clean of weeds and disease-free.*
*An electric car would be pollution-free.*
*It is perfectly possible to live healthily on a meat-free diet.*

Here are some examples of words with this meaning:

| | | | |
|---|---|---|---|
| accident-free | dust-free | meat-free | risk-free |
| additive-free | duty-free | nuclear-free | stress-free |
| carefree | guilt-free | oxygen-free | symptom-free |
| crime-free | ice-free | pain-free | tax-free |
| debt-free | interest-free | pollution-free | trouble-free |
| disease-free | lead-free | rent-free | weed-free |

**-free** also combines in this way with the adjective 'nuclear'.

*...proposals to create European nuclear-free zones.*

# fresh-

PRODUCTIVE USE: **fresh-** combines with the past participles of transitive verbs to form adjectives. Adjectives formed in this way describe something which has been made or done recently. For example, if bread is 'fresh-baked', it has been baked recently; if land is 'fresh-ploughed', it has just been ploughed.

*...the smell of fresh-baked bread.*
*...a vase of fresh-cut flowers.*
*...delicious fresh-fried doughnuts.*
*...several fresh-made jellies.*

Here are some examples of words with this meaning:

| | | | |
|---|---|---|---|
| fresh-baked | fresh-cut | fresh-ironed | fresh-planted |
| fresh-chopped | fresh-fried | fresh-made | fresh-ploughed |

# -ful

## 1 Amounts and measurement

PRODUCTIVE USE: **-ful** combines with nouns that refer to things that can contain or carry things in order to form new nouns. Nouns formed in this way refer to the amount that the container mentioned can hold. For example, a 'teaspoonful' is the amount of a powder or liquid that a teaspoon will hold; an 'armful' of something is the amount of it you can carry in one or both of your arms.

*Add half a teaspoonful of salt to each pint of corn.*
*My school-teacher gave me a bagful of sweets.*

# -ful

*Pour a bucketful of cold water on top of the ash.*
*He drank a mouthful of cold black coffee.*

Here are some examples of words with this meaning:

| | | | |
|---|---|---|---|
| armful | fistful | mouthful | saucerful |
| bagful | glassful | panful | spoonful |
| bottleful | handful | plateful | tablespoonful |
| boxful | houseful | pocketful | tankful |
| bucketful | jugful | roomful | teaspoonful |
| cupful | ladleful | sackful | thimbleful |

## 2 Characteristics and qualities

**-ful** also combines with nouns that refer to a particular
characteristic or quality in order to form adjectives. Adjectives
formed in this way describe someone or something as having a lot of
the characteristic or quality mentioned. For example, if someone or
something is 'beautiful', they are very attractive and pleasing to
look at; if someone is 'deceitful', they tell a lot of lies.

*...a charming boy with the most beautiful hair.*
*It is a large, meaty and flavourful fungus.*
*The vicar called in and said what delightful news it was about John*
*Parr.*
*...a shocking and shameful story.*

Here is a list of words with this meaning:

| | | | | |
|---|---|---|---|---|
| beautiful | dutiful | helpful | peaceful | tactful |
| boastful | flavourful | hopeful | playful | thankful |
| cheerful | forceful | joyful | powerful | useful |
| deceitful | graceful | merciful | shameful | youthful |
| delightful | harmful | painful | successful | |

### Words with other meanings

| | | | | |
|---|---|---|---|---|
| awful | brimful | eyeful | fruitful | rueful |
| baleful | doleful | fateful | grateful | wistful |
| bashful | earful | fitful | lawful | wrongful |

# full-

## 1 Degree or extent

**full-** combines with nouns and adjectives to form words which
describe someone or something that has performed a particular
action, or that has a particular quality, to the greatest extent
possible. For example, if a person or animal is 'full-grown', they
have reached their adult size and have grown as much as they are
going to; if a vehicle is travelling at 'full-speed', it is travelling as
fast as it possibly can.

*...a full-grown adult in mind as well as body.*
*Hostilities had erupted into full-scale war.*
*...the manufacturer of a full-strength beer.*

Here is a list of words with this meaning:

| | | | |
|---|---|---|---|
| full-blast | full-flavoured | full-grown | full-strength |
| full-blooded | full-force | full-scale | full-throated |
| full-blown | full-frontal | full-speed | full-volume |

## 2 Whole

**full-** also combines with nouns to form words which describe
something which occupies or includes the whole of the thing
referred to by the original noun. For example, if you have a 'full-
time' job, you do it for the whole of a working week; a 'full-page'
advertisement in a magazine or newspaper covers a whole page.

*We would have to pay a full-time man £100 a week.*
*On display inside the exhibition are full-size drawings of many early
Ferraris.*
*ICI pleased the market with full-year figures showing profits of
£1.47 billion.*
*...profits of £2 million for the full-year to February 1990.*

Here is a list of words with this meaning:

| | | | | |
|---|---|---|---|---|
| full-colour | full-page | full-size | full-time | full-year |

'Full-time' can also be used with this meaning as an adverb.

*Jenny and I worked full-time.*

**full-** also combines with this meaning with 'colour' to describe
something which is printed entirely in colour.

*...full-colour advertisements for hi-fi equipment.*

### Words with other meanings

| | | | |
|---|---|---|---|
| full-back | full-face | full-length | full-up |
| full-bodied | full-fledged | full-stop | |

# geo-

**geo-** occurs in words which have 'earth' as part of their meaning.
For example, 'geography' is the study of the different land
formations, seas, regions, and climates of the earth; 'geopolitics' is

# geo-

the study of the effects of the position and other features of a country on that country's politics.

Here is a list of words with this meaning:

| | | | |
|---|---|---|---|
| geocentric | geological | geophysics | geothermal |
| geographical | geology | geopolitical | |
| geography | geophysical | geopolitics | |

# -gon

-gon occurs in words which have 'angles' as part of their meaning. For example, a 'pentagon' is a geometric shape with five sides and five angles.

Here is a list of words with this meaning:

| | | | |
|---|---|---|---|
| decagon | hexagon | octagon | polygon |
| heptagon | nonagon | pentagon | |

# -gram

## 1 Written or drawn

-gram occurs in nouns which refer to something that is written or drawn. For example, a 'diagram' is a simple drawing that is used to show how something works; an 'anagram' is a word or phrase which is formed by changing the order of the letters in another word or phrase.

Here is a list of words with this meaning:

| | | |
|---|---|---|
| anagram | hologram | pentagram |
| diagram | monogram | pictogram |
| epigram | parallelogram | telegram |

## 2 Weight

-gram also occurs in nouns that refer to weights in the metric system. For example, a 'kilogram' is a unit of weight that is equal to a thousand grams.

Here is a list of words with this meaning:

| | | |
|---|---|---|
| kilogram | microgram | milligram |

# -graph

-graph occurs in words which have 'writing', 'record', or 'drawing' as part of their meaning. For example, a 'paragraph' is a section of a piece of writing and consists of a sentence or a series of sentences; a 'photograph' is a visual record produced by exposing film to light.

Here is a list of words with this meaning:

| | | | |
|---|---|---|---|
| autograph | holograph | paragraph | pictograph |
| chronograph | monograph | photograph | telegraph |

# great-

**great-** combines with nouns that refer to members of a family in order to form new nouns. Nouns formed in this way refer to a relative who is two or more generations away from you. For example, your 'great-uncle' is the uncle of your mother or father. Someone's 'great-grandchild' is the child of one of their grandchildren.

*His grandfather and great-uncle had both been merchants.*
*They may muddle up your parents' names with those of your great-uncles and great-aunts.*
*The two men may have been related, perhaps great-uncle and great-nephew.*

Here is a list of words with this meaning:

| | | |
|---|---|---|
| great-aunt | great-grandmother | great-niece |
| great-grandchild | great-grandparent | great-uncle |
| great-granddaughter | great-grandson | |
| great-grandfather | great-nephew | |

**great-** sometimes occurs twice before a noun to refer to a relative who is three or more generations away from you.

*Previous MP's in his family included his grandfather and a great-great-grandfather.*

# haem-

**haem-** occurs in words which have 'blood' as part of their meaning. For example, a 'haemorrhage' is serious bleeding from broken blood vessels; 'haemophilia' is an inherited disease in which a person's blood does not clot properly so that they bleed for a long time when they cut themselves.

Here is a list of words with this meaning:

| | | | |
|---|---|---|---|
| haematologist | haemoglobin | haemophiliac | haemorrhoids |
| haematology | haemophilia | haemorrhage | |

# half-

## 1 Almost happening or partly true

PRODUCTIVE USE: **half-** combines with verbs, participles, adjectives, and nouns, to form new verbs, adjectives, and nouns. Words formed in this way express the idea that something almost happens, is partly the case, or is only partly true. For example, if something is 'half-finished', the work on it has not been completed; if someone is 'half-asleep', they are almost asleep.

*...half-finished attempts at different jobs and studies.*
*The girl was half-smiling with a rather enigmatic, teasing expression.*
*The theatre was half-empty and there was nobody in the row they were in.*
*Benson sat with his eyes closed, half-brooding, half-listening.*
*James told us a deliberate half-truth.*
*A creature that lives half-buried in the sand of the sea floor.*

Here are some examples of words with this meaning:

| | | | |
|---|---|---|---|
| half-afraid | half-dressed | half-full | half-promise |
| half-asleep | half-eaten | half-grown | half-realize |
| half-brooding | half-empty | half-hearted | half-smiling |
| half-buried | half-fearful | half-listening | half-starved |
| half-cooked | half-finished | half-melted | half-truth |
| half-dead | half-forgotten | half-open | half-wild |

**half-** occasionally combines with this meaning with adverbs.

*The writer half-playfully suggested that Jimmie's problem might be his good looks.*

For more information on prefixes which mean 'half', see **demi-** and **semi-**.

## 2 Part of something

PRODUCTIVE USE: **half-** also combines with nouns to form new nouns. Nouns formed in this way refer to something that is one of two equal, or approximately equal, parts that together make up the whole of the thing referred to. For example, two 'half-inches' are equal to one inch; if something is 'half-price', it costs only half of what it usually costs.

*...a half-inch chain.*
*There is a glaring half-moon in the sky.*
*...the half-page advertisement for a new line of dresses.*

*The young men sat in a half-circle.*

Here are some examples of words with this meaning:

| | | | |
|---|---|---|---|
| half-acre | half-dozen | half-measure | half-pay |
| half-bottle | half-gram | half-mile | half-pint |
| half-century | half-hour | half-million | half-pound |
| half-circle | half-inch | half-minute | half-price |
| half-cup | half-length | half-moon | half-strength |
| half-distance | half-marathon | half-page | half-year |

## 3 Race and nationality

PRODUCTIVE USE: **half-** combines with adjectives of nationality to form new adjectives. Adjectives formed in this way describe someone whose parents come from different countries. For example, if someone is 'half-German' one of their parents is German.

*...a half-French, half-German civilian who had deserted from the Army.*
*Annabel was of mixed parentage: half-English, half-Dutch.*
*...this half-Irish, half-Indian young man.*

## 4 Brothers and sisters

Your 'half-brother' is the son of either your mother or father by another partner; your 'half-sister' is the daughter of either your mother or father by another partner.

### Words with other meanings

| | | | |
|---|---|---|---|
| half-back | half-caste | half-holiday | half-wit |
| half-baked | half-cock | half-past | |
| half-board | half-day | half-term | |
| half-breed | half-hearted | half-time | |

# hand-

## 1 Made, done, or operated by a person

**hand-** combines with verbs and participles to form words which indicate that something is done by a person, without the help of a machine. For example, if you 'hand-wash' your clothes, you wash them yourself in a sink rather than in a washing machine; someone's 'hand-writing' is their style of writing which they do with a pen or pencil rather than with a typewriter.

**Spelling:** Words formed in this way are usually written with a hyphen, but some of the more common ones are written as one word.

# hand-

*Hand-wash woollens in lukewarm water using a mild detergent.*
*Hand-weeding must go on incessantly so that weeds do not have*
*time to seed.*
*...lacy hand-crocheted shawls.*
*...hand-made paper of a quality unfindable today.*

Here is a list of words with this meaning:

| | | | |
|---|---|---|---|
| hand-built | hand-made | hand-sew | hand-weeding |
| hand-crocheted | hand-operated | hand-stitched | hand-woven |
| hand-finished | hand-painted | hand-wash | handwriting |
| hand-knitted | hand-printed | hand-washing | handwritten |

## 2 Carried or operated with your hands

**hand-** combines with nouns that refer to objects such as tools,
machines, or vehicles in order to form new nouns. Nouns formed in
this way refer to something that is designed to be operated
manually rather than automatically, or that is small enough to be
carried by hand and used easily. For example, a 'hand-mirror' is a
mirror that is small enough to hold in your hand; a 'handgun' is a
gun that is small enough to carry, hold, and fire with one hand.

*She was sitting on a stool looking at herself in a hand-mirror.*
*I'd been allowed to carry it on to the plane as hand-baggage.*
*Mr Boggis climbed back into the car and released the handbrake.*

Here is a list of words with this meaning:

| | | | |
|---|---|---|---|
| handbag | handbrake | handgun | hand-luggage |
| hand-baggage | handcart | handkerchief | hand-mirror |
| hand-bell | hand-grenade | handloom | |

### Words with other meanings

| | | |
|---|---|---|
| handbill | handhold | handsome |
| handbook | handmaiden | handspring |
| handcuffs | handshake | handstand |

# -hand

## 1 Holding something

PRODUCTIVE USE: **-hand** combines with nouns which refer to
something which is being held in order to form new nouns. Nouns
formed in this way refer to the hand that is holding the thing
mentioned. For example, your 'cup-hand' is the hand you are using
to hold a cup.

*He waved introductions with his cup-hand.*

*She pushed at the bracelet with the wrist of her flashlight-hand.*
*He signed the cheque against the wall, holding it there with his phone-hand.*
*The blond man held his bloody knife-hand over the young man.*

Here are some examples of words with this meaning:

| | | | |
|---|---|---|---|
| cup-hand | gun-hand | napkin-hand | racket-hand |
| flashlight-hand | knife-hand | phone-hand | weapon-hand |

## 2 Jobs

**-hand** also combines with nouns that refer to the place where someone works, or to the animals they work with, in order to form new nouns. Nouns formed in this way refer to a person who does a particular job. For example, a 'farm-hand' is someone who works on a farm; a 'cow-hand' is someone who works with cows.

*...a disease that would have killed any healthy farm-hand.*
*She works as a fieldhand.*
*He had been working as a garage-hand in Los Angeles.*

Here is a list of words with this meaning:

| | | |
|---|---|---|
| cowhand | factory-hand | fieldhand |
| deckhand | farm-hand | garage-hand |

## 3 Position

**-hand** combines with 'left' and 'right' to form adjectives that describe the position of something. For example, a 'left-hand' seat is towards the left of a row, and a 'right-hand' seat is towards the right.

*She opened the desk's left-hand bottom drawer and got out the folder of photos.*
*The aircraft did have a problem with the left-hand engine.*
*You'll find a bookcase in the right-hand corner near the window.*

# -head

## 1 Disapproval

**-head** combines with nouns and adjectives to form new nouns. Nouns formed in this way refer to someone you disapprove of or disagree with. For example, if you call someone a 'muddlehead', you think they are behaving in a muddled or confused way; if you call someone a 'hothead', you think that they are acting hastily, without thinking of the consequences of what they are doing.

Note that words formed in this way are informal and often rude.

# -head

*You're a bit of a muddlehead and lack organizational ability.*
*The question was addressed to the other squarehead.*
*...cracking a joke about the questions some pinhead had asked him.*

Here is a list of words with this meaning:

| | | |
|---|---|---|
| airhead | hothead | sleepyhead |
| egghead | muddlehead | sorehead |
| fathead | pinhead | squarehead |

## 2 The top part of something

**-head** also combines with nouns to form new nouns that refer to the top part of something, or to the part of an object that resembles a head. For example, a 'bed-head' is a board fixed to the top part of a bed behind your head; a 'thistle-head' is the large, top part of a thistle, where the flower is.

*...his coat of arms carved on the bed-head behind him.*
*...the seed-head of a poppy.*
*...a razor-sharp spearhead.*

Here is a list of words with this meaning:

| | | | |
|---|---|---|---|
| bed-head | flower-head | pinhead | spearhead |
| clubhead | masthead | seed-head | thistlehead |

## 3 An entrance or source

**-head** also combines with nouns which refer to a place in order to form new nouns. Nouns formed in this way refer to the entrance or the start of something. For example, a 'wellhead' is the point at which a well is accessible, or the structure around the top of a well; a 'railhead' is the point at which a railway starts or stops.

*...a well with a carved wellhead.*
*I waved the envelope at her and she immediately recognized the letterhead.*
*A loud bawl brought him to the stairhead. 'Somebody want me?' he roared.*

Here is a list of words with this meaning:

| | | | |
|---|---|---|---|
| bridgehead | pithead | road-head | wellhead |
| letterhead | railhead | stairhead | |

### Words with other meanings

| | | | | |
|---|---|---|---|---|
| beachhead | bulkhead | figurehead | forehead | warhead |

# -headed

## 1 Characteristics

**-headed** combines with adjectives to form new adjectives. Adjectives formed in this way describe someone's attitudes or the way they behave. For example, if someone is 'big-headed', they are arrogant and think that they are very clever; if someone is 'clear-headed', they think and behave in a sensible or logical fashion.

*They told us off for being big-headed.*
*He was industrious, ambitious and hard-headed.*
*...hot-headed young soldiers.*

Here is a list of words with this meaning:

| | | | |
|---|---|---|---|
| big-headed | even-headed | level-headed | thick-headed |
| clear-headed | fuzzy-headed | light-headed | woolly-headed |
| cool-headed | hard-headed | muddle-headed | wrong-headed |
| empty-headed | hot-headed | soft-headed | |

## 2 Appearance

PRODUCTIVE USE: **-headed** also combines with adjectives and nouns to form new adjectives which describe the head of a person or animal, or the top part of something. For example, if someone is 'bald-headed', they have very little or no hair on the top of their head; if something is 'wooden-headed', the top of it is made of wood.

*...a bald-headed man in a short overcoat.*
*Many black-headed gulls have arrived from Eastern Europe.*
*After a moment the shaven-headed soldier spoke to Miss Ryan.*
*...a gold-headed cane.*

Here are some examples of words with this meaning:

| | | | |
|---|---|---|---|
| bald-headed | curly-headed | heavy-headed | silver-headed |
| bareheaded | elephant-headed | ivory-headed | sleek-headed |
| black-headed | flat-headed | redheaded | small-headed |
| blond-headed | flaxen-headed | round-headed | stubble-headed |
| blunt-headed | gold-headed | shaven-headed | white-headed |
| crop-headed | grey-headed | shock-headed | wooden-headed |

# hetero-

**hetero-** occurs in words which have 'other', 'another', or 'different' as part of their meaning. For example, a group of things that are

## hetero-

'heterogeneous' are all different; a 'heterosexual' relationship is a
sexual relationship between people of different sexes.

Here is a list of words with this meaning:

heterodox          heterogeneity          heterogeneous          heterosexual

# hom-

**hom-** occurs in words which have 'same' as part of their meaning.
For example, if something is 'homogeneous', it has parts or
members which are all the same or which consist of only one
substance.

Here is a list of words with this meaning:

homeopathy          homogenous          homosexual
homogeneous          homonym

# home-

## 1 In the home

PRODUCTIVE USE: **home-** combines with past participles of transitive
verbs to form adjectives. Adjectives formed in this way describe
something as being made in someone's home rather than in a shop,
factory or office. For example, if something is 'home-made', it was
made in someone's home; 'home-grown' fruit and vegetables have
been grown in your own garden.

*I bought some home-made toffee.*
*Don't wash home-dyed articles with biological washing powder.*
*...biscuits baked in the wood stove and spread with home-churned
butter.*
*...a fortnight's supply of home-frozen food.*

Here are some examples of words with this meaning:

| | | | |
|---|---|---|---|
| home-baked | home-churned | home-frozen | home-prepared |
| home-bottled | home-cooked | home-grown | home-produced |
| home-bred | home-distilled | home-made | home-woven |
| home-brewed | home-dyed | home-painted | |

'Home-grown' and 'home-produced' can also be used to describe
something that comes from or was made in someone's own area or
country.

*It was hoped that home-grown food would meet Britain's needs.*
*Buyers will not give preference to home-produced goods if imported
goods are cheaper.*

## 2 Related to someone's home

**home-** combines with nouns and participles to form new nouns and adjectives. Words formed in this way refer to or describe something or someone that is related to the home. For example, a 'home-buyer' is someone who is in the process of buying a house; if someone is 'home-loving', they like their home and are happy to spend a lot of time there.

*First-time home-buyers are handicapped by the high cost of a mortgage.*
*Home-owners are bracing themselves for another rise in interest rates.*
*...home-based social lives.*

Here is a list of words with this meaning:

| | | |
|---|---|---|
| home-based | home-centred | homemaker |
| home-builder | home-improvement | home-owner |
| home-buyer | home-loving | |

### Words with other meanings

| | | | |
|---|---|---|---|
| homecoming | homesick | home-time | homework |
| homeland | homespun | hometown | |

# -hood

PRODUCTIVE USE: **-hood** combines with nouns that refer to people in order to form new nouns. Nouns formed in this way refer to states, conditions, or the periods of time in which something is experienced. For example, your 'childhood' is the time of your life when you are a child; 'motherhood' is the state of being a mother.

*...the passage of individuals from childhood to adolescence and parenthood.*
*He had written several books on the pleasures of bachelorhood.*
*He began to talk to me about his boyhood in London.*

Here are some examples of words with this meaning:

| | | | |
|---|---|---|---|
| adulthood | fatherhood | nationhood | widowerhood |
| babyhood | girlhood | parenthood | widowhood |
| bachelorhood | guesthood | selfhood | wifehood |
| boyhood | maidenhood | slobhood | womanhood |
| childhood | manhood | spinsterhood | |
| daughterhood | motherhood | studenthood | |

'Manhood' and 'womanhood' can also be used to refer to all the men or women of a particular nation or community.

# -hood

*...everything that was good and clean and manly in French young manhood.*
*...a perfect specimen of English womanhood.*

### Words with other meanings

| | |
|---|---|
| brotherhood | neighbourhood |
| knighthood | sisterhood |

# hydr-

**hydr-** occurs in words which have 'water' as part of their meaning. For example, a 'hydrant' is a pipe that is connected to the main water system and provides water for emergencies; 'hydro-electricity' is electricity produced from the energy of running water.

Here is a list of words with this meaning:

| | | | |
|---|---|---|---|
| hydrant | hydro-electric | hydrofoil | hydrophobia |
| hydraulic | hydro-electricity | hydrology | hydro-power |
| hydrocarbon | hydro-energy | hydrometer | hydrothermal |

# hyper-

PRODUCTIVE USE: **hyper-** combines with adjectives to form new adjectives. Adjectives formed in this way describe someone as having too much of a particular quality. For example, if someone is 'hyperactive', they are unable to relax and always seem to be in a state of great agitation or activity; if someone is 'hyper-alert', they are extremely alert, often in a way which affects the rest of their behaviour.

**Spelling:** Words formed in this way can be written with a hyphen or as one word.

*...the problems of the hyper-active child.*
*The man became hypersensitive to the slightest movement around him.*
*He was a hyper-cautious commander who never took risks.*
*Even her hyperdevoted mother had criticized her.*

Here are some examples of words with this meaning:

| | | | |
|---|---|---|---|
| hyperactive | hyper-conscious | hyperdevoted | hypersensitive |
| hyper-alert | hypercreative | hyper-modern | |
| hyper-cautious | hypercritical | hypernatural | |

**hyper-** occasionally combines with nouns to form new nouns. Nouns formed in this way refer to something that is a lot larger than usual.

*...a new hypermarket often causes the closure of local supermarkets. Hyperinflation could cause a collapse of the currency.*

# hypo-

**hypo-** occurs in medical words which have 'below' or 'lower' as part of their meaning. For example, 'hypodermic' needles are used to give injections beneath the skin; 'hypothermia' is an abnormally low body temperature.

Here is a list of words with this meaning:

| | | | |
|---|---|---|---|
| hypodermic | hypoglycaemia | hypothalamus | hypothermia |

# -ial

See **-al.**

# -ian

## 1 A job or hobby

**-ian** combines with nouns and adjectives to form new nouns. Nouns formed in this way refer to a person whose job or hobby involves the thing referred to by the original noun. For example, an 'electrician' is a person whose job is to install and repair electrical equipment; a 'historian' is a person who specializes in the study of history.

Note that 'dietician' is formed from 'diet', and 'beautician' is formed from 'beauty'.

*Water heaters should be removed only by a qualified electrician.*
*The magician tossed the rabbit across the stage.*
*She worked as a beautician in an expensive salon.*

Here is a list of words with this meaning:

| | | | |
|---|---|---|---|
| beautician | historian | obstetrician | politician |
| comedian | magician | optician | technician |
| dietician | mathematician | paediatrician | theologian |
| electrician | musician | physician | |

## 2 Connected with a particular person

PRODUCTIVE USE: **-ian** combines with the names of famous people to form words which describe something or someone as being connected with the work of the person mentioned or the time at which they lived. For example, 'Wordsworthian' describes the type of poetry written by Wordsworth; 'Victorian' describes things that

# -ian

happened or were made in Britain during the reign of Queen Victoria.

**Spelling:** Names ending in 'e' usually combine with 'an' rather than **-ian**; 'an' also occasionally occurs in more established forms such as 'Elizabethan'.

*The writer's determination gives the poem a Wordsworthian force.*
*...the great Shakespearean tragedy Othello.*
*...a lovely Elizabethan house in Somerset.*
*...the gloomy Dickensian image of funeral parlours.*
*...the Freudian movement.*

Here are some examples of words with this meaning:

| | | | |
|---|---|---|---|
| Chaucerian | Elizabethan | Keynesian | Wordsworthian |
| Darwinian | Freudian | Orwellian | \|Wagnerian |
| Dickensian | Georgian | Shakespearean | |
| Edwardian | Jungian | Victorian | |

## Words with other meanings

| | | | |
|---|---|---|---|
| amphibian | civilian | metropolitan | republican |
| Anglican | custodian | ovarian | suburban |
| bohemian | equestrian | pedestrian | urban |
| caesarean | guardian | Presbyterian | utopian |
| Christian | mammalian | reptilian | |

# -iana

**-iana** combines with nouns which refer to a person or place in order to form new nouns. Nouns formed in this way refer to a collection of objects or information relating to the person or place mentioned. For example, objects which were made in the time of Queen Victoria are referred to as 'Victoriana'; objects such as books or documents associated with the politician Sir Winston Churchill are referred to as 'Churchilliana'.

**Spelling: -iana** only combines with nouns that end in a consonant. When the noun combined with ends in a vowel, the final vowel is replaced by 'ana'.

PRODUCTIVE USE: It is possible to form new words with this meaning by adding **-iana** to nouns, particularly if they refer to people. However, words formed in this way are not very common and few of them occur frequently.

*You may not be able to put ornate Victoriana in a modern flat.*
*...the middle-class disdain for Americana.*

*...the display of Wellingtoniana.*

Here are some examples of words with this meaning:

| | | | |
|---|---|---|---|
| Americana | Churchilliana | Victoriana | Wellingtoniana |
| Australiana | Freudiana | Virginiana | |

# -ibility

PRODUCTIVE USE: **-ibility** combines with adjectives that end in 'ible' in order to form nouns. Nouns formed in this way refer to the state or quality described by the adjective, or to something which is characterized by that state or quality. For example, 'accessibility' is the state of being accessible; a 'possibility' is something that is possible or might happen.

**Spelling:** 'ible' is replaced by **-ibility.**

*...increasing the accessibility of art to all sorts of men and women.*
*The women had been enthusiastic about the possibility of a longer stay.*
*No one has admitted responsibility for Colonel Rowe's murder.*

Here are some examples of words with this meaning:

| | | | |
|---|---|---|---|
| accessibility | eligibility | legibility | susceptibility |
| audibility | feasibility | plausibility | tangibility |
| compatibility | flexibility | possibility | visibility |
| credibility | invincibility | responsibility | |

Note that 'sensibility' is not the noun formed from 'sensible'. Someone's 'sensibility' is their ability to experience deep feelings and often to express their understanding of those feelings.

# -ible

**-ible** combines with verbs to form adjectives. Adjectives formed in this way describe something to which the action or process referred to by the verb can be done. For example, if something is 'digestible', it can be digested; if something is 'comprehensible', it can be easily understood.

**Spelling:** A final 'e' is replaced by **-ible.** A final 'd' or 'de' is replaced by 's' before adding **-ible.** A final 'it' is replaced by 'iss' before adding **-ible.**

*Raw meat is perfectly digestible, although it can be tough.*
*...a collapsible canvas bucket.*
*The cliffs were easily discernible.*

# -ible

*I understood that it was permissible to ask a question.*

Here is a list of words with this meaning:

| | | |
|---|---|---|
| accessible | corruptible | discernible |
| collapsible | deductible | divisible |
| comprehensible | defensible | permissible |
| convertible | digestible | resistible |

Note that the use of **-ible** is not productive. **-able** is used to form new adjectives with this meaning. For more information see **-able**.

There are also a number of adjectives ending in **-ible** that are formed from stems which are not current words in English.

*It was a hot day, with every object on the sea's surface visible for miles.*
*Any sounds of pursuit would be clearly audible among the thickets of the ruined garden.*
*I want to make the game as safe as possible.*

Here is a list of words formed in this way:

| | | | | |
|---|---|---|---|---|
| audible | edible | flexible | perceptible | reversible |
| compatible | eligible | horrible | plausible | sensible |
| credible | fallible | legible | possible | terrible |
| destructible | feasible | negligible | responsible | visible |

# -ic

**-ic** combines with nouns to form adjectives. Adjectives formed in this way describe something as resembling, involving, or being connected with the thing referred to by the original noun. For example, 'photographic' equipment and objects are connected with photographs and photography; if someone is 'enthusiastic' about something, they show a lot of enthusiasm for it.

*...distributing photographic products to retailers.*
*He took a carving knife from a magnetic board on the wall.*
*Daniel laughed with idiotic pleasure.*
*The machine made a soft, rhythmic pulsing sound.*

Here is a list of words with this meaning:

| | | | |
|---|---|---|---|
| acidic | cubic | idiotic | mythic |
| acrobatic | democratic | idyllic | patriotic |
| alcoholic | demonic | ironic | pedantic |
| angelic | diplomatic | linguistic | photographic |
| atomic | enthusiastic | magnetic | poetic |
| autocratic | gymnastic | meteoric | rhythmic |
| bureaucratic | heroic | moronic | symbolic |

PRODUCTIVE USE: **-ic** also combines with this meaning with nouns ending in '-ist' that refer to people. For example, if someone is 'optimistic', they have a lot of optimism about the future.

*I was curiously happy and optimistic.*
*Gerald Brooke was a young and idealistic lecturer at a London technical college.*
*I was getting more and more journalistic work.*

Here are some examples of words with this meaning:

| | | | |
|---|---|---|---|
| anarchistic | chauvinistic | nationalistic | pessimistic |
| antagonistic | idealistic | naturalistic | socialistic |
| artistic | journalistic | opportunistic | traditionalistic |
| capitalistic | moralistic | optimistic | |

A number of words ending in **-ic** combine with **-al** to form adjectives. For more information, see **-al.**

## Words with other meanings

| | | |
|---|---|---|
| automatic | manic | periodic |
| classic | organic | prophetic |
| graphic | panic | systemic |

# -ics

**-ics** occurs in uncount nouns which refer to a subject or an area of study. For example, 'physics' is the scientific study of the behaviour of matter and energy; 'acoustics' is the scientific study of sound.

Note that nouns formed in this way usually take the third person singular form of the verb.

*Physics is a means of understanding the way the world is designed.*
*Economics is the oldest of the social sciences.*
*...amazing developments in biochemistry and genetics.*

Here is a list of words with this meaning:

| | | | |
|---|---|---|---|
| acoustics | classics | linguistics | physics |
| aerobics | economics | logistics | politics |
| aeronautics | electronics | mathematics | |
| athletics | genetics | obstetrics | |

Some of these nouns are occasionally used as plural nouns, especially when you are talking about a particular person's work or activities. When they are used in this way they take the third person plural of the verb.

*I don't know what your politics are.*

# -ide

-ide occurs in nouns that refer to chemical compounds. For example, an 'oxide' is a compound of oxygen and another chemical element; a 'chloride' is a compound of chlorine and another substance.

Here is a list of words with this meaning:

| | | | |
|---|---|---|---|
| bromide | fluoride | oxide | sulphide |
| chloride | hydroxide | peroxide | |
| cyanide | iodide | phosphide | |

# -ify

-ify occurs in verbs that describe the process by which a state, quality, or condition is brought about. For example, if one thing 'dignifies' another, it makes it seem more impressive; if you 'beautify' something, you make it look more beautiful.

*They stood admiring the broad steps that dignified the front of the mansion.*
*The local authority has promised to simplify planning procedures.*
*'Concentrate,' said Lucas, without specifying on what.*
*I was terrified by the bull and wanted to run out of the field.*

Here is a list of words with this meaning:

| | | | | |
|---|---|---|---|---|
| amplify | diversify | intensify | personify | simplify |
| beautify | falsify | justify | purify | solidify |
| clarify | glorify | magnify | qualify | specify |
| classify | horrify | modify | satisfy | terrify |
| dignify | identify | notify | signify | |

# il-, im-, in-, ir-

il-, im-, in-, and ir- combine with adjectives, and with nouns related to adjectives, in order to form new adjectives and nouns. Words formed in this way have the opposite meaning to the original adjective or noun. For example, if someone's actions are 'illogical', there is no logical reason for them; if you refer to someone's 'inability' to do something, you are referring to the fact that they cannot do it.

*I have been possessed by a wild and entirely illogical unrest.*
*The robot is doing something which would otherwise be impossible.*
*It was stupid and irrational to feel frightened.*

*...the prolonged insecurity of an unhappy marriage.*

Here is a list of words with this meaning:

| | | |
|---|---|---|
| illegal | impossible | informal |
| illegible | impractical | injustice |
| illegitimate | improbable | insecurity |
| illiterate | inability | irrational |
| illogical | inadequate | irregular |
| immature | inaudible | irrelevant |
| impatient | incapable | irreplaceable |
| imperceptible | incomprehensible | irresistible |
| imperfect | independent | irresponsible |

Adjectives formed in this way can be used to form **-ly** adverbs.

For more information on **-ly** adverbs, see **-ly**.

*The men behaved irrationally, acting against their own interest.*
*He was informally dressed, wearing slacks and an open-necked shirt.*

For more information on prefixes with a negative meaning, see **de-**, **dis-**, **non-**, and **un-**.

## Words with other meanings

| | | | |
|---|---|---|---|
| inborn | indifferent | ingrained | inset |
| inbred | infamous | ingrowing | invaluable |
| inbuilt | inflammable | inlaid | |

# ill-

## 1 Done badly

PRODUCTIVE USE: **ill-** combines with past participles to form adjectives. Words formed in this way describe an action as having been done badly or inadequately. For example, if something is 'ill-timed', it happens or is done at the wrong time, so that it is inappropriate or rude; if you are 'ill-informed', the information you have been given is wrong or inadequate.

*I find your jokes singularly ill-timed.*
*There was some ill-concealed laughter behind me.*
*Parents have always maintained that the headmaster was ill-advised.*
*The schools are understaffed, ill-equipped, and in poor repair.*

Here are some examples of words with this meaning:

| | | | |
|---|---|---|---|
| ill-adapted | ill-concealed | ill-educated | ill-paid |
| ill-advised | ill-conceived | ill-equipped | ill-prepared |
| ill-assorted | ill-considered | ill-founded | ill-suited |
| ill-chosen | ill-designed | ill-informed | ill-timed |

## ill-

Note that **ill-** occasionally combines in this way with present participles.

*A tall man with ill-fitting glasses that kept slipping to the end of his nose.*

## 2 Unpleasantness

**ill-** combines with nouns and adjectives to form new nouns and adjectives. Words formed in this way refer to or describe something that is unpleasant or bad. For example, if someone is 'ill-tempered', they have a bad temper; if you have 'ill-fortune', you are unlucky.

*Victoria Station was full of anxious, ill-tempered travellers.*
*Alice recounted the story of her ill-fated boating expedition.*
*He bore ill-health with considerable fortitude.*

Here is a list of words with this meaning:

| | | | |
|---|---|---|---|
| ill-bred | ill-fortune | ill-mannered | ill-tempered |
| ill-disposed | ill-health | ill-natured | ill-treatment |
| ill-fated | ill-humour | ill-omened | ill-will |
| ill-feeling | ill-luck | ill-starred | ill-wisher |

**ill-** occasionally combines in this way with verbs.

*...the type of minder who may ill-treat children in her care.*

## im-

See **il-**.

## in-

See **il-**.

## Indo-

**Indo-** occurs in words which have 'Indian' or 'India' as part of their meaning. For example, 'Indo-China' is a geographical region in Southeast Asia between India and China.

## infra-

**infra-** occurs in words which have 'below' or 'beneath' as part of their meaning. For example, the 'infrastructure' of a country, society, or business is its underlying structure or organization.

Here is a list of words with this meaning:

| | | | |
|---|---|---|---|
| infra-red | infrasonic | infrasound | infrastructure |

# -ing

## 1 Forming present participles

**-ing** combines with the base form of verbs to form the present participle.

*A lady came slowly walking across the field.*
*We sat in the hotel lounge drinking.*
*I turned to Elaine to make sure she was watching.*

## 2 Present participles used as nouns

Some present participles are used as nouns to refer to the activity described by the verb. For example, if you dance, you can say that you like 'dancing'.

*We celebrated with music and dancing.*
*He managed to find time for reading.*
*She simply loathed cooking.*

## 3 Present participles used as adjectives

When the present participles of transitive verbs are used as adjectives, they describe the effect that something has on someone's feelings and ideas. For example, if you find something 'disgusting', it disgusts you.

*The beer at the Rugby Club was disgusting.*
*...a brilliantly amusing novel.*
*...one of the most frightening sights I have ever seen.*

When the present participles of intransitive verbs are used as adjectives, they describe a continuing process or state. For example, a 'recurring' problem is one that occurs repeatedly.

*...the nation's recurring industrial crises.*
*...currents driven by the prevailing wind.*
*...a small ageing man in an elderly car.*

Note that there are a number of adjectives ending in **-ing** that are formed from stems that are not current words in English.

*He woke up in the night with an excruciating pain.*
*...the announcement of Flight Two's impending departure.*
*...a cunning solution to the problem.*

Here is a list of words formed in this way:

| | | | |
|---|---|---|---|
| appetizing | cunning | excruciating | scathing |
| balding | enterprising | impending | unwitting |

For more information about the present participle of verbs, see the Collins Cobuild English Grammar.

## -in-law

-in-law combines with nouns which refer to members of your family in order to form new nouns. Nouns formed in this way refer to someone who is related to you by marriage. For example, your 'father-in-law' is the father of your husband or wife; your 'daughter-in-law' is your son's wife.

*He wondered if he should put his elderly father-in-law in a home.*
*He took his sister-in-law home to England.*
*My daughter and son-in-law led a hard life.*

Here is a list of words with this meaning:

| | | | |
|---|---|---|---|
| brother-in-law | father-in-law | parents-in-law | son-in-law |
| daughter-in-law | mother-in-law | sister-in-law | |

# inter-

## 1 Between

PRODUCTIVE USE: **inter-** combines with nouns and adjectives that refer to a person, place, or thing in order to form new adjectives. Adjectives formed in this way describe something as existing or happening between two or more people or things. For example, an 'inter-city' train goes from one city to another; an 'international' competition involves two or more nations.

**Spelling:** Words formed in this way are usually written with a hyphen, but some of the more common ones are written as one word.

*...inter-city phone calls.*
*...an inter-continental flight back to England.*
*...the building of the interstate highways.*
*...inter-racial relations.*

Here are some examples of words with this meaning:

| | | |
|---|---|---|
| inter-city | international | interseasonal |
| intercontinental | inter-office | interstate |
| inter-department | interpersonal | inter-stellar |
| inter-family | interplanetary | interterritorial |
| inter-government | inter-racial | inter-union |
| interlanguage | inter-school | inter-university |

## 2 Connection

**inter-** also combines with verbs, and with nouns and adjectives related to verbs, in order to form words which indicate that two or more people or things are related or connected in some way. For example, things that 'interconnect' are connected to each other; if people or things are 'intermingled', they have become mixed together.

*...a complicated network of interconnecting parts.*
*There was a quick interchange of information between the men.*
*...a beautiful sari interwoven with a pattern of red and gold.*

Here is a list of words with this meaning:

| | | | |
|---|---|---|---|
| interact | interdependence | interlock | interrelate |
| interbreeding | interknit | intermarriage | intersection |
| interchange | interlace | intermingled | intertwine |
| interconnect | interlink | interplay | interweave |

# intra-

PRODUCTIVE USE: **intra-** combines with nouns and adjectives to form new adjectives. Adjectives formed in this way describe one thing as existing or taking place within another. For example, 'intra-Community' trade is carried out within the European Community.

Note that adjectives formed in this way are formal and occur infrequently.

*...intra-Community police co-operation.*
*Modern Pan-Africanism starts from quite new intra-African bases.*
*...intra-party groupings such as the chartist-socialists.*

Here are some examples of words with this meaning:

| | | |
|---|---|---|
| intra-African | intra-European | intra-racial |
| intracellular | intra-generation | intra-regional |
| intra-class | intramuscular | intra-uterine |
| intra-Community | intra-party | intravenous |

# -ion

**-ion** combines with verbs to form nouns. Nouns formed in this way refer to the state or process described by the verb, or to an instance of that process. For example, if you give someone 'protection', you protect them or keep them safe from unpleasant effects and events; an 'explanation' is something which explains or gives a reason for a particular event or situation.

**Spelling:** There are a number of variations of the spelling of **-ion**. The most common ones are 'ation', 'ition', 'sion', and 'tion'. Examples of all of these are given below.

# -ion

*...protection against the sun's rays.*
*...the realization of how close I had been to death.*
*...the great Picasso exhibition at the Museum of Modern Art in New York.*
*...a fifty-percent reduction in staff.*
*I think that I made the wrong decision.*

Here is a list of words with this meaning:

| | | | |
|---|---|---|---|
| action | contribution | exhibition | production |
| addition | creation | explanation | protection |
| collection | decision | imagination | reaction |
| combination | direction | information | realization |
| conclusion | education | operation | reduction |
| connection | examination | organization | situation |

## Words with other meanings

| | | | | |
|---|---|---|---|---|
| affection | attention | disposition | edition | mission |

# -ious

See -ous.

# ir-

See il-.

# -ise

See -ize.

# -ish

## 1 Nationality or language

-ish occurs in words which refer to or describe the people, language, or characteristics of a particular country or region. For example, if someone is 'Irish', they come from Ireland; 'Danish' is the language spoken in Denmark; the 'English' refers to all the people who come from England.

*...Irish workers based in London.*
*...a tall youth who spoke only Polish.*
*...a cheery bedroom with Swedish furniture.*

*California inherited much of its law from the Spanish.*

Here is a list of words with this meaning:

| | | | | |
|---|---|---|---|---|
| British | English | Irish | Moorish | Spanish |
| Cornish | Finnish | Jewish | Polish | Swedish |
| Danish | Flemish | Kurdish | Scottish | Turkish |

## 2 With adjectives

PRODUCTIVE USE: **-ish** combines with adjectives to form new adjectives. Adjectives formed in this way describe something as having a small amount of the characteristic or quality described by the original adjective. For example, if something is 'longish', it is fairly long; if someone is 'tallish', they are fairly tall; if something is 'greenish', it is slightly green in colour.

Note that words formed in this way are informal.

**Spelling:** A final 'e' is replaced by **-ish**. If a word of one syllable ends in a 'b', 'd', 'g', 't', or 'n' preceded by a single vowel, the 'b', 'd', 'g', 't', or 'n' is doubled before adding **-ish**.

*After tea he wrote a longish letter to Hilda.*
*The early sky was a pale whitish blue.*
*He was a biggish fellow.*
*...three yellowish wooden armchairs.*
*Mr and Mrs Bixby lived in a smallish apartment.*

Here are some examples of words with this meaning:

| | | | | |
|---|---|---|---|---|
| biggish | darkish | greenish | plumpish | warmish |
| blackish | dullish | largish | reddish | wettish |
| bluish | fattish | longish | smallish | whitish |
| brownish | flattish | lowish | tallish | youngish |
| dampish | goodish | oldish | thinnish | |

## 3 With nouns

PRODUCTIVE USE: **-ish** combines with nouns to form adjectives. Adjectives formed in this way describe one person or thing as being like another. For example, if a man is 'boyish', he is very youthful in appearance and behaviour and looks like a boy; if someone is 'foolish', they behave like a fool.

**Spelling:** A final 'e' is replaced by **-ish**. If a word of one syllable ends in a 'b', 'd', 'g', 't', or 'n' preceded by a single vowel, the 'b', 'd', 'g', 't', or 'n' is doubled before adding **-ish**.

*His boyish charm was irresistible.*
*...childish misbehaviour.*
*As a plot it was amateurish beyond belief.*

# -ish

*...his low womanish round shoulders.*
*...an American girl with an owlish, spectacled face.*

Here are some examples of words with this meaning:

| | | | |
|---|---|---|---|
| amateurish | coquettish | hellish | priggish |
| babyish | devilish | impish | prudish |
| bearish | feverish | kittenish | slavish |
| boyish | fiendish | mannish | sluttish |
| brutish | foolish | monkish | snobbish |
| bullish | girlish | nightmarish | wolfish |
| childish | hawkish | owlish | womanish |

**-ish** occasionally combines in this way with names.

*He was a nice enough boy—rather Jimmy Olsenish I thought.*
*...the air-conditioned Disneylandish shopping centre.*

## 4 Age or time

PRODUCTIVE USE: **-ish** combines with words referring to times, dates, or ages in order to form words which indicate that the number or time mentioned is approximate. For example, if someone is 'fortyish', they are about forty years old; if you say you will do something around 'noonish', you mean that you will do it at about noon.

**Spelling:** Words formed in this way can be written with a hyphen or as one word.

*Mrs Hoyland Leach was a florid, fortyish lady.*
*Shall I ring you about nine-ish?*

## Words with other meanings

| | | | |
|---|---|---|---|
| bookish | peckish | sharpish | sluggish |
| feverish | rakish | sheepish | stylish |
| outlandish | selfish | shrewish | ticklish |

# -ism

## 1 Beliefs and behaviour

**-ism** occurs in nouns which refer to particular beliefs, or to behaviour based on these beliefs. For example, 'feminism' is the belief that women should have the same rights, power, and opportunities as men; 'pessimism' is the belief that bad things will happen or are happening, or that a particular thing will be unsuccessful or bad.

*The popular image of feminism unfortunately tends to repel many women.*

*He was accused of impiety and atheism.*
*There was a definite air of optimism at the headquarters.*

Here is a list of words with this meaning:

| | | |
|---|---|---|
| atheism | feminism | pacificism |
| fascism | optimism | pessimism |

PRODUCTIVE USE: **-ism** combines with this meaning with nouns and adjectives in order to form new nouns. Nouns formed in this way refer to beliefs and behaviour based on the thing referred to or described by the original noun or adjective. For example, 'cynicism' is the attitude that cynics have towards people and things in which they always expect the worst of them; 'modernism' is the ideas and methods of modern art and literature.

*...a growing cynicism about politics.*
*The Labour movement wanted more democracy, socialism and unity.*
*...plans to counter hooliganism.*
*In some schools, malaria is estimated to cause high absenteeism rates.*
*The founder of Methodism lived here for the last years of his life.*

Here are some examples of words with this meaning:

| | | |
|---|---|---|
| absenteeism | Hinduism | opportunism |
| alcoholism | hooliganism | patriotism |
| anarchism | humanism | perfectionism |
| barbarism | idealism | professionalism |
| capitalism | Impressionism | Protestantism |
| Catholicism | industrialism | realism |
| Communism | internationalism | scepticism |
| consumerism | Judaism | socialism |
| cynicism | liberalism | symbolism |
| expressionism | Methodism | terrorism |
| extremism | modernism | totalitarianism |
| heroism | nationalism | vandalism |

**-ism** occasionally combines in this way with names.

*...the intellectual influence of Marxism.*
*...the analysis of eleven years of Thatcherism.*
Note that **-ism** also combines in this way with some nouns to form new nouns that refer to a form of discrimination based on the thing described by the original noun. For example, 'sexism' is the idea or belief that the members of one sex are less intelligent or less capable than those of the other sex.

*...an organization set up to counter sexism in the Church.*

# -ism

*Older women encouraged back to work still face ageism.*

Here is a list of words with this meaning:

ageism          racism          sexism

The ending **-ism** can often change to **-ist** to form words which refer
to or describe people who have particular beliefs or behaviour based
on these beliefs. For more information, see **-ist**.

## 2 Actions and ceremonies

**-ism** combines with some verbs ending in 'ize' or 'ise' in order to
form nouns. Nouns formed in this way refer to the process described
by the verb, or to an instance of that process. For example, if you
make a 'criticism' of someone, you criticize them because you
disapprove of them or their behaviour; 'baptism' is the religious
ceremony during which someone is baptized.

*Teachers are intensely sensitive to any sort of criticism.*
*Patricia began to ask him about hypnotism and how it worked.*
*...exorcism of the harmful spirits.*

Here is a list of words with this meaning:

| | | | |
|---|---|---|---|
| baptism | exorcism | magnetism | plagiarism |
| criticism | hypnotism | mechanism | specialism |

For more information on verbs ending in 'ize' or 'ise', see **-ize**.

### Words with other meanings

| | | | |
|---|---|---|---|
| euphemism | mannerism | tourism | witticism |
| journalism | organism | truism | |

# iso-

**iso-** occurs in words which have 'equal' or 'identical' as part of their
meaning. For example, 'isotopes' are atoms which have the same
atomic number but have a different number of neutrons; an
'isosceles' triangle is a triangle which has two sides that are the
same length.

Here is a list of words with this meaning:

isobar          isometric          isosceles          isotope

# -ist

## 1 Beliefs and behaviour

**-ist** occurs in nouns which refer to a person whose behaviour is
based on a particular set of beliefs. For example, a 'feminist' is

someone who believes that women should have the same rights, power, and opportunities as men; a 'pessimist' is someone who believes that bad things will happen or are happening, or that a particular thing will be unsuccessful or bad.

*Claudia thought of herself as a feminist.*
*He is a convinced atheist.*
*I'm an optimist by nature.*

Here is a list of words with this meaning:

| | | |
|---|---|---|
| atheist | feminist | pacificist |
| fascist | optimist | pessimist |

PRODUCTIVE USE: **-ist** combines with this meaning with nouns and adjectives in order to form new nouns. Nouns formed in this way refer to someone whose beliefs and behaviour are based on the thing referred to or described by the original noun or adjective. For example, if someone is an 'idealist', they try to base their behaviour on their ideals; a 'terrorist' attack is an attack by people who use violence to achieve their political aims.

*You don't have to be an idealist to realise that there's something wrong with this society.*
*...a vigorous civil rights activist.*
*Mr Morris was always a perfectionist.*
*...a leading industrialist with business interests in Germany.*
*...the history of the socialist movement in Europe.*

Here are some examples of words with this meaning:

| | | | |
|---|---|---|---|
| activist | expressionist | internationalist | realist |
| anarchist | extremist | Methodist | socialist |
| capitalist | humanist | modernist | terrorist |
| communist | idealist | nationalist | |
| conformist | Impressionist | opportunist | |
| elitist | industrialist | perfectionist | |

**-ist** occasionally combines in this way with names.

*Would you call yourself a Marxist?*
*...Jansenist repression.*

Note that **-ist** also combines in this way with some nouns to form new nouns that refer to a form of discrimination based on the thing referred to by the original noun. For example, if you describe someone, especially a man, as a 'sexist', you mean that you think they have ideas based on sexism.

*We had to sit through a cabaret full of sexist jokes.*
*The consequences of being a racist are serious.*

Here is a list of words with this meaning:

| | | |
|---|---|---|
| ageist | racist | sexist |

# -ist

The ending **-ist** can often change to **-ism** to form words which refer to the beliefs or behaviour mentioned. For more information, see **-ism**.

## 2 Occupations or study

**-ist** also combines with nouns to form new nouns that refer to someone whose work or study involves the thing referred to by the original noun. For example, a 'novelist' is someone who writes novels; a 'scientist' is someone whose work or study is connected with one of the sciences.

*How would George Eliot compare with a novelist like Jane Austen?*
*A good cartoonist can capture a face in a few lines.*
*She was chief physiotherapist at Massachusetts Memorial Hospital.*

Here is a list of words with this meaning:

| | | |
|---|---|---|
| anaesthetist | educationalist | physiotherapist |
| artist | educationist | psychiatrist |
| botanist | environmentalist | satirist |
| cartoonist | historicist | scientist |
| columnist | lyricist | soloist |
| dentist | novelist | therapist |
| dramatist | pharmacist | tourist |
| economist | physicist | typist |

**-ist** also combines in this way with nouns ending in **-ology**. For example, a 'biologist' is someone whose job involves the study of biology.

*...a developmental biologist at the Institute for Cancer Research.*
*Geologists noticed very odd shapes in the ancient sandstone.*
*...an ancient burial site discovered by archaeologists.*

Here is a list of words with this meaning:

| | | | |
|---|---|---|---|
| anthropologist | ecologist | meteorologist | psychologist |
| archaeologist | geologist | microbiologist | sociologist |
| biologist | graphologist | neurologist | technologist |
| climatologist | gynaecologist | ornithologist | zoologist |

## 3 Musicians

**-ist** also combines with nouns that refer to a musical instrument in order to form new nouns. Nouns formed in this way refer to someone who plays the instrument mentioned, especially if they do it as their profession. For example, a 'guitarist' is someone who plays the guitar; a 'pianist' is someone who plays the piano.

*...the rhythm guitarist of Cliff Richard's old backing group.*
*His father, a violinist, obtained work in small orchestras.*

*The student oboist began to play Delius.*

Here is a list of words with this meaning:

| | | | | |
|---|---|---|---|---|
| accordionist | bassoonist | flautist | oboist | trombonist |
| altoist | cellist | guitarist | pianist | tympanist |
| bassist | clarinettist | keyboardist | saxophonist | violinist |

**Words with other meanings**

| | | | |
|---|---|---|---|
| chemist | cyclist | naturalist | specialist |

# Italo-

**Italo-** occurs in words which have 'Italian' or 'Italy' as part of their meaning. For example, an 'Italophile' is someone who admires Italy and the Italians.

# -ite

PRODUCTIVE USE: **-ite** combines with names to form new nouns. Nouns formed in this way refer to someone who is a follower or supporter of the person mentioned. For example, a 'Trotskyite' is someone who believes in the political ideas of Leon Trotsky; 'Lawsonite' policies are based on the ideas put forward by the British politician Nigel Lawson.

Note that words formed in this way are often used to suggest that you disagree with or disapprove of someone's beliefs.

*...a wealthy American Trotskyite.*
*He didn't want to be labelled a Baldwinite.*
*The long Thatcherite nightmare is coming to an end.*
*Harold Wilson condemned the exercise as McCarthyite.*

# -ition

See **-ion**.

# -itis

## 1 Illness

**-itis** occurs in some nouns which refer to an illness. For example, you suffer from 'tonsillitis' when your tonsils are swollen and sore; 'hepatitis' is a serious disease that affects the liver.

*It was last winter when he had tonsillitis.*

# -itis

*Her fingers were badly swollen with arthritis.*
*Do you ever get rashes, dermatitis or spots?*

Here is a list of words with this meaning:

| | | | |
|---|---|---|---|
| appendicitis | bronchitis | hepatitis | tonsillitis |
| arthritis | dermatitis | meningitis | |

## 2 Obsession

**-itis** combines with nouns to form new nouns. Nouns formed in this way refer to an unusual obsession or preoccupation with the thing referred to by the original noun. For example, 'weddingitis' refers to an unusual preoccupation with weddings.

PRODUCTIVE USE: It is possible to form new words with this meaning by adding **-itis** to nouns. However, words formed in this way are very informal and usually intended to be humorous. Few of them occur frequently.

*Weddingitis is now at fever pitch.*
*She was now obviously suffering from auctionitis.*

Here are some examples of words with this meaning:

| | | |
|---|---|---|
| auctionitis | consumeritis | weddingitis |
| campaignitis | relationitis | |

# -ity

**-ity** combines with adjectives to form nouns. Nouns formed in this way refer to the state or condition described by the adjective. For example, 'immunity' is the state of being immune to something; 'anonymity' is the state of being anonymous.

*Babies receive immunity to a variety of infections through breast feeding.*
*The war had brought prosperity to Port Philip.*
*...the growing equality of women.*

Here is a list of words with this meaning:

| | | | |
|---|---|---|---|
| abnormality | creativity | generosity | productivity |
| absurdity | curiosity | hostility | prosperity |
| anonymity | diversity | immunity | security |
| authenticity | equality | intensity | sensitivity |
| brutality | familiarity | originality | simplicity |
| complexity | formality | popularity | superiority |

## Words with other meanings

| | | | |
|---|---|---|---|
| locality | minority | personality | priority |
| majority | morality | principality | publicity |

94

# -ive

## 1 Adjectives

-ive occurs in a large number of adjectives, some of which are formed from stems which are not current words in English. For example, if someone is 'creative', they have the ability to create and develop new ideas; if an activity or business is 'lucrative', it earns someone a lot of money or makes large profits.

*A youngster has more time to be creative.*
*Rumours will make you feel even more nervous and apprehensive.*
*Most tinned fruits contain excessive amounts of sugar.*

Here is a list of words with this meaning:

| | | | |
|---|---|---|---|
| active | comprehensive | effective | lucrative |
| aggressive | constructive | excessive | massive |
| alternative | creative | expensive | negative |
| apprehensive | decisive | extensive | offensive |
| attractive | defensive | imaginative | productive |
| competitive | destructive | intensive | protective |

## 2 Nouns

-ive also occurs in nouns. For example, a 'detective' is someone whose job is to find out what happened in a particular crime and to find the people involved; an 'additive' is something which is added in small amounts to something such as food or petrol in order to improve it or to make it last longer.

*He sent a detective upstairs to examine Mrs Wilt's clothes.*
*...you need initiative and willingness to work to improve your education.*
*Her narrative began uncertainly with a rambling account of her childhood.*

Here is a list of words with this meaning:

| | | | |
|---|---|---|---|
| additive | executive | missive | prerogative |
| archive | incentive | motive | preservative |
| collective | initiative | narrative | relative |
| conservative | invective | objective | representative |
| contraceptive | laxative | offensive | sedative |
| detective | locomotive | perspective | |

# -ize

## 1 Actions

-ize combines with nouns to form verbs. Verbs formed in this way refer to actions that involve or are related to the original noun. For example, if you 'apologize' to someone, you give them an apology and tell them you are sorry for something you have done or said; if you 'sympathize' with someone, you have sympathy for them and share their feelings, often when they have had some misfortune.

*He apologized for being late.*
*The events of the wedding were characterized by muddle.*
*Lorries and trains have revolutionized the entire pattern of moving goods.*

Here is a list of words with this meaning:

| | | | |
|---|---|---|---|
| apologize | epitomize | moralize | subsidize |
| characterize | fantasize | philosophize | summarize |
| criticize | jeopardize | pressurize | symbolize |
| emphasize | memorize | revolutionize | sympathize |

## 2 Bringing about a state or condition

**-ize** also combines with nouns and adjectives that refer to a state or condition in order to form verbs. Verbs formed in this way describe the process by which the state or condition mentioned is brought about. For example, if someone 'terrorizes' you, they make you feel terror by threatening you in some way; if you 'tenderize' meat, you make it more tender by preparing it in a particular way.

*Forbes allowed his dog to terrorize the officer on duty.*
*...farm workers victimized for joining a trade union.*
*...an act to legalize abortion.*
*The Prime Minister wants Nato to modernize short-range nuclear weapons.*

Here is a list of words with this meaning:

| | | | |
|---|---|---|---|
| colonize | harmonize | modernize | standardize |
| democratize | hospitalize | neutralize | sterilize |
| dramatize | industrialize | personalize | tenderize |
| equalize | institutionalize | publicize | terrorize |
| generalize | legalize | rationalize | victimize |
| glamorize | mobilize | stabilize | visualize |

## 3 -ise

'ise' is often used as an alternative spelling of **-ize** in British English but there are some verbs which always end in 'ise' rather than **-ize.** Most of these are formed from stems which are not current words of English.

Here is a list of words written in this way:

| | | | |
|---|---|---|---|
| advertise | compromise | exercise | supervise |
| advise | despise | improvise | surmise |
| arise | devise | practise | surprise |
| comprise | disguise | promise | televise |

## Words with other meanings

| | | | |
|---|---|---|---|
| agonize | civilize | materialize | scandalize |
| authorize | economize | organize | scrutinize |
| capitalize | fertilize | realize | specialize |

# kilo-

**kilo-** occurs in nouns that refer to things which have a thousand parts. For example, a 'kilogram' is a metric unit of weight of a thousand grams; a 'kilometre' is a measurement of length containing a thousand metres.

Here is a list of words with this meaning:

| | | | |
|---|---|---|---|
| kilobyte | kilogram | kilolitre | kilowatt |
| kilocalorie | kilohertz | kilometre | |

# -kind

**-kind** combines with nouns that refer to people in order to form new nouns. Nouns formed in this way refer to a group of the people mentioned. For example, you can refer to all women as 'womankind' when you are considering them as a group.

*The present day Hottentot and Bushmen females are the last remnants of the original shape of womankind.*
*...mankind will seek to explore and exploit space.*
*Ecology teaches us that humankind is not the centre of life on the planet.*

Here is a list of words with this meaning:

humankind    mankind    womankind

For more information on words that refer to people, see **-folk, -man, -people, -person,** and **-woman.**

# -led

PRODUCTIVE USE: **-led** combines with nouns and adjectives of nationality in order to form new adjectives. Adjectives formed in this way describe people or things that are controlled, organized, or influenced by whatever the original nouns and adjectives refer to or describe. For example, if an activity is 'student-led', students are responsible for it; if production of something is 'demand-led', the amount produced of that thing is controlled by the size of the demand for it.

*...the student-led pro-democracy movement.*

# -led

*...Comecon, the Soviet-led trading organisation.*
*...a community-led partnership of local people.*
*...a market-led economy.*

Here are some examples of words with this meaning:

| | | | |
|---|---|---|---|
| American-led | earnings-led | labour-led | Soviet-led |
| communist-led | employee-led | market-led | state-led |
| community-led | employer-led | moderate-led | student-led |
| consumer-led | government-led | Muslim-led | teacher-led |
| demand-led | investment-led | opposition-led | worker-led |

# -less

## 1 Lacking something

PRODUCTIVE USE: **-less** combines with nouns to form adjectives.
Adjectives formed in this way describe people or things that do not
have or do whatever is referred to. For example, if something is
'harmless', it cannot harm you; if something is 'meaningless', it has
no meaning.

*Most people think of measles as harmless.*
*The injustice of it all left me speechless.*
*The room was characterless, a clean neat room with oddments of
furniture.*
*He hummed a tuneless song to himself.*
Note that some adjectives formed in this way are used in a non-
literal way. For example, if you describe somebody as 'brainless',
you mean that you think that they are stupid and silly.

*'You're brainless. You can't even count.'*
*He was a spineless coward.*

Here are some examples of words with this meaning:

| | | | |
|---|---|---|---|
| airless | flawless | meaningless | speechless |
| beltless | harmless | motherless | spineless |
| brainless | heartless | motionless | spotless |
| characterless | helpless | nameless | tactless |
| childless | hopeless | powerless | thoughtless |
| effortless | humourless | restless | tuneless |
| endless | lifeless | seedless | useless |

Adjectives formed in this way can be used to form **-ly** adverbs.

For more information on **-ly** adverbs, see **-ly.**

*At the airport there were refugees, desperate to get out, milling
hopelessly around.*
*Agrot had studied the text, and studied it endlessly.*

## 2 Exceeding a category

**-less** also combines with nouns or verbs to form adjectives.
Adjectives formed in this way describe people or things whose
qualities cannot be measured in terms of whatever the noun or verb
refers to. For example, if a group of things is 'countless', it is so big
that it is almost impossible to count them; if a work of art is
'priceless', it is so valuable that it is impossible to put a price on it
that matches its worth.

*...sausages, pork pies, hamburgers, chips, ice cream, cakes and
countless other products.*
*A small, spry, ageless nun dragged the gate open.*

Here is a list of words with this meaning:

| ageless | countless | numberless | priceless | timeless |
|---------|-----------|------------|-----------|----------|

### Words with other meanings

| artless | regardless | shiftless | wireless |
|---------|------------|-----------|----------|
| listless | relentless | stainless | |

# -let

## 1 Smaller things

**-let** combines with nouns to form new nouns. Words formed in this
way describe things that are smaller examples of whatever the
noun refers to. For example, a 'droplet' is a very small drop of
liquid; a 'booklet' is a book that has only a very few pages.

*Into this aperture a droplet of mercury was poured.*
*They found a piglet caught in a curtain of creepers.*
*Shrubs and roots of huge trees watered by the rivulet fill the crevice.*

Here is a list of words with this meaning:

| booklet | droplet | islet | rivulet |
|---------|---------|-------|---------|
| coverlet | eaglet | owlet | starlet |
| cutlet | froglet | piglet | streamlet |

PRODUCTIVE USE: It is possible to form new words with this meaning
by adding **-let** to nouns. However, words formed in this way are
fairly informal and few of them occur frequently.

*Daisy's flatlet consisted of one room, with a sink and a gas oven.*
*They each contributed their own ploy or ploylet and passed it on.*

## 2 Jewellery

**-let** also occurs in nouns that refer to jewellery. For example, a
'bracelet' is a piece of jewellery you wear around your wrist or arm;
an 'anklet' is a piece of jewellery you wear around your ankle.

# -let

*A gold bracelet watch was ripped from the bound wrist of Mrs Ross.*
*...a circlet of nine pearls.*

Here is a list of words with this meaning:

| anklet | armlet | bracelet | circlet | wristlet |
|--------|--------|----------|---------|----------|

## Words with other meanings

| ballet | bullet | gullet | triplet |
|--------|--------|--------|---------|
| billet | couplet | leaflet | |

# -like

PRODUCTIVE USE: **-like** combines with nouns to form adjectives.
Adjectives formed in this way describe things that are similar to
whatever the nouns refer to. For example, if someone is 'childlike',
they are similar to a child in the way they look and behave; if a
building is 'prison-like', it looks like a prison.

**Spelling:** Words formed in this way are usually written with a
hyphen, but some of the more common ones are written as one
word.

*She has a sweet and childlike nature.*
*Tigers have sharp, dagger-like claws.*
*The flowers of mature lime trees have a delicious honey-like*
*fragrance.*
*He pulled himself through between the smooth pillar-like rocks.*

Here are some examples of words with this meaning:

| animal-like | claw-like | daisy-like | flower-like | owl-like |
|-------------|-----------|------------|-------------|----------|
| baby-like | clock-like | desert-like | fox-like | pillar-like |
| bird-like | clown-like | dog-like | honey-like | prison-like |
| cat-like | cowlike | doll-like | hook-like | vice-like |
| childlike | dagger-like | dreamlike | ladylike | |

Note that **-like** is often used in this way with names.

*He looked away from the Barry-like young man.*
*...a Proust-like scheme.*

## Words with other meanings

| businesslike | lifelike | suchlike | warlike |
|--------------|----------|----------|---------|

# -logue

**-logue** occurs in words which have 'speaking' or 'discussion' as part
of their meaning. For example, a 'dialogue' is a conversation or

discussion between two or more people; a 'travelogue' is a talk or film about travel.

Here is a list of words with this meaning:

| | | | |
|---|---|---|---|
| catalogue | dialogue | epilogue | prologue |
| decalogue | duologue | monologue | travelogue |

# -ly

## 1 Forming adverbs

PRODUCTIVE USE: **-ly** combines with adjectives to form adverbs. Adverbs formed in this way express the idea that something is done in the way described by the adjective. For example, if somebody smiles 'happily', they smile in a way that looks happy; if you do something 'rapidly', you do it in a rapid way. Adverbs formed in this way can often be used with adverbs of degree such as 'very' to show the extent to which the qualities described are true.

**Spelling:** A final 'y' is replaced by 'i' before adding **-ly**.

*My sister was singing very happily.*
*They walked quickly between the lines of houses.*
*...an opportunity to buy oil cheaply.*
*Her voice and manner changed suddenly; she became critical and dogmatic.*

Here are some examples of words with this meaning:

| | | | |
|---|---|---|---|
| badly | exactly | naturally | rapidly |
| cheaply | finally | normally | recently |
| clearly | frequently | obviously | seriously |
| directly | gradually | perfectly | slowly |
| easily | happily | properly | suddenly |
| equally | immediately | quickly | usually |

Note that the adverb formed from 'good' is 'well'.

## 2 Forming adjectives

**-ly** combines with nouns and occasionally adjectives to form new adjectives. Adjectives formed in this way describe things or people that have the qualities or characteristics which are typical of the original nouns and adjectives. For example, if someone is 'lively', they are very active, enthusiastic, and cheerful; if someone is 'friendly', they behave in a pleasant and kind way as if they are or would like to be your friend.

*They are bright, alert and lively.*

# -ly

*They were beautiful, lovely people.*

Here is a list of words with this meaning:

| | | | | |
|---|---|---|---|---|
| brotherly | fatherly | lonely | orderly | westerly |
| costly | friendly | lovely | saintly | womanly |
| deadly | heavenly | lowly | shapely | worldly |
| earthly | kindly | manly | sickly | |
| easterly | leisurely | motherly | sisterly | |
| elderly | lively | northerly | southerly | |

**Spelling:** A final 'y' is replaced by 'i' before adding 'er' and 'est' to form the comparative and superlative forms of these adjectives. For more information, see **-er** and **-est**.

*The officer guarding me was one of the friendlier ones.*
*He tends to choose the costliest solution rather than the least-costly.*

Here is a list of comparative and superlative adjectives:

| | | | |
|---|---|---|---|
| costlier | kindlier | lonelier | lowlier |
| costliest | kindliest | loneliest | lowliest |
| friendlier | livelier | lovelier | sicklier |
| friendliest | liveliest | loveliest | sickliest |

PRODUCTIVE USE: **-ly** combines with nouns that refer to people in order to form adjectives. For example, 'soldierly' skills are skills that a soldier typically has; 'musicianly' interests are interests that a musician is likely to have.

*To prove their soldierly abilities they started cutting off the knot of hair the Navahos wore.*
*She was on neighbourly terms with the Woods.*

# 3 Frequency

**-ly** combines with nouns that refer to periods of time in order to form words which indicate how often something happens or is done. For example, 'weekly' shopping trips happen once a week; if you wash you hair 'daily', you wash it every day.

**Spelling:** The adjective formed from 'day' is 'daily'.

*...a weekly payment of seven shillings.*
*Kate visited him daily, sometimes twice daily.*
*...an excellent hourly train service to London.*

Here is a list of words with this meaning:

| | | | |
|---|---|---|---|
| daily | hourly | quarterly | yearly |
| fortnightly | monthly | weekly | |

## Words with other meanings

| | | | |
|---|---|---|---|
| chiefly | highly | namely | timely |
| fully | mainly | nearly | utterly |
| hardly | merely | only | virtually |

# macro-

**macro-** occurs in words which refer to or describe things which are large in size or scope. Words formed in this way are usually technical or scientific. For example, 'macroeconomics' is the study of economics on a national scale.

*In macroeconomics it is necessary to have both planning and freedom.*
*...the macrocosm of the outer world.*
*...macro-scale correlations.*

Here is a list of words with this meaning:

| | | | |
|---|---|---|---|
| macrobiotic | macroeconomics | macromolecular | macro-scale |
| macrocosm | macro-graph | macro-objectives | macro-structure |

# -made

PRODUCTIVE USE: **-made** combines with nouns and adjectives, especially those that refer to people, places, or nationalities, in order to form new adjectives. Words formed in this way describe things which have been produced in a particular way or place, or by a particular group of people. For example, if food is 'home-made', it was cooked in someone's home rather than bought in a shop; if a product is 'British-made', it was produced in Britain.

*...Grandmother's home-made brown bread.*
*The line of boulders looked quite like the foundations of a man-made wall.*
*...hand-made items from skilled craftsmen.*
*...a mass-produced, machine-made article.*

Here are some examples of words with this meaning:

| | | |
|---|---|---|
| American-made | French-made | new-made |
| British-made | fresh-made | purpose-made |
| Chinese-made | German-made | ready-made |
| country-made | hand-made | Soviet-made |
| custom-made | Hollywood-made | tailor-made |
| European-made | home-made | US-made |
| factory-made | machine-made | |
| foreign-made | man-made | |

Note that a 'self-made' man is someone who started life without money, education, or social position and who has become rich and successful by his own efforts.

# mal-

**mal-** combines with nouns, adjectives, and verbs to form new nouns, adjectives, and verbs. Words formed in this way refer to or describe things that are bad or unpleasant, or that are unsuccessful or imperfect in some way. For example, if someone suffers from 'malnutrition', they have not eaten enough good food; if a machine 'malfunctions', it doesn't work properly.

*Malnutrition lowers resistance to illness.*
*The child is thoroughly maladjusted.*
*...the criminal maldistribution of the world's food resources.*

Here is a list of words with this meaning:

| | | |
|---|---|---|
| malabsorption | maldistribution | malnutrition |
| maladjusted | malformation | malodorous |
| maladjustment | malfunction | malpractice |
| maladministration | malnourished | maltreatment |

For more information on words with this meaning, see **mis-**.

### Words with other meanings

| | | | |
|---|---|---|---|
| maladroit | malaria | malice | malignant |
| malaise | malevolent | malign | malinger |

# man-

**man-** combines with nouns and participles that refer to or describe an action in order to form new nouns and adjectives. Words formed in this way refer to or describe things which affect or are affected by people, or actions affecting people. For example, if something is 'man-made', it is made by people rather than being formed naturally; 'man-management' is the control and organization of the people involved in a business or similar concern.

Note that words formed in this way relate to people of either sex, and not just men in particular.

*Man-made materials are preferable to natural materials.*
*Man-devised processes work reliably only when applied to non-living materials.*

*All leopards everywhere are under attack as potential man-killers.*

Here is a list of words with this meaning:

| | | |
|---|---|---|
| man-destroying | man-killer | man-watching |
| man-devised | man-made | man-worshipping |
| man-eating | man-management | |
| man-hunt | man-powered | |

## Words with other meanings

| | | | |
|---|---|---|---|
| manhandle | man-hour | manpower | manslaughter |
| manhole | mankind | manservant | |

# -man

## 1 Occupation or interests

**-man** combines with nouns to form new nouns. Nouns formed in this way refer to people whose job or occupation involves whatever the original noun refers to. For example, a 'clergyman' is a member of the clergy and works for the Christian church; a 'fireman' is someone whose job is to put out fires.

*...the college clergyman, the Reverend Rigger.*
*Dixon paid the garage-man and the taxi moved off.*
*He started in television as a cameraman, but progressed to directing.*
*When the barman set their glasses in front of them, they drank to Mary Jane.*

Here is a list of words with this meaning:

| | | | |
|---|---|---|---|
| barman | dairyman | gunman | salesman |
| businessman | deliveryman | milkman | seaman |
| cameraman | fireman | policeman | stuntman |
| clergyman | fisherman | postman | taxman |
| coalman | garage-man | railwayman | tradesman |
| committeeman | gasman | repairman | weatherman |

PRODUCTIVE USE: **-man** combines with nouns that describe a place of work, a piece of equipment, or the thing that someone works with.

*He was the best camel-man in town.*
*The lighting-man is a highly experienced old pro.*
Note that words formed in this way are often used generally to refer to people of either sex. Many people think this is wrong, however, and prefer to use '-woman' when the person referred to is a woman, and '-person' or '-people' when the sex of a person or group of people is not known or is not thought to be important.

For more information on words that refer to people, see **-folk, -kind, -people, -person,** and **-woman**.

## 2 People's origins

-man combines with the names of places and with adjectives describing nationality in order to form new nouns. Nouns formed in this way refer to a man who comes from the particular town, county, or country named. For example, a 'Yorkshireman' is a man who comes from, or lives in, Yorkshire; a 'Welshman' is somebody who comes from Wales. Words formed in this way are never used to refer to women.

*Even though the Yorkshireman finished two seconds outside his best, the race was no anti-climax.*
*In Wungong, there is a single general store, run by a Chinaman.*
*The greatest of Scotsmen was the first economist, Adam Smith.*
*McCalden is an Ulsterman who trained as a teacher.*

Here is a list of words with this meaning:

| | | | |
|---|---|---|---|
| Chinaman | Englishman | Scotsman | Yorkshireman |
| Cornishman | Frenchman | Ulsterman | |
| Dutchman | Irishman | Welshman | |

PRODUCTIVE USE: -man combines with any noun which describes a place.

*Although my parents have always lived in towns, I feel like a countryman.*
*They are as amazed and delighted as an Earthman would be on learning that Martians cook by gas.*

## 3 Numbers of people

PRODUCTIVE USE: -man combines with any number to show that something involves or is intended for use by the number of people mentioned. For example, football is played by an 'eleven-man' team; a 'two-man' tent is designed for two people to sleep in. Man- is usually used in this way to refer to people of either sex.

*The organization secured a majority on the eleven-man National Committee.*
*...the sound of an eighty-man orchestra playing the overture.*
*The Rooikat is a four-man, eight-wheel vehicle.*
*Behind Crown counsel are three rows of seats for the fifteen-man jury.*

### Words with other meanings

| | | | |
|---|---|---|---|
| batsman | footman | gentleman | marksman |
| bushman | foreman | handyman | nobleman |
| caveman | freshman | highwayman | ombudsman |
| chairman | frogman | hitman | spokesman |
| con-man | front-man | layman | statesman |
| everyman | gamesman | linesman | yes-man |

# -mania

**-mania** occurs in nouns which refer to unusual behaviour caused by a compulsion to do a particular thing. For example, 'kleptomania' is a strong and uncontrollable desire to steal things; 'pyromania' is an uncontrollable urge to set fire to things.

*A teacher unaided by a child's parents can seldom cure kleptomania.*
*Kawukji was obsessed with himself; his egomania knew no bounds.*
*Kennedy's assassination was the greatest act of megalomania in modern crime.*

Here is a list of words with this meaning:

| | | |
|---|---|---|
| egomania | kleptomania | monomania |
| erotomania | megalomania | nymphomania |

# -mate

**-mate** combines with nouns that refer to a place or activity in order to form new nouns. Nouns formed in this way refer to a person who shares that place with someone or who helps them with that particular activity. For example, your 'flatmate' is the person who shares a flat with you; a 'workmate' is someone you work with.

**Spelling:** Words formed in this way are usually written as one word, but some of the less common ones can be written with a hyphen.

*Laura clearly felt that her flatmate had been in the way.*
*I sought permission to swap shifts with a workmate.*
*He met an old schoolmate of his from Umtata.*
*His cabin-mate, Sandy, was still feeling under the weather.*

Here is a list of words with this meaning:

| | | | |
|---|---|---|---|
| bedmate | clubmate | roommate | team-mate |
| cabin-mate | flatmate | schoolmate | workmate |
| classmate | playmate | shipmate | |

PRODUCTIVE USE: **-mate** combines with any noun that describes a place or activity that you share with someone.

*Anne, a cheerful nine-year-old, seemed Linda's best desk-mate.*
*Otto's watch-mate was due to make his appearance just at that moment.*
*..her tent-mate of the previous summer.*

## Words with other meanings

| | | | |
|---|---|---|---|
| checkmate | inmate | soul-mate | stalemate |

107

# matri-

**matri-** or **matr-** occurs in words which have 'mother' or 'woman' as part of their meaning. For example, a 'matriarch' is the female head of a society, family, or organization; a 'matron' can be either a middle-aged married woman, a woman who looks after the health and hygiene of children in boarding schools, or a very senior nurse in a hospital.

Here is a list of words with this meaning:

| | | | |
|---|---|---|---|
| matriarch | matriarchal | matricide | matron |

# mega-

## 1 Size

PRODUCTIVE USE: **mega-** combines with nouns to form new nouns. Nouns formed in this way refer to things which are extremely large or important. For example, 'megabucks' refers to a great deal of money; a 'megaloss' is the loss of a very large amount of money.

**Spelling:** Words formed in this way can be written with a hyphen or as one word.

*Megabucks are there for the taking.*
*...another massive mega-acquisition.*
*...these megablocks of flats.*
*...Italy's megastar, Giorgio Armani.*
Here are some examples of words with this meaning:

| | | |
|---|---|---|
| mega-acquisition | mega-bureaucracy | megaloss |
| mega-bid | mega-buyout | mega-production |
| megablock | mega-documentary | megarock |
| megabucks | mega-fantasy | megastar |

Note that words formed in this way are very informal. They occur frequently in conversation, especially amongst young people, and tend to sound exaggerated. **mega** is also often used as a word by itself in informal conversation to mean extremely large or extremely good.

## 2 Measurement

**mega-** combines with nouns that refer to units of measurement in order to form new nouns that refer to units that are a million times bigger. For example, a 'megahertz' is a unit of frequency, especially radio frequency. One 'megahertz' equals one million cycles per second.

*Hydrogen has a characteristic frequency of 1,420 megahertz.*
*...500,000 megatons of TNT.*

Here is a list of words with this meaning:

| | | |
|---|---|---|
| megabyte | megahertz | megawatt |
| megacycle | megaton | |

## Words with other meanings

| | | |
|---|---|---|
| megalithic | megalomania | megalomaniac | megaphone |

# -ment

**-ment** combines with verbs to form nouns. Nouns formed in this way refer to the process of making or doing something, or to the result of this process. For example, if you are proud of an 'achievement', you are proud of something you have achieved or caused to happen; you make an 'adjustment' when you adjust something or adjust to something; 'excitement' is the emotion you feel when you are excited.

*...the achievement of equality for women.*
*...the rapid development of British industry.*
*The weather showed signs of improvement.*
*Fanny saw with amazement that the letter was addressed to her.*

Here is a list of words with this meaning:

| | | |
|---|---|---|
| abandonment | assessment | improvement |
| accomplishment | assignment | investment |
| achievement | attachment | involvement |
| acknowledgement | attainment | management |
| adjustment | commitment | movement |
| advertisement | deployment | payment |
| agreement | development | punishment |
| amazement | discouragement | puzzlement |
| amusement | employment | replacement |
| announcement | enjoyment | requirement |
| argument | entertainment | resentment |
| arrangement | excitement | retirement |

## Words with other meanings

| | | | |
|---|---|---|---|
| apartment | detriment | government | sentiment |
| armament | document | instrument | settlement |
| basement | element | monument | shipment |
| comment | embankment | ointment | statement |
| compartment | environment | parliament | supplement |
| complement | equipment | pavement | temperament |
| compliment | establishment | placement | testament |
| department | experiment | secondment | treatment |

109

# -meter

**-meter** occurs in words which refer to instruments or devices that measure things, particularly for scientific purposes. For example, a 'speedometer' is an instrument that measures the speed of a car or other vehicle; a 'mileometer' is an instrument that measures the distance in miles that a vehicle has travelled.

Here is a list of words with this meaning:

| | | | |
|---|---|---|---|
| acidimeter | calorimeter | hydrometer | speedometer |
| altimeter | chronometer | mileometer | thermometer |
| barometer | colorimeter | pedometer | voltmeter |

# -metre

**-metre** occurs in nouns that refer to units of length that are either greater or smaller than a metre. For example, there are a hundred 'centimetres' in a metre; a 'kilometre' is a thousand metres long.

Here is a list of words with this meaning:

| | | | |
|---|---|---|---|
| centimetre | kilometre | millimetre | nanometre |

# micro-

**micro-** occurs in nouns that have 'very small' as part of their meaning. For example, a 'micro-organism' is a very small organism which cannot be seen with the naked eye; a 'microscope' is an instrument which magnifies very small objects so you can look at them and study them. Nouns formed with **micro-** are often used in technical or scientific language.

**Spelling:** Words formed in this way are usually written as one word, but some of the less common ones can be written with a hyphen.

Here is a list of words with this meaning:

| | | |
|---|---|---|
| microbiology | micro-environment | microscope |
| microcomputer | microfilm | microsecond |
| micro-economics | microgram | microstructure |
| microelectronics | micro-organism | microsurgery |

## Words with other meanings

| | | | |
|---|---|---|---|
| microlight | microphone | microprocessor | microwave |

# mid-

## 1 Time

PRODUCTIVE USE: **mid-** combines with nouns that refer to months, years, and particular parts of the day in order to form new nouns. Nouns formed in this way refer to the middle part of a particular period of time. For example, if something happens in 'mid-June', it happens in the middle of June; if something happens at 'midnight', it happens at twelve o'clock in the middle of the night. **mid-** does not combine with nouns that refer to days of the week or to precise times.

**Spelling:** Words formed in this way are usually written with a hyphen, but some of the more common ones are written as one word.

*Although it was mid-June, the weather outside was a fine chill drizzle.*
*It was a Saturday in midsummer.*
*They run out of energy in mid-evening at the end of each busy day.*
*The Promenade Concerts have been organized by the BBC since the mid-1920s.*
*They were huddled into two or three coats against the mid-October chill.*

Here are some examples of words with this meaning:

| | | | |
|---|---|---|---|
| mid-afternoon | mid-evening | mid-morning | mid-week |
| mid-century | mid-hour | midnight | midwinter |
| midday | mid-month | midsummer | |

Note that **mid-** is sometimes used in this way with expressions which refer to someone's age.

*...a portly gentleman in his mid-fifties.*
*...a boy in his mid-teens.*

## 2 Position

PRODUCTIVE USE: **mid-** combines with nouns that refer to a particular place or area in order to form new nouns. Nouns formed in this way refer to the central part of that place or area. For example, if something happens in 'mid-ocean', it happens in the middle of an ocean; 'mid-America' is the central part of America.

*He saw it glide past him, as a ship passes another in mid-ocean.*
*The ship backed into mid-harbour and dropped anchor.*
*The taxi, in mid-road, was just beginning to reverse.*

# mid-

*...a mid-air collision in British airspace.*
*...the Ratgoed Valley, near Machynlleth in mid-Wales.*

Here are some examples of words with this meaning:

| | | | |
|---|---|---|---|
| mid-air | mid-channel | mid-Europe | mid-road |
| mid-America | mid-court | mid-harbour | mid-stairs |
| mid-Atlantic | mid-Devon | mid-ocean | mid-Wales |

## 3 Actions

PRODUCTIVE USE: **mid-** also combines with nouns that refer to or involve an action in order to form new nouns. Nouns formed in this way are usually used in prepositional phrases beginning with 'in', but can also be used to modify other nouns. Words formed in this way express the idea that the action referred to is not completed. For example, if someone stops in 'mid-bite', they stop in the middle of biting something; if someone stops talking in 'mid-sentence', they stop before they have finished what they are saying.

*Mr. Solomon and Mrs. Babcock froze guiltily in mid-bite.*
*Boon, frozen in mid-stride, glared at me.*
*A commotion out in the hall stopped Meadows in mid-sentence.*
*She was playing Chopin on the piano; I heard her stop in mid-prelude.*
*...a mid-flight shutdown of a perfectly good engine.*

Here are some examples of words with this meaning:

| | | | |
|---|---|---|---|
| mid-banter | mid-guffaw | mid-race | mid-syllable |
| mid-bite | mid-life | mid-section | mid-term |
| mid-career | mid-lunge | mid-sentence | mid-verse |
| mid-composition | mid-page | mid-session | mid-voyage |
| mid-flight | mid-passage | mid-step | mid-whirl |
| mid-flow | mid-prelude | mid-stride | mid-yawn |

### Words with other meanings

| | | |
|---|---|---|
| midpoint | midstream | midwife |
| midriff | midway | |

# milli-

**milli-** occurs in words which have 'thousand' or 'thousandth' as part of their meaning. For example, a 'millilitre' is a metric unit of volume for liquids and gases which is equal to one thousandth of a litre.

Here is a list of words with this meaning:

| | | | |
|---|---|---|---|
| milliamp | milligram | millimetre | milli-rad |
| millidegree | millilitre | millipede | millisecond |

# -minded

## 1 Attitudes and characteristics

PRODUCTIVE USE: **-minded** combines with adjectives to form new adjectives. Adjectives formed in this way describe the character, attitudes, or opinions of particular people. For example, if someone is 'single-minded', they have only one aim or purpose and are determined to achieve it; if someone is 'narrow-minded', they are unwilling to consider new ideas or opinions.

**Spelling:** Words formed in this way are written with a hyphen with the exception of 'broadminded', which is written as one word.

*He loved India with the single-minded devotion that some men give to their work.*
*She was possibly even more serious-minded than her father.*
*Johan became more broadminded about race the longer he stayed in England.*
*...an attractive, strong-minded Scots girl.*
*She is very obedient, but so absent-minded, careless and untidy.*

Here are some examples of words with this meaning:

| | | |
|---|---|---|
| absent-minded | liberal-minded | right-minded |
| bloody-minded | like-minded | serious-minded |
| broadminded | literal-minded | single-minded |
| dirty-minded | mean-minded | small-minded |
| evil-minded | narrow-minded | strong-minded |
| fair-minded | open-minded | tidy-minded |
| generous-minded | petty-minded | tough-minded |
| high-minded | practical-minded | weak-minded |

## 2 Interests and aims

PRODUCTIVE USE: **-minded** combines with nouns to form adjectives that describe people who are interested in or concerned with a particular thing. For example, if someone is 'community-minded', they are interested in and take account of the needs of the community; if someone is 'career-minded', they are committed to their career and want to make a success of it.

*Some community-minded seniors had left us.*

## -minded

*...liberal and reform-minded governments.*
*The Americans are the most sports-minded nation in the world.*

Here are some examples of words with this meaning:

| | | |
|---|---|---|
| acquisition-minded | expansion-minded | reform-minded |
| career-minded | future-minded | security-minded |
| church-minded | management-minded | sports-minded |
| civic-minded | marriage-minded | war-minded |
| community-minded | nuclear-minded | |
| economy-minded | peace-minded | |

## 3 Intelligence

**-minded** also combines with adjectives to form new adjectives that describe someone's intellectual qualities. For example, if you describe someone as 'simple-minded', you mean that they are not very clever and cannot think intelligently; if someone is 'lively-minded', they are intelligent and able to think quickly.

*He is simple-minded and totally unable to understand anyone more complicated than himself.*
*...a beautiful, sharp-minded actress.*
*Never have so many people been as bright-minded, as curious and as critical as the young today.*

Here is a list of words with this meaning:

| | | | |
|---|---|---|---|
| bright-minded | feeble-minded | lively-minded | simple-minded |
| empty-minded | fuzzy-minded | sharp-minded | woolly-minded |

# mini-

PRODUCTIVE USE: **mini-** combines with nouns to form new nouns that refer to a smaller version of a particular thing. For example, a 'minibus' is a small bus; a 'mini-skirt' is a very short skirt.

**Spelling:** Words formed in this way are written with a hyphen with the exception of 'minibus', which is written as one word.

*They would be providing minibuses to carry staff to and from work.*
*...the most successful company in the mini-computer field.*
*...a mini-expedition to Everest with just four climbers and a few sherpas.*
*Promotion is based on mini-exams or teachers' assessment of performance.*

*The drums of chemicals were located by an unmanned mini-submarine.*

Here are some examples of words with this meaning:

| | | |
|---|---|---|
| mini-budget | mini-dress | mini-scooter |
| minibus | mini-exam | mini-series |
| mini-cab | mini-expedition | mini-skirt |
| mini-camera | mini-explosion | mini-submarine |
| mini-city | mini-golf | mini-summit |
| mini-computer | mini-lecture | mini-team |
| mini-cruise | mini-market | mini-tour |
| mini-documentary | mini-rugby | mini-version |

## Words with other meanings

| | | | |
|---|---|---|---|
| miniature | minimal | minimize | minimum |

# mis-

**mis-** combines with verbs and nouns to form new verbs and nouns. Words formed in this way describe or refer to things that are done wrongly or badly. For example, if you 'mishear' what someone says to you, you think that they said something different from what they actually said; a 'misunderstanding' occurs when someone fails to understand something properly.

*I was sure I had misheard the question.*
*He jumped at what he thought was the right moment, misjudged, and fell to the bottom of the boat.*
*I was wondering where I'd picked up this piece of blatant misinformation.*
*...the enormity of the student's misconception.*

Here is a list of words with this meaning:

| | | |
|---|---|---|
| misapprehension | mishear | mispronunciation |
| misbehave | misinform | misquotation |
| misbehaviour | misinformation | misquote |
| miscalculate | misinterpret | misread |
| miscalculation | misjudge | misrepresentation |
| misconception | misjudgement | mistreat |
| misconduct | mismanage | mistrust |
| misconstrue | mismanagement | misunderstand |
| misdirect | misplace | misunderstanding |
| misfortune | misprint | misuse |

For more information on words with this meaning see **mal-**.

## Words with other meanings

| | | | |
|---|---|---|---|
| misadventure | misdeed | misguided | mistake |
| miscarriage | misdemeanour | mislay | mistook |
| mischance | misfit | mislead | |
| mischief | misgiving | misshape | |

# mock-

PRODUCTIVE USE: **mock-** combines with nouns and adjectives to form new nouns and adjectives. Words formed in this way refer to or describe things that are an imitation or copy of something else. For example, if someone displays 'mock-aggression', they are pretending to be aggressive; if a house is described as 'mock-Tudor', it has been made to look like the houses built in Tudor times.

*She spoke quietly, with none of her usual mock-aggression.*
*...a mock-English public-house.*
*Instead of honest, simple crafts, he prefers mock-expensive products.*
*...a deliberately mock-provocative look.*

Here are some examples of words with this meaning:

| | | |
|---|---|---|
| mock-aggression | mock-fight | mock-sadness |
| mock-attack | mock-flirtatious | mock-savage |
| mock-childish | mock-heroics | mock-style |
| mock-Chippendale | mock-imperial | mock-sulk |
| mock-courtesy | mock-innocent | mock-surprise |
| mock-discomfort | mock-Latin | mock-Tudor |
| mock-English | mock-modesty | mock-wrestling |
| mock-expensive | mock-provocative | mock-yawn |

### Words with other meanings

| | | |
|---|---|---|
| mockery | mocking | mock-up |

# -monger

**-monger** occurs in nouns that have 'trader' or 'dealer' as part of their meaning. For example, a 'fishmonger' is a person who sells fish; an 'ironmonger' is someone who works in a shop selling tools, nails and other things made out of metal. **-monger** also occurs in some words which refer to people who start or encourage rumours of some kind. For example, a 'warmonger' encourages people to expect war or tries to get a war started.

Here is a list of words with this meaning:

| | | | |
|---|---|---|---|
| fishmonger | rumourmonger | tattle-monger | whoremonger |
| ironmonger | scaremonger | warmonger | |

# mono-

**mono-** occurs in words which have 'one' or 'single' as part of their meaning. For example, 'monogamy' is the custom of being married to only one person at a time; if you speak in a 'monosyllabic' way you use words that have only one syllable.

Here is a list of words with this meaning:

| | | | |
|---|---|---|---|
| monocentric | monocracy | monologue | monotheism |
| monochrome | monoculture | monoplane | monotone |
| monocle | monogamy | monosyllabic | monoxide |

# -most

**-most** combines with adjectives that describe position in order to form new adjectives. Adjectives formed in this way describe things that are situated further in a particular direction than other things of the same kind. For example, the 'topmost' sheet of paper is the one that is highest or nearest the top; the 'northernmost' part of a country is the area that is farthest towards the north.

*Families of cranes nested in the topmost branches of the tree.*
*...the innermost room of the castle.*
*They hurled themselves from sleighs on to the rearmost carriages.*

Here is a list of words with this meaning:

| | | | |
|---|---|---|---|
| easternmost | lowermost | outermost | topmost |
| hindmost | nethermost | rearmost | uppermost |
| innermost | northernmost | southernmost | westernmost |

### Words with other meanings

| | | |
|---|---|---|
| foremost | utmost | uttermost |

# much-

PRODUCTIVE USE: **much-** combines with past participles to form adjectives. Adjectives formed in this way express the idea that the qualities or states they describe are true to a great extent. For example, a 'much-respected' person is someone who is respected a great deal; a 'much-needed' thing is something there is a great need for.

*He was a long serving and much-respected member of staff.*
*Schools raise much-needed cash by letting their facilities in the evening.*
*...the author of a much-acclaimed book.*
*For a young child, the death of a much-loved pet can be a terrible blow.*

## much-

*...Hearst's own account of her much-publicized kidnapping.*

Here are some examples of words with this meaning:

| | | |
|---|---|---|
| much-abused | much-criticized | much-prized |
| much-acclaimed | much-discussed | much-publicized |
| much-admired | much-improved | much-quoted |
| much-appreciated | much-loved | much-respected |
| much-beloved | much-maligned | much-travelled |
| much-changed | much-married | much-tried |
| much-complimented | much-needed | much-vaunted |
| much-copied | much-praised | much-worn |

# multi-

PRODUCTIVE USE: **multi-** combines with nouns and adjectives to form new adjectives. Adjectives formed in this way express the idea that there is a large number of a particular thing, or a large amount of a particular quality. For example, a 'multinational' company is one which operates in a number of countries; a 'multi-purpose' tool is a tool that can be used for more than one purpose.

**Spelling:** Words formed in this way are usually written with a hyphen, but some of the more common ones are written as one word.

*...the dismantling of the economic system from the multinational companies downwards.*
*...commitment to human rights and multi-racial harmony.*
*...a manifesto for next year's multi-party elections.*
*...a multi-flavoured white wine.*

Here are some examples of words with this meaning:

| | | |
|---|---|---|
| multi-candidate | multi-family | multi-million |
| multi-children | multi-flavoured | multinational |
| multi-choice | multilateral | multi-party |
| multi-coloured | multi-layered | multi-purpose |
| multicultural | multi-legged | multi-racial |
| multi-dimensional | multi-level | multi-screen |
| multi-faceted | multilingual | multi-storey |
| multi-faith | multi-media | multi-talented |

### Words with other meanings

| | |
|---|---|
| multiplication | multiply |
| multiplicity | multitude |

# -naut

**-naut** occurs in nouns that refer to people who navigate or control a vehicle of some kind. For example, an 'astronaut' is a person who is trained to fly in a spacecraft; an 'aeronaut' is the pilot of a hot-air balloon or airship.

Here is a list of words with this meaning:

aeronaut          cosmonaut
astronaut

Note that a 'juggernaut' is a type of very large lorry and not the person who drives it.

# near-

PRODUCTIVE USE: **near-** combines with nouns and adjectives to form new nouns and adjectives. Words formed in this way express the idea that something has almost all of the qualities usually associated with the original noun or adjective. For example, if you describe something as 'near-perfect', you mean that you think there is so little wrong with it that it is almost perfect; a 'near-accident' is an incident which could easily have led to an accident but did not.

*We completed the climb in near-perfect conditions.*
*The inexperience of the pilots produced near-disaster.*
*...all shades from pink to near-black.*
*The tree was a hardy, near-wild variety.*
*Mick and I collapsed into near-hysterical laughter.*

Here are some examples of words with this meaning:

| | | | |
|---|---|---|---|
| near-accident | near-crisis | near-landless | near-silence |
| near-bankrupt | near-disaster | near-miraculous | near-slum |
| near-black | near-equal | near-monopoly | near-vacuum |
| near-capacity | near-hysterical | near-panic | near-vertical |
| near-certainty | near-identical | near-perfect | near-white |
| near-chaos | near-impossible | near-permanent | near-wild |

## Words with other meanings

| | | |
|---|---|---|
| near-neighbour | nearside | near-term |
| near-relative | near-sighted | |

# neo-

PRODUCTIVE USE: **neo-** combines with nouns and adjectives to form new nouns and adjectives. Words formed in this way refer to or describe things or people that follow a previous example of something, but that are slightly different because they have been changed, adapted, or brought up to date. For example, 'neo-classical' architecture uses designs based upon classical Greek and

# neo-

Roman architecture and art; a 'neo-Freudian' is someone whose beliefs are based on the teachings of Freud.

Note that words formed in this way are fairly formal and few of them occur frequently.

*To the left is a neo-classical church, St John's.*
*...a kind of neo-Stalinism.*
*To some, this appeal for a form of neo-populism will no doubt seem naive.*
*...real Tudor chimneys, and neo-Tudor turrets beyond.*

Here are some examples of words with this meaning:

| | | |
|---|---|---|
| neo-Aristotelian | neo-Darwinism | neo-Nazi |
| neo-baroque | neo-expressionism | neo-Nazism |
| neo-bourgeoisie | neo-Freudian | neo-Platonic |
| neo-classical | neo-Georgian | neo-populism |
| neo-classicism | neo-Gothic | neo-Stalinism |
| neo-colonialism | neo-Liberal | neo-Tudor |
| neo-colonialist | neo-Marxist | |

## Words with other meanings

| | | | |
|---|---|---|---|
| neocortex | neolithic | neo-natal | neotechnic |

# -ness

PRODUCTIVE USE: **-ness** combines with adjectives to form nouns that refer to the state or quality described by the adjective. For example, 'gentleness' is the quality of being gentle; 'happiness' is the state of being happy.

**Spelling:** A final 'y' is replaced by 'i' before adding **-ness.**

*There was a gentleness about his face.*
*He took advantage of my utter helplessness.*
*...an awareness of the child's real needs.*
*My disbelief gave way to sadness.*
*...the Sunday emptiness of the streets.*

Here are some examples of words with this meaning:

| | | | |
|---|---|---|---|
| aggressiveness | consciousness | happiness | permissiveness |
| attractiveness | deafness | helplessness | rudeness |
| awareness | drunkenness | illness | sadness |
| awkwardness | effectiveness | kindness | sickness |
| bitterness | emptiness | loneliness | sweetness |
| blindness | foolishness | loveliness | tenderness |
| boldness | friendliness | madness | ugliness |
| carelessness | gentleness | nervousness | weakness |
| cleverness | goodness | openness | youthfulness |

### Words with other meanings

business       forgiveness      likeness      witness

# neur-, neuro-

**neur-** or **neuro-** occurs in words which have 'nerve' or 'nervous system' as part of their meaning. For example, 'neuralgia' is a very severe pain along the whole length of a nerve; 'neurology' is the study of the nervous system. Words formed in this way are formal and medical uses.

Here is a list of words with this meaning:

| | | |
|---|---|---|
| neuralgia | neurology | neuro-physiology |
| neurectomy | neuromuscular | neuropsychiatry |
| neuroanatomy | neuron | neurosurgeon |
| neurobiologist | neuro-pharmacology | neurotoxin |

# new-

## 1 Recently done

PRODUCTIVE USE: **new-** combines with past participles to form adjectives. Adjectives formed in this way describe things that have been made or done very recently. For example, 'new-baked' bread is bread that has been made very recently; a 'new-found' ability is one you have discovered recently.

**Spelling:** Words formed in this way are written with a hyphen with the exception of 'newborn', which is written as one word.

*Mothers now have six weeks off from work to nurse their newborn babies.*
*...the new-built palace of St. James.*
*New-hatched frogs hopped about like flies.*
*...new-baked bread.*
*...his short strong hands with hairy fingers and new-clipped nails.*

Here are some examples of words with this meaning:

| | | | |
|---|---|---|---|
| new-baked | new-cut | new-hatched | new-pointed |
| newborn | new-fashioned | new-laid | new-skinned |
| new-built | new-fledged | new-made | new-washed |
| new-clipped | new-floored | new-minted | new-wedded |
| new-coined | new-found | new-mown | new-won |

## 2 Recent

**new-** combines with nouns and present participles to form new nouns and adjectives. Words formed in this way refer to or describe

## new-

things that have been made or come into existence recently. For
example, 'new-generation' technology is technology which makes
use of the most recent developments; something that is 'new-
smelling' smells as though it is new.

*...new-generation pressurized water reactor stations.*
*...a former Kremlin leader, running for election to a new-style*
*parliament.*
*...inside, among the new-smelling oak panels.*
*His suitcase was new-looking but cheap.*

Here is a list of words with this meaning:

| | | |
|---|---|---|
| new-age | new-look | new-smelling |
| new-generation | new-looking | new-style |

## news-

**news-** combines with nouns to form new nouns. Nouns formed in
this way refer to things that are connected with the news in some
way. For example, a 'newspaper' is a publication printed on large
sheets of paper giving information about recent events; a
'newsletter' is made up of a small number of printed sheets
containing recent information about a group or organization.

**Spelling:** Words formed in this way are usually written as one
word, but some of the less common ones can be written with a
hyphen.

*...a journalist on an anti-Government newspaper.*
*...a small tobacconist and newsagent shop in Paddington.*
*...the newsroom where the reporters were clattering on typewriters.*

Here is a list of words with this meaning:

| | | | |
|---|---|---|---|
| newsagent | newsfilm | newsman | newsreel |
| newsboy | newsflash | newspaper | newsroom |
| newscast | newsletter | newsprint | news-sheet |
| newsdesk | news-magazine | newsreader | news-stand |

**News-** is also used with this meaning to form the adjective
'newsworthy'. If something is 'newsworthy', it is sufficiently
interesting to be reported in the news.

*...a particularly macabre and newsworthy crime.*

## non-

PRODUCTIVE USE: **non-** combines with nouns and adjectives to form
new nouns and adjectives. Words formed in this way express the

122

idea that a person or thing does not have the qualities or characteristics referred to. For example, a 'non-smoker' is someone who does not smoke; if you take up a 'non-aggressive' position, you approach something in a way that is not aggressive. **Non-** also combines with nouns that refer to a particular kind of action to express the idea that that action has not been taken. For example, if you refer to the 'non-acceptance' of something, you are referring to the fact that it has not been accepted.

**Spelling:** Words formed in this way are usually written with a hyphen, but some of the more common words are written as one word.

*He chain smoked, which isn't very pleasant for a non-smoker like me.*
*If the landlord is non-resident, the landlord does not have right of access.*
*The answer is not non-change, but a different kind of change.*
*...simple non-economic values like beauty, health, or cleanliness.*

Here are some examples of words with this meaning:

| | | | |
|---|---|---|---|
| non-academic | non-classical | non-payment | non-target |
| non-aggressive | non-committal | non-problem | non-verbal |
| non-athletic | non-competitive | non-profit | non-violence |
| non-believer | non-economic | non-reader | non-violent |
| non-binding | non-essential | non-resident | non-virtue |
| non-biological | non-fatal | non-smoker | |
| non-change | non-human | non-specialist | |

Note that **non-** also combines with adverbs that derive from the adjectives given above.

*Eighty percent of the meaning in a conversation passes non-verbally.*
*In 1975 his son succeeded non-violently to the leadership.*

For more information on prefixes with a negative meaning, see **de-, dis-, il-,** and **un-**.

### Words with other meanings

| | | |
|---|---|---|
| non-drip | nonentity | nonsense |

# -ocracy, -ocrat

**-ocracy** occurs in nouns which refer to a particular type of ruling body or powerful class of people. For example, a 'democracy' is a system of government in which people choose their rulers by voting for them in elections; the 'aristocracy' is a class of people whose families have a high social rank and, in some countries, special titles.

Here is a list of words with this meaning:

| | | |
|---|---|---|
| aristocracy | bureaucracy | technocracy |
| autocracy | democracy | |

**-ocrat** occurs in nouns which refer to someone who is a member of one of these groups. For example, a 'democrat' is someone who believes in the ideals of democracy; an 'aristocrat' is someone whose family belongs to the aristocracy.

Here is a list of words with this meaning:

| | | |
|---|---|---|
| aristocrat | bureaucrat | technocrat |
| autocrat | democrat | |

# octa-, octo-

**octa-** and **octo-** occur in words which indicate that something has eight parts. For example, an 'octagon' is a geometrical shape which has eight straight sides; an 'octopus' is a sea creature with eight limbs.

Here is a list of words with this meaning:

| | | |
|---|---|---|
| octagon | octave | octopus |
| octahedron | octogenarian | octosyllabic |

# off-

## 1 Position

PRODUCTIVE USE: **off-** combines with nouns which refer to a place in order to form words which are used in front of other nouns. Words formed in this way describe places, things, or events which are not situated or do not happen in a particular place or the expected place. **off-** is only used in this way when the noun it combines with is usually used with the preposition 'on'. For example, if students live in 'off-campus' accommodation, they do not live on the campus of their college or university; if there are 'off-stage' noises in a play, they do not happen on the stage, but in the part of the theatre that is just behind or to the side of the stage.

**Spelling:** Words formed in this way are written with a hyphen with the exception of 'offshore', which is written as one word.

*...off-campus social life.*
*...offshore oil production.*

*...the off-field pressures of captaincy.*
Words formed in this way are occasionally used as adverbs.

*Tina, a Swedish girl, wanted to live off-campus with a friend.*

Here are some examples of words with this meaning:

| | | | |
|---|---|---|---|
| off-Broadway | off-field | off-screen | off-stage |
| off-campus | off-piste | offshore | off-track |
| off-court | off-road | off-site | |

## 2 Showing that something is not the case

**off-** also combines with some other nouns to form words which express the idea that whatever is referred to by the noun is not the case. For example, if you are 'off-balance', you are standing in a way that is not properly balanced and can easily fall or be knocked over; if something is 'off-centre', it is not exactly in the middle of a space or surface.

*There was a stone under his boot, and he was off-balance.*
*...cheap, or off-peak electricity.*
*It is easy to be taken off-guard.*

Words formed in this way are occasionally used as adverbs.

*The music was slow now; a single fiddle played a mournful solo off-key.*
Here is a list of words with this meaning:

| | | |
|---|---|---|
| off-balance | off-guard | off-peak |
| off-centre | off-key | off-season |

### Words with other meanings

| | | | |
|---|---|---|---|
| offbeat | off-day | off-limits | offshoot |
| off-chance | off-duty | off-load | offside |
| off-colour | off-hand | off-putting | offspring |
| offcut | off-licence | offset | off-white |

# -off

**-off** combines with adverbs to form adjectives which describe how much money someone has. For example, if someone is 'well-off', they have plenty of money; if someone is 'badly-off', they do not have very much money.

*They were evidently well-off enough to throw away a perfectly good kitchen chair.*
*There were many comfortably-off business or professional people.*
Words formed in this way are occasionally used as nouns.

# -off

*The better-off obtain the best housing.*

Here is a list of words with this meaning:

badly-off          comfortably-off          worse-off
better-off         well-off

# -oholic

See **-aholic**.

# -oid

**-oid** occurs in words which express the idea that something resembles or is related to something else. For example, if something is 'humanoid', it resembles a human being in some way; if something is 'cuboid', it is shaped like a cube.

Here is a list of words with this meaning:

cuboid          fungoid          humanoid          spheroid          tabloid

# -old

PRODUCTIVE USE: **-old** combines with nouns and noun groups which refer to a period of time in order to form words which indicate how old something is. Words formed in this way usually consist of a number and the singular form of a noun such as 'week' or 'year' followed by **-old.** For example, a 'six-month-old' animal was born six months ago; a 'five-year-old' is a child who is five years old.

*They were taking the six-month-old seal from Thief Sand, where it lay bleeding.*
*A double engine failure on the twelve-week-old jet had been ruled out.*
*The killers had murdered a ten-year-old girl.*
*A seventy-year-old seldom sprints upstairs.*
*...a good teacher who can inspire and stimulate the eight-year-olds.*

The expressions 'age-old' and 'centuries-old' are used to indicate that something is extremely old, or that it has existed for a long time.

*...the age-old suspicion between parents and children.*
*...square-cut Norman churches surrounded by centuries-old grey stone houses.*

# -ological, -ology

**-ology** occurs in nouns which refer to an area of study or a system. For example, 'biology' is the study of living things such as plants and animals; 'methodology' is a system of methods or principles for doing a particular thing.

*He went to Manchester University in 1961 to study biology.*
*...the enthusiasm for astrology and the occult.*
*...the sort of phraseology used by some journalists.*
*...modern theories of child psychology.*

Here is a list of words with this meaning:

| | | | |
|---|---|---|---|
| anthropology | graphology | neurology | technology |
| archaeologist | gynaecology | ornithology | terminology |
| astrology | ideology | pathology | theology |
| biology | meteorology | phraseology | zoology |
| climatology | methodology | physiology | |
| ecology | microbiology | psychology | |
| geology | mythology | sociology | |

Adjectives are formed from these nouns by replacing **-ology** with **-ological**.

*Soak the garments overnight in lukewarm water and biological washing powder.*
*...an archaeological expedition to Turkey.*

### Words with other meanings

| | | |
|---|---|---|
| anthology | apology | tautology |

# omni-

**omni-** occurs in words which have 'all' as part of their meaning. For example, if someone is 'omnipotent', they have complete power over things or people; if a person or animal is an 'omnivore', they eat all kinds of food, including meat and plants.

Here is a list of words with this meaning:

| | | | |
|---|---|---|---|
| omnipotent | omnipresent | omniscience | omnivore |

# on-

**on-** combines with nouns which refer to a place in order to form words which describe the place where something happens or exists. For example, 'onshore' oil is found on land rather than at sea; 'on-stage' dancing takes place on a stage.

*The oil fields of Oman are primarily onshore.*
*He showed the same on-court flair that had carried him to a semi-final victory.*
*...the problem of how to organize on-site inspection.*

## on-

Words formed in this way are occasionally used as adverbs.

*...the gates will be built onshore.*

Here is a list of words with this meaning:

| | | |
|---|---|---|
| on-court | on-screen | on-site |
| on-field | onshore | on-stage |

### Words with other meanings

| | | | |
|---|---|---|---|
| on-board | ongoing | onside | onwards |
| oncoming | on-line | onward | |

## once-

PRODUCTIVE USE: **once-** combines with adjectives to form new adjectives. Adjectives formed in this way describe someone or something that used to have a particular quality or characteristic but no longer has. For example, a 'once-famous' person used to be famous but is not famous any more.

*...the ruins of a once-famous castle.*
*The once-great man was treated as a buffoon.*
*...the once-powerful unions controlling the broadcasting industry.*
*A once-thriving badger population has been reduced to just a few individuals.*
*Hundreds of other once-common species have similarly become rarities.*

Here are some examples of words with this meaning:

| | | |
|---|---|---|
| once-celebrated | once-great | once-powerful |
| once-common | once-happy | once-private |
| once-famous | once-lively | once-respected |
| once-fashionable | once-lovely | once-thriving |
| once-feared | once-luxurious | |
| once-forgotten | once-popular | |

## -or

**-or** combines with verbs to form nouns. Nouns formed in this way refer to people who do the action described by the original verb, usually because it is their job. For example, an 'actor' is someone whose occupation is acting in plays and films; a 'supervisor' is a person who supervises people or activities.

*He was an extremely fine actor.*
*...conductor of the Bach Society Orchestra.*

*He has become a frequent visitor to our house.*

Here is a list of words with this meaning:

| | | | |
|---|---|---|---|
| actor | conductor | inspector | oppressor |
| adjudicator | conspirator | instructor | possessor |
| administrator | contractor | inventor | prosecutor |
| advisor | contributor | investigator | protector |
| agitator | coordinator | investor | sailor |
| auditor | counsellor | invigilator | spectator |
| collaborator | creator | manipulator | speculator |
| collator | director | moderator | supervisor |
| collector | distributor | narrator | visitor |
| commentator | editor | navigator | |
| competitor | governor | operator | |

**-or** also combines with verbs to form nouns that refer to things rather than people. For example, a 'calculator' is a small electronic device that you use for doing calculations.

*Pupils are expected to learn how to use a pocket calculator.*
*She went in and took the small elevator to the fourth floor.*

Here is a list of words with this meaning:

| | | |
|---|---|---|
| applicator | compressor | escalator |
| aspirator | detector | reactor |
| calculator | elevator | refrigerator |

Note that the use of **-or** is not productive. **-er** is used to form new nouns with this meaning.

For more information see **-er**.

# -osis

## 1 A process or state

**-osis** occurs in nouns which refer to a process or state. For example, 'metamorphosis' is an event or process in which someone or something changes into something completely different; 'hypnosis' is a state of unconsciousness in which a person seems to be asleep but can see or hear things and respond to things said to them.

*...the metamorphosis of the Viscount into Count Dracula.*
*Joan's fever led to a diagnosis of pneumonia.*

Here is a list of words with this meaning:

| | | |
|---|---|---|
| diagnosis | metamorphosis | prognosis |
| hypnosis | osmosis | |

## 2 Illness or disease

**-osis** also occurs in nouns which refer to an illness or disease. For example, 'tuberculosis' is a serious infectious disease which affects

# -osis

someone's lungs; 'neurosis' is a mental illness which causes people to have continual, unreasonable fears and worries.

*...deaths from whooping cough, measles and tuberculosis.*
*Twenty-nine million people died of cirrhosis of the liver.*

Here is a list of words with this meaning:

| | | | |
|---|---|---|---|
| cirrhosis | neurosis | sclerosis | tuberculosis |
| myxomatosis | psychosis | thrombosis | |

# -ous

**-ous** occurs in adjectives which describe someone or something as having a particular quality. For example, if someone is 'adventurous', they are willing to take risks and try new methods; if food is 'delicious', it has a very pleasant taste or smell.

**Spelling:** There are a number of variations of the spelling of **-ous**. The most common ones are 'eous', 'ious', and 'uous'. Examples of all of these are given below.

*I can't help wishing that Sinclair had been a bit more adventurous.*
*The work was arduous and poorly paid.*
*She was superstitious and believed firmly in ghosts.*
*...a grave, courteous man in late middle age.*
*I was furious and told them to get out of my house.*

Here is a list of words with this meaning:

| | | | |
|---|---|---|---|
| advantageous | contemptuous | impetuous | serious |
| adventurous | continuous | marvellous | simultaneous |
| ambiguous | courageous | mysterious | spacious |
| ambitious | courteous | nervous | spontaneous |
| anonymous | curious | nutritious | superstitious |
| anxious | dangerous | obvious | suspicious |
| arduous | enormous | previous | tenacious |
| cautious | famous | religious | tremendous |
| conscious | furious | righteous | various |
| conspicuous | gracious | sensuous | virtuous |

# out-

**out-** combines with verbs, nouns, and adjectives to form new verbs. Verbs formed in this way describe someone or something as doing a particular action much better or to a greater extent than another person or thing. For example, if you 'outrun' someone, you succeed in running somewhere faster than they do; if you 'outdo' someone, you are a lot more successful than they are at a particular activity; if one thing 'outgrows' another, it grows until it is bigger than the other thing.

*...no one was able to outrun this incredible athlete.*
*England were outplayed in the second Test.*
*English ships easily outmanoeuvred the lumbering galleons of the Spanish fleet.*

Here is a list of words with this meaning:

| | | | |
|---|---|---|---|
| outbid | outlast | outsell | out-talk |
| outclass | outlive | outsmart | out-walk |
| outclimb | outmanoeuvre | outsprint | outwit |
| outdo | outpace | outstare | |
| outgrow | outplay | outstrip | |
| outjump | outrun | outswim | |

## Words with other meanings

| | | |
|---|---|---|
| outrage | out-vote | outweigh |

# over-

## 1 Excess

**over-** combines with adjectives, verbs, and nouns to form new adjectives, verbs, and nouns. Words formed in this way indicate that a quality exists or an action is done to too great an extent. For example, if you 'overload' something, you put too large a load on it; if someone is 'overweight', they weigh more than they should do.

*The pilot warned him that the plane was overloaded and wouldn't fly.*
*Men and women of squarer build, if they overeat, are very likely to become obese.*
*Do not over-react if your child gets into trouble at school.*
*Every ledge of the cliff is overgrown with vegetation.*
*He took an overdose of seasickness pills and slept through it all.*
*He was over-anxious to keep an appointment.*

Here is a list of words with this meaning:

| | | | |
|---|---|---|---|
| overabundance | overcrowd | overexposure | overrate |
| over-anxious | over-demanding | overfill | over-react |
| overawe | over-developed | overgrown | oversize |
| overburden | overdo | overheat | oversized |
| over-cautious | overdose | over-indulgence | oversleep |
| overcharge | overdue | overload | overspend |
| overcompensate | over-eager | over-populated | overweight |
| over-confident | overeat | overproduce | overwork |
| overcook | overestimate | over-protective | over-worried |

# over-

## 2 Age

PRODUCTIVE USE: **over-** combines with numbers to form nouns. Nouns formed in this way are always used in the plural form and refer to people who are older than the number mentioned.

*...daycare for over-fives.*
*The over-sixties want to do something that the community values.*

## 3 Power

**over-** also combines with verbs and nouns to form new verbs. Verbs formed in this way express the idea that one person or group of people has power or authority over another. For example, if a group of people 'overthrow' a leader or government, they remove them by force and take power for themselves; if one thing 'overrides' another, it replaces the other thing or reduces its importance.

*...a secret group that helped him overthrow the King.*
*Thieves dressed as policemen overpowered guards at a Boston museum.*
*The European Court of Justice has the power to overrule statutes.*

Here is a list of words with this meaning:

| | | | |
|---|---|---|---|
| overcome | override | overrun | overturn |
| overpower | overrule | overthrow | overwhelm |

### Words with other meanings

| | | | |
|---|---|---|---|
| overall | overhear | overshadow | overtime |
| overalls | overkill | overshoot | overtone |
| overbalance | overlook | oversight | overture |
| overcoat | overnight | overspill | overview |
| overflow | overseas | overstatement | |
| overhang | oversee | overtake | |

# pan-

PRODUCTIVE USE: **pan-** combines with adjectives which describe a nation or a particular group of people in order to form new adjectives. Adjectives formed in this way describe something that is connected with or involves the whole of the nation or group of people mentioned. For example, a 'pan-African' project is one which involves the whole of Africa; a 'pan-continental' airline is one which serves the whole of a particular continent.

*...pan-African nationalism.*
*The companies mentioned tended to be large pan-American companies.*
*...broadcasting live sports coverage via the satellite to a pan-European audience.*

...a pan-Indian institution.

Here are some examples of words with this meaning:

| | | | |
|---|---|---|---|
| pan-African | pan-continental | pan-Hellenic | pan-Slavic |
| pan-American | pan-European | pan-Indian | |
| pan-Arab | pan-German | pan-national | |

# para-

## 1 Similarity

**para-** combines with nouns and adjectives to form new nouns and adjectives. Words formed in this way refer to or describe one thing which is very similar to another. For example, a 'paramilitary' organization is similar to an army, but is not the official army of a country; a 'paramedic' is a person whose training is similar to that of a nurse and who helps to do medical work.

*They were jailed for organizing, training and equipping a paramilitary organization.*
*Not all ambulance staff were trained paramedics.*
*Paratyphoid is a highly infectious form of food poisoning.*

Here is a list of words with this meaning:

| | |
|---|---|
| paramedic | para-professional |
| paramilitary | paratyphoid |

## 2 Activities involving parachutes

**para-** occurs in nouns which refer to activities connected with parachutes, or to the people who use them. For example, 'paragliding' is a sport in which you use a specially designed parachute; a 'paratrooper' is a soldier who is trained to be dropped by parachute into battle or enemy territory.

*The paratroopers and glider-borne infantry would launch the assault.*
*...there are water-skiing and paragliding facilities on the main beach.*

Here is a list of words with this meaning:

| | | |
|---|---|---|
| parachute | parasailing | paratrooper |
| paragliding | parascending | |

### Words with other meanings

| | | | |
|---|---|---|---|
| paradigm | paralyse | parapet | parasites |
| paradise | parameter | paraphernalia | parasol |
| paradox | paramount | paraphrase | |
| paragraph | paranoid | paraplegic | |
| parallel | paranormal | parapsychology | |

# part-

PRODUCTIVE USE: **part-** combines with past participles and nouns to form new adjectives and nouns. Words formed in this way describe or refer to something which is partly but not completely the thing mentioned by the original past participle or noun. For example, if you are the 'part-owner' of something such as a business, you share it with one or more other people; if someone gives you a 'part-explanation' of something, they tell you some things about it, but not everything.

*John Robinson was editor and part-owner of the Natal Mercury.*
*He handed me the rest of his part-cooked meal.*
*The mountain was part-concealed by snow.*

Here are some examples of words with this meaning:

| | | | |
|---|---|---|---|
| part-assembled | part-concealed | part-cooked | part-ownership |
| part-boarded | part-constructed | part-owner | part-payment |

## Words with other meanings

| | | |
|---|---|---|
| part-exchange | part-time | part-work |
| part-singing | part-way | |

# penta-

**penta-** occurs in words which indicate that something has five parts. For example, a 'pentagon' is a geometrical shape with five straight sides; a 'pentathlon' is a sporting competition which has five events.

Here is list of words with this meaning:

| | | | | |
|---|---|---|---|---|
| pentagon | pentagram | pentameter | pentangle | pentathlon |

# -people

**-people** combines with nouns to form new nouns which refer to groups of people who live in a particular place, or who are involved in a particular activity. For example, the 'townspeople' of a town are the people who live there; 'salespeople' are people who make their living by selling goods.

*The soldiers posted notices ordering the townspeople to stay indoors.*
*The tribespeople of Bomvanaland lived on hills and in valleys.*
*Ibbett denied that the salespeople had been told.*

Here is a list of words with this meaning:

| | | | |
|---|---|---|---|
| country-people | townspeople | tradespeople | tribespeople |

Note that words formed in this way are not used in the singular. For example, you would not refer to someone as a 'townsperson'.

For more information on words that refer to people, see **-folk**, **-kind**, **-man**, **-person**, and **-woman**.

# -person

## 1 Occupation or involvement

**-person** combines with nouns to form new nouns which refer to someone who carries out a particular role or has a particular job. For example, a 'spokesperson' is someone who speaks or issues statements on behalf of a particular organization; a 'chairperson' is someone who chairs a committee.

**-person** is often used instead of '-man' or '-woman' in order to avoid specifying what sex somebody is.

*Her spokesperson told me that about ten manuscripts arrive each day.*
*The chairperson asked for volunteers to participate in the various subcommittees.*
*...his decision to speak to no newsperson.*

Here is a list of words with this meaning:

chairperson          newsperson          ombudsperson          spokesperson

Note that words formed in this way are seldom used in the plural, but when they are they combine with **-persons** rather than **-people**.

*The members of The Advisory Council include sixty chairpersons of smaller councils.*

## 2 Numbers

PRODUCTIVE USE: **-person** combines with numbers to form words which describe how many people a particular object or activity is intended for. For example, a 'twelve-person' caravan is one that has enough room and beds for twelve people to sleep in; a 'four-person' game is played by four people.

*...a four-person self-catering holiday flat.*
*...a £63-a-week pay claim for driving one-person operated trains.*
*...two-person board games such as chess and draughts.*

For more information on words that refer to people, see **-folk**, **-kind**, **-man**, **-people**, and **-woman**.

# -phile

**-phile** occurs in nouns which refer to or describe someone who likes a particular place or thing very much. For example, a 'Francophile' is someone who has a great liking for and admiration of France and the French people; a 'bibliophile' is someone who likes books very much.

Here is a list of words with this meaning:

| | | | | |
|---|---|---|---|---|
| Anglophile | bibliophile | Europhile | Francophile | Italophile |

# -phobia, -phobic

**-phobia** occurs in nouns and **-phobic** occurs in adjectives which have 'fear' or 'dread' as part of their meaning. For example, if someone suffers from 'agoraphobia', they are afraid of open spaces and dislike leaving their home; if someone is 'claustrophobic', they have a fear of being in small, narrow, or enclosed places.

Here is a list of words with this meaning:

| | | |
|---|---|---|
| agoraphobia | claustrophobic | technophobia |
| agoraphobic | homophobia | xenophobia |
| claustrophobia | hydrophobia | xenophobic |

# phon-

**phon-** occurs in words which have 'sound' or 'voice' as part of their meaning. For example, 'phonology' is the study of speech sounds in a particular language; a 'phoneme' is one of the possible speech sounds in a language.

Here is a list of words with this meaning:

| | | |
|---|---|---|
| phoneme | phonetics | phonograph |
| phonetic | phonic | phonology |

# -phone

**-phone** occurs in words which refer to instruments which produce, amplify, or transmit sound. For example, the 'telephone' is an electrical instrument that makes it possible for you to talk to someone else in a different place; a 'saxophone' is a musical instrument played by blowing and pressing keys.

Here is a list of words with this meaning:

| | | |
|---|---|---|
| dictaphone | megaphone | telephone |
| earphone | microphone | vibraphone |
| gramophone | saxophone | xylophone |

**-phone** is also used as an abbreviation of 'telephone' and it occurs in words which have this as part of their meaning. For example, an 'answerphone' is a machine that answers the telephone and records messages.

Here is a list of words with this meaning:

| | | |
|---|---|---|
| answerphone | cellphone | payphone |
| carphone | freephone | |

# photo-

**photo-** occurs in words which indicate that something relates to or is produced by light. For example, a 'photograph' is a picture made when light falls onto a film in a camera.

Here is a list of words with this meaning:

| | | |
|---|---|---|
| photocell | photograph | photosensitive |
| photochemical | photokinesis | photosynthesis |

**photo-** is also used as an abbreviation of 'photograph' and it occurs in words which have photography as part of their meaning. For example, a 'photocopier' is a machine that quickly copies documents by photographing them.

Here is a list of words with this meaning:

| | | |
|---|---|---|
| photocopier | photofit | photo-journalist |
| photocopy | photogenic | photo-novel |

# physio-

**physio-** occurs in words which have 'physical' as part of their meaning. For example, 'physiology' is the study of the way the bodies of people and animals function; 'physiography' is another name for physical geography.

Here is a list of words with this meaning:

| | |
|---|---|
| physiography | physiotherapist |
| physiology | physiotherapy |

# -piece

## 1 Numbers

PRODUCTIVE USE: **-piece** combines with numbers to form words which describe the number of members or pieces in a particular

# -piece

group. For example, a 'forty-two-piece' dinner service is made up of forty-two plates, cups, saucers, and so on.

*My sitting room has a three-piece suite and a desk.*
*... two-piece dresses.*
*...her one-piece swimming costume.*

## 2 Use or position

**-piece** combines with nouns to form new nouns. Nouns formed in this way refer to something which is part of a larger object and which serves a particular purpose or is situated in a particular position. For example, an 'eyepiece' is part of something that you put near your eye to look through; a 'side-piece' is located at the side of a larger object.

*The cameraman peered into the eyepiece.*
*The centrepiece of the picture was a representation of the King.*
*It was on the stone slab beneath the chimney-piece.*

Here is a list of words with this meaning:

| | | | |
|---|---|---|---|
| altar-piece | chimney-piece | eyepiece | side-piece |
| centrepiece | earpiece | mouthpiece | |

Note that 'mouthpiece' and 'centrepiece' both have another common meaning. The 'mouthpiece' of an organization is the person who publicly states their policies and opinions. The 'centrepiece' of a set of things is something that you show as the best example of that set.

### Words with other meanings

| | | | |
|---|---|---|---|
| frontispiece | mantlepiece | masterpiece | showpiece |

# politico-

**politico-** combines with adjectives to form new adjectives which describe something which involves politics. For example, a 'politico-religious' ideal involves both political and religious concerns; if a country or group of countries is subject to 'politico-economic' domination, it is controlled and influenced, both politically and economically, by another country or group of countries.

Note that adjectives formed in this way are fairly formal and occur infrequently.

*...a politico-religious ideal as old as Christianity itself.*
*The politico-administrative systems had different characteristics.*

Here is a list of words with this meaning:

| | | |
|---|---|---|
| politico-administrative | politico-military | politico-strategic |
| politico-economic | politico-religious | |

# poly-

**poly-** occurs in words which have 'many' as part of their meaning. For example, a 'polygon' is a geometrical shape with three or more straight sides; 'polyphonic' music is made up of many different parts and melodies.

Here is a list of words with this meaning:

| | | | |
|---|---|---|---|
| polyglot | polygraph | polyphonic | polytechnic |
| polygon | polyhedron | polyphony | polytheism |
| polygram | polymath | polysyllabic | |

# -poor

**-poor** combines with nouns to form adjectives which describe something that does not have enough of a desirable or valuable substance. For example, if food is 'nutrient-poor' it is a bad source of nutrients; if soil is 'nitrogen-poor', it does not contain enough nitrogen.

PRODUCTIVE USE: It is possible to form new words with this meaning by adding **-poor** to nouns, particularly if they refer to chemical or organic substances. However, words formed in this way are not very common and they are normally used in formal language, for example in books and articles on subjects of scientific interest.

*...nutrient-poor, permanently waterlogged pastures.*
*...a foul, oxygen-poor atmosphere.*
*...resource-poor countries.*

Here are some examples of words with this meaning:

| | | |
|---|---|---|
| nitrogen-poor | oxygen-poor | sulphur-poor |
| nutrient-poor | resource-poor | |

# post-

## 1 After

PRODUCTIVE USE: **post-** combines with nouns and adjectives which refer to or describe a particular event or development in order to form new nouns and adjectives. Words formed in this way indicate that one thing that takes place after another. For example, a 'post-election' survey is conducted after an election has taken place; a 'post-feminist' movement is based on ideas which developed out of the original feminist movement.

**Spelling:** Words formed in this way are usually written with a

# post-

hyphen, but some of the more common ones are written as one word.

*...the post-election confusion.*
*...the post-ceremony luncheon.*
*We live in a post-religious era.*
*Public confidence has fallen dramatically, according to a post-budget poll.*
*...an instant post-race reaction.*

Here are some examples of words with this meaning:

| | | |
|---|---|---|
| post-budget | post-independence | post-natal |
| post-ceremony | post-liberation | post-race |
| post-election | post-Marxist | post-religious |
| post-examination | post-match | post-renaissance |
| post-feminist | post-medieval | post-structuralism |
| post-Freudian | post-menopausal | |
| post-impressionism | post-modernism | |

**post-** also combines in this way with dates.

*...post-1960's society.*
*He began to study some of the post-sixth-century portraits.*

## 2 Postal services

**post-** also combines with nouns to refer to something that is connected with the postal service. For example, a 'postman' is someone who delivers letters and parcels; a 'postcode' is a code or short sequence of letters and numbers at the end of an address which makes sorting mail easier.

*The postman handed me my letters through the window.*
*Mary sent her husband many postcards and one real letter from Istanbul.*
*A post-box in Rome is emptied, on average, every three days.*

Here is a list of words with this meaning:

| | | | |
|---|---|---|---|
| postbag | postcode | postmaster | post-service |
| post-box | postman | postmistress | |
| postcard | postmark | post-office | |

### Words with other meanings

| | |
|---|---|
| postgraduate | postscript |

# pre-

## 1 Before

PRODUCTIVE USE: **pre-** combines with nouns and adjectives which refer to or describe a particular event or development in order to

form words which are used in front of nouns. Words formed in this way describe one thing that takes place before another. For example, a footballer might suffer from 'pre-match' nerves before playing a football match; you have a 'pre-dinner' drink just before you eat dinner.

**Spelling:** Words formed in this way are usually written with a hyphen, but some of the more common ones are written as one word.

For more information on words that have 'before' as part of their meaning, see **ante-**.

*The squad will go to Shaw Hill for pre-match training.*
*He found himself opposing Chamberlain in the pre-war years.*
*...pre-industrial Britain.*
*...pre-job education or training schemes.*

Here are some examples of words with this meaning:

| | | |
|---|---|---|
| pre-adolescent | pre-examination | pre-reformation |
| pre-birth | pre-game | pre-retirement |
| pre-budget | pre-glasnost | pre-revolution |
| pre-capitalist | prehuman | pre-Roman |
| pre-Christian | pre-independence | pre-school |
| pre-Christmas | pre-industrial | pre-transmission |
| pre-dawn | pre-lunch | pre-trial |
| pre-delivery | premarital | pre-war |
| pre-dinner | pre-match | |
| pre-election | pre-race | |

**pre-** combines in this way with dates.

*More than eighty pre-1939 sports cars took part in the rally.*
*...information extracted from pre-fourteenth century documents.*

**pre-** also combines in this way with verbs to form new verbs. For example, if you 'prejudge' a situation, you form an opinion about it before you know all the facts.

*Party organizations inevitably prejudge proposals from their opponents.*
*He married late and his wife predeceased him.*

Here is a list of words with this meaning:

| | | |
|---|---|---|
| pre-date | predetermine | prejudge |
| predecease | prefigure | preview |

# 2 Already

PRODUCTIVE USE: **pre-** also combines with nouns and past participles to form new nouns and adjectives. Words formed in this way refer to or describe an action which has already been done. For

## pre-

example, a 'preconception' is a belief that you already have about something before you know enough about it to form a fair opinion of it; if something is 'prepaid', it has already been paid for.

**Spelling:** Words formed in this way are usually written with a hyphen, but some of the more common ones are written as one word.

*He tries to deny information which challenges his preconceptions.*
*Fuel was provided at pre-arranged stores along the routes.*
*The door of his study was open, and without premeditation he turned into it.*
*Cover the dish and bake in a preset oven.*
*The food is pre-prepared but not pre-cooked.*

Here are some examples of words with this meaning:

| | | | |
|---|---|---|---|
| pre-arranged | predestination | premeditation | pre-planned |
| pre-booked | predestined | preordained | pre-prepared |
| preconceived | pre-digested | preordination | pre-recorded |
| preconception | prefabricated | pre-packed | pre-selected |
| pre-cooked | pre-heated | pre-paid | pre-selection |
| pre-cut | premeditated | pre-payment | preset |

### Words with other meanings

| | | | |
|---|---|---|---|
| preamble | predominate | prehistoric | prepossessing |
| precaution | pre-eminent | prejudice | prerequisite |
| predispose | pre-empt | premature | presentiment |
| predominant | prefix | preoccupy | pretext |

## pro-

PRODUCTIVE USE: **pro-** combines with nouns and adjectives which refer to or describe a person, system, philosophy, or policy in order to form words which describe someone or something that strongly supports the person or thing mentioned. For example, if someone is 'pro-democracy', they support democracy; if a magazine is 'pro-feminist', it contains articles which support feminism.

*Demonstrators carrying pro-democracy banners.*
*...a pro-government rally outside the Presidential Palace.*
*...the prospect of a pro-Western country on its borders.*

Here are some examples of words with this meaning:

| | | |
|---|---|---|
| pro-allies | pro-conservation | pro-monarchy |
| pro-authority | pro-democracy | pro-nationalist |
| pro-business | pro-exercise | pro-nuclear |
| pro-capitalist | pro-family | pro-union |
| pro-choice | pro-feminist | pro-West |
| pro-church | pro-government | pro-Western |
| pro-communist | pro-liberal | |

# -proof

PRODUCTIVE USE: -**proof** combines with nouns which refer to things which might be considered harmful or undesirable in order to form adjectives. Adjectives formed in this way describe something that cannot be harmed or that is unaffected by a particular thing. For example, if clothing is 'waterproof', it does not let water pass through it; if a dish is 'ovenproof', it can be used in an oven without being damaged by the heat.

**Spelling:** Words formed in this way are usually written with a hyphen, but some of the more common ones are written as one word.

*A pair of waterproof trousers will prevent a wet backside.*
*...secure from random snipers behind my bullet-proof windows.*
*The film tins were stacked ceiling high in the two fireproof store rooms.*
*The camp in the woods was well sheltered and storm-proof.*

Here are some examples of words with this meaning:

| | | | |
|---|---|---|---|
| accident-proof | fireproof | leakproof | storm-proof |
| bullet-proof | flameproof | ovenproof | vandal-proof |
| burglar-proof | foolproof | rainproof | waterproof |
| child-proof | frost-proof | rot-proof | weatherproof |
| damp-proof | greaseproof | rust-proof | windproof |
| dishwasherproof | heatproof | shower-proof | |
| dust-proof | inflation-proof | soundproof | |

-**proof** occasionally combines with verbs to form adjectives which indicate that something is resistant to a particular action.

*The shatterproof windows had held up to the attack.*

# proto-

**proto-** combines with nouns to form new nouns. Nouns formed in this way refer to something which comes from the early stages in the development of a particular thing. For example, a 'prototype' is the first model that is made of something, usually the basis for later improved models; a 'proto-fascist' was an influential member of the early fascist movement whose ideas were used as the basis for later developments.

**Spelling:** Words formed in this way are usually written with a hyphen with the exception of 'prototype', which is written as one word.

PRODUCTIVE USE: It is possible to form new words with this meaning by adding **proto-** to nouns, particularly if they refer to things

## proto-

which have developed in some way, such as animals or plants. However, words formed in this way are not very common and they are normally used in formal language, for example in books and articles on subjects of scientific interest.

*...the building and testing of prototype cars and engines.*
*...without jaws, the proto-fish could not prey upon shelled molluscs.*
*...protohumans who lived one-and-a-half million years ago.*

Here are some examples of words with this meaning:

| | | | |
|---|---|---|---|
| proto-coalition | proto-fish | protohuman | prototype |
| proto-fascist | proto-horse | protoplanet | |

## pseudo-

PRODUCTIVE USE: **pseudo-** combines with nouns and adjectives in order to form new nouns and adjectives. Words formed in this way refer to or describe something which is not really what it seems or claims to be. For example, if a building is 'pseudo-rustic', it does not come from the countryside but is designed to look as if it does. **pseudo-** is often used to show disapproval. For example, if you describe someone as a 'pseudo-friend', you think that although they appear to be friendly they are not genuinely your friend.

*...a pretty, pseudo-rustic bistro.*
*He undid his coat and slung it over the back of a pseudo-oak settee.*
*...pseudo-modern patterns and plain colours.*

Here are some examples of words with this meaning:

| | | |
|---|---|---|
| pseudo-creativity | pseudo-metal | pseudo-oak |
| pseudo-democratic | pseudo-military | pseudo-parent |
| pseudo-fact | pseudo-modern | pseudo-religious |
| pseudo-friend | pseudo-natural | pseudo-rustic |
| pseudo-literary | pseudo-noble | pseudo-science |

## psych-

**psych-** occurs in words which have 'mind' or 'mental processes' as part of their meaning. For example, 'psychiatry' is the branch of medicine concerned with the study and treatment of mental illness; a 'psychopath' is someone who is mentally disturbed with the result that they often do very violent or destructive things.

Here is a list of words with this meaning:

| | | |
|---|---|---|
| psychiatrist | psychoanalysis | psychology |
| psychiatry | psychoanalyst | psychopath |
| psychic | psychological | psychotic |

# quad-

**quad-** occurs in words which indicate that something has four parts. For example, a 'quadrilateral' is a geometrical shape with four straight sides; a 'quadruped' is an animal with four legs.

Here is a list of words with this meaning:

| | | | |
|---|---|---|---|
| quadrangle | quadriceps | quadrilateral | quadruped |

# quasi-

**quasi-** combines with adjectives to form new adjectives. Adjectives formed in this way describe a person or thing that is almost, but not quite, the thing described by the adjective. For example, a 'quasi-academic' book is written in the style of an academic book but its content is not considered to be properly academic; a 'quasi-religious' experience is almost, but not quite, the same as a religious experience.

PRODUCTIVE USE: It is possible to form new words by adding **quasi-** to adjectives. However, words formed in this way are fairly formal or literary and do not occur frequently.

*...academic and quasi-academic literature.*
*...a mystical or quasi-religious experience.*
*...quasi-human automation.*

Here are some examples of words with this meaning:

| | | |
|---|---|---|
| quasi-academic | quasi-human | quasi-military |
| quasi-attractive | quasi-industrial | quasi-moderate |
| quasi-autonomous | quasi-judicial | quasi-moral |
| quasi-diplomatic | quasi-legal | quasi-official |
| quasi-divine | quasi-magical | quasi-religious |

**quasi-** occasionally combines in this way with nouns.

*They have turned their countries into quasi-republics.*

# radio-

**radio-** occurs in words which have 'radiation' or 'radio waves' as part of their meaning. For example, a 'radioactive' substance produces energy in the form of radiation; a 'radio-telescope' is an instrument which receives radio waves from space and uses them to find the position of stars.

Here is a list of words with this meaning:

| | | |
|---|---|---|
| radioactive | radiogram | radio-telescope |
| radio-car | radiography | radio-transmitter |
| radiocarbon | radio-operator | |
| radio-controlled | radio-telephone | |

# re-

PRODUCTIVE USE: **re-** combines with verbs and their related nouns to form new verbs and nouns. Words formed in this way describe or refer to the fact that an action or process is done or happens a second time, sometimes in a different way. For example, if you 'rewrite' something, you make changes to something you have already written in order to improve it; if a person or thing 'reappears', they appear again after previously disappearing or being away; if a person or thing makes a 'reappearance', they reappear.

**Spelling:** Words formed in this way are usually written as one word, but some of the less common ones can be written with a hyphen, especially when **re-** combines with a word that begins with a vowel.

*...a comedy well worth re-reading.*
*...Grosvenor Road, now renamed Millbank.*
*The theatre was founded in 1720, but rebuilt in 1820.*
*...a re-examination of the purposes of education.*
*...the redistribution of government spending.*

Here are some examples of words with this meaning:

| | | | |
|---|---|---|---|
| re-allocate | recreate | re-examine | reopening |
| re-allocation | recreation | refreeze | repossess |
| reappear | redefine | regenerate | repossession |
| reappearance | redefinition | regeneration | reprint |
| rebuild | rediscover | remarriage | re-read |
| reconsider | rediscovery | remarry | re-reading |
| reconsideration | redistribute | rename | restart |
| reconstruct | redistribution | renaming | reunite |
| reconstruction | re-examination | reopen | rewrite |

Note that 'rewrite' and 'reprint' can be used as either verbs or nouns and that 'recreation' also has another meaning and is listed below.

## Words with other meanings

| | | |
|---|---|---|
| react | release | reserve |
| reactor | relive | resignation |
| reassure | remark | resolution |
| rebound | remove | resolve |
| recollection | repay | resort |
| recommendation | replace | restore |
| recover | represent | restrain |
| recreation | reproduce | retirement |
| recycle | reproduction | retrace |
| redress | reprove | retreat |
| reform | research | return |
| relay | reservation | review |

146

# -related

PRODUCTIVE USE: **-related** combines with nouns to form adjectives that describe one thing as being connected with another. For example, if tax is 'income-related', the amount of tax someone pays is linked to the size of their income; if a project is 'school-related', it is connected with school.

*...a campaign for income-related Family Credit.*
*He spent a lot of time away as a result of job-related travel.*
*The benefits for children were age-related.*
*The project could create 120,000 new City-related jobs.*
*...extensive limitations on tobacco-related advertising.*

Words formed in this way are often used to describe the cause of an illness or accident. For example, if a disease is 'smoking-related', it is caused by smoking cigarettes.

*...the threat of lung and other smoking-related cancers.*
*...the toll from drink-related road accidents.*
*...a high incidence of drug-related crimes.*

Here are some examples of words with this meaning:

| | | | |
|---|---|---|---|
| age-related | drink-related | job-related | smoking-related |
| alcohol-related | drug-related | leisure-related | stress-related |
| career-related | earnings-related | oil-related | tax-related |
| city-related | income-related | race-related | tobacco-related |
| disaster-related | injury-related | school-related | work-related |

# retro-

**retro-** occurs in words which have 'back' or 'backwards' as part of their meaning. For example, if a decision is 'retroactive', it is intended to take effect from a date in the past; if you form an opinion about something in 'retrospect', you look back on it and base your opinion on what actually happened.

Here is a list of words with this meaning:

| | | | |
|---|---|---|---|
| retroactive | retrograde | retrogressive | retrospective |

# -rich

PRODUCTIVE USE: **-rich** combines with nouns to form adjectives. Adjectives formed in this way describe things which contain a large amount or high concentration of whatever the nouns refer to. **-rich** is often used in this way with nouns which refer to chemical or organic substances. For example, if a food is 'fibre-rich', it contains

# -rich

a high amount of fibre; if something is 'energy-rich', it is a good source of energy.

Note that words formed in this way are fairly formal; they usually occur in books or articles on subjects of scientific interest.

*...fibre-rich foods, such as wholemeal bread, cereals, and vegetables.*
*...sacks of protein-rich groundnuts.*
*The big buyers have been cash-rich companies and investment trusts.*
*...carbon-rich compounds.*
*...chocolates, sweet drinks, and other sugar-rich foods.*

Here are some examples of words with this meaning:

| | | | |
|---|---|---|---|
| asset-rich | fibre-rich | nutrient-rich | resource-rich |
| carbon-rich | information-rich | oil-rich | rubber-rich |
| cash-rich | lead-rich | oxygen-rich | species-rich |
| energy-rich | mineral-rich | phosphate-rich | sugar-rich |
| fat-rich | nitrate-rich | protein-rich | vitamin-rich |

# -ridden

PRODUCTIVE USE: **-ridden** combines with nouns to form adjectives. Adjectives formed in this way describe people or things that suffer from a large or excessive amount of something unpleasant or unwanted. For example, if someone is 'guilt-ridden', they are suffering so much from guilt that it affects the way they behave; if a country or culture is 'class-ridden', it is affected by the class system in many unpleasant and restrictive ways.

*...his cold, overwrought, guilt-ridden childhood.*
*...a sprawling tension-ridden slum.*
*This served only to cause further confusion in a rumour-ridden Peking.*
*...the flood- and cyclone-ridden islands of the Ganges delta.*
*...a filthy, mouse-ridden jail.*

Here are some examples of words with this meaning:

| | | | |
|---|---|---|---|
| bullet-ridden | draught-ridden | maggot-ridden | scandal-ridden |
| class-ridden | drought-ridden | mouse-ridden | storm-ridden |
| cliche-ridden | fear-ridden | penalty-ridden | strike-ridden |
| cyclone-ridden | flood-ridden | plague-ridden | tension-ridden |
| debt-ridden | guilt-ridden | priest-ridden | terror-ridden |
| disease-ridden | lice-ridden | rumour-ridden | vermin-ridden |

# Russo-

**Russo-** occurs in words which have 'Russian' or 'Russia' as part of their meaning. For example, the 'Russo-Japanese' war was fought between Russia and Japan.

# -scape

PRODUCTIVE USE: **-scape** combines with nouns that refer to a particular feature in the physical world to form new nouns. Nouns formed in this way refer to the view of an area which is characterized by that feature. For example, a 'landscape' is a view of a particular area of land; a 'waterscape' is a landscape containing a large area of water, such as a river or lake. Words formed in this way can also be used to refer to paintings of these areas.

*The Clee Hills dominate a landscape where the soil is red.*
*The dusty moonscape lay before them, glimmering in the earthlight.*
*...a little townscape of roofs and chimneys.*
*The riverscape has a weird and romantic starkness.*
*...a deep blue seascape showing three yachts making their way among rocks.*

Here are some examples of words with this meaning:

| | | | | |
|---|---|---|---|---|
| cityscape | landscape | riverscape | skyscape | starscape |
| cloudscape | moonscape | roofscape | snowscape | townscape |
| lakescape | mudscape | seascape | spirescape | waterscape |

# self-

## 1 Actions done to or by yourself

PRODUCTIVE USE: **self-** combines with nouns to form new nouns or with past and present participles in order to form adjectives. Words formed in this way refer to or describe actions that people do to or by themselves. For example, 'self-government' is the government of a country by its own people rather than by another country; someone who is 'self-taught' has learnt a subject on his or her own.

*...the desire for self-government and independence.*
*Single children are always intensely self-absorbed.*
*They took up karate partly for self-protection and partly to keep fit.*

## self-

*...a self-service petrol station.*
*...a four-person self-catering holiday flat.*

Here are some examples of words with this meaning:

| | | |
|---|---|---|
| self-absorbed | self-discipline | self-interest |
| self-analysis | self-doubt | self-knowledge |
| self-appointed | self-educated | self-love |
| self-approval | self-employed | self-management |
| self-awareness | self-expression | self-pity |
| self-catering | self-government | self-portrait |
| self-control | self-hate | self-preservation |
| self-criticism | self-help | self-protection |
| self-deception | self-image | self-reliance |
| self-defeating | self-imposed | self-restraint |
| self-defence | self-indulgence | self-service |
| self-denial | self-inflicted | self-taught |

**self-** also combines with present participles to form adjectives and nouns. Words formed in this way describe or refer to an object, especially a machine, that performs an action automatically. For example, a 'self-locking' door is a door that locks itself automatically without needing a key; a 'self-loading' gun reloads itself automatically after firing a bullet.

*He closed the self-locking flat door behind him.*
*...a self-winding watch.*
*...a self-cleaning oven.*

Here is a list of words with this meaning:

| | | | |
|---|---|---|---|
| self-cleaning | self-heating | self-propelled | self-starting |
| self-destruction | self-locking | self-regulating | self-winding |

Note that 'self-destruct' is a verb formed from the noun 'self-destruction'. If something 'self-destructs', it destroys itself, often in a violent way, for example by blowing itself up.

## 2 Attitudes

**self-** also combines with nouns and adjectives to form new nouns and adjectives that refer to or describe how people feel about themselves. For example, if someone is 'self-confident', they are very confident of their own ability and judgement; if someone is 'self-opinionated', they believe very firmly that their own ideas or opinions are right.

*She was remarkably self-confident and dependable for her age.*
*He addressed the Board with his usual self-assurance.*

150

*Patrick is self-conscious about his thinness.*

Here is a list of words with this meaning:

| | | |
|---|---|---|
| self-assertive | self-conscious | self-possession |
| self-assertiveness | self-esteem | self-respect |
| self-assurance | self-importance | self-respecting |
| self-assured | self-important | self-righteous |
| self-confidence | self-opinionated | self-satisfaction |
| self-confident | self-possessed | self-satisfied |

Note that words formed in this way also often combine with '-ly' to form adverbs.

## Words with other meanings

| | | |
|---|---|---|
| self-addressed | self-evident | self-styled |
| self-centred | self-explanatory | self-sufficiency |
| self-confessed | selfish | self-sufficient |
| self-contained | selfless | self-will |
| self-determination | self-made | self-willed |
| self-effacement | self-same | |
| self-effacing | self-serving | |

# semi-

## 1 Describing something only partly true

PRODUCTIVE USE: **semi-** combines with nouns and adjectives to form new nouns and adjectives. Words formed in this way refer to or describe something that almost happens or is only partly true. For example, if a place is in 'semi-darkness', it is almost but not entirely dark; if someone is 'semi-retired', they have not completely retired but still work occasionally.

*They stared forward into the semi-darkness of the undergrowth.*
*There is an enormous demand for skilled and semi-skilled labour.*
*The semi-liquid clay is then called 'slip'.*
*He was back in Glasgow again, this time on a semi-permanent basis.*

Here are some examples of words with this meaning:

| | | | |
|---|---|---|---|
| semi-automatic | semi-divine | semi-mystical | semi-precious |
| semi-conscious | semi-human | semi-naked | semi-retired |
| semi-dark | semi-invalid | semi-official | semi-skilled |
| semi-darkness | semi-liquid | semi-organic | semi-soft |
| semi-derelict | semi-literate | semi-permanent | semi-synthetic |

**semi-** also occasionally combines with verbs to form other verbs. For example, if someone 'semi-smiles', they smile slightly. Verbs formed in this way do not occur very often and should be used only with extreme care.

# semi-

## 2 Half

**semi-** also combines with nouns and adjectives to form new nouns and adjectives. Words formed in this way express the idea that something is equal to one half of something else. For example, a 'semicircle' is one half of a circle, or something that has the shape of half a circle; a 'semi-annual' event happens every half year.

*The Romans always made the arch as a semicircle.*
*The musicians were afraid of missing a single semi-quaver.*

Here is a list of words with this meaning:

| | | |
|---|---|---|
| semi-annual | semicircular | semi-quaver |
| semicircle | semi-detached | semi-tone |

For more information on prefixes that mean 'half', see **demi-** and **half-**.

### Words with other meanings

| | | | |
|---|---|---|---|
| semi-colon | semiconductor | semiology | semiotics |

# -ship

## 1 Occupation and position

PRODUCTIVE USE: **-ship** combines with nouns that refer to people in a particular occupation or position in order to form new nouns. Nouns formed in this way refer to the state or experience of having that occupation or position. For example, 'ownership' is the state of being the owner of something; the 'editorship' of a newspaper or magazine is the position and status of its editor.

*Kenya has encouraged the development of private land ownership.*
*Mitterrand has just taken over the chairmanship of the European Community.*
*He applied for the rectorship of Upton-on-Severn.*
*She concealed her authorship to ensure fair criticism of her work.*
*He was offered a professorship in mathematics.*

Here are some examples of words with this meaning:

| | | | |
|---|---|---|---|
| ambassadorship | deanship | leadership | professorship |
| apprenticeship | directorship | lectureship | proprietorship |
| authorship | doctorship | librarianship | rectorship |
| chairmanship | editorship | membership | stewardship |
| chancellorship | governorship | ownership | studentship |
| citizenship | headmastership | premiership | traineeship |

## 2 Skills and ability

**-ship** also combines with nouns that refer to people with a particular job or occupation in order to form new nouns. Nouns formed in this way refer to the skill those people use when doing the job or occupation referred to. For example, 'marksmanship' is the ability to shoot a gun accurately; 'statesmanship' is the skill and ability a statesman needs to carry out his duties.

*His room bore plentiful evidence of his marksmanship in the form of stuffed animals.*
*England set a high standard of sportsmanship.*
*The workmanship of the dresses was unmistakably French.*
*It was a marvellous example of oarsmanship.*

Here is a list of words with this meaning:

| | | | |
|---|---|---|---|
| craftsmanship | marksmanship | salesmanship | sportsmanship |
| draftsmanship | musicianship | seamanship | statesmanship |
| horsemanship | oarsmanship | showmanship | workmanship |

## 3 Connections

**-ship** combines with nouns to form new nouns that refer to a relation between two or more people and things. For example, a 'friendship' is the relationship between two or more people who are friends; 'companionship' is the state of having a companion rather than being alone.

*That evening a strong friendship between the two women began.*
*...a cosy new relationship between the two countries.*
*The overwhelming mood was one of comradeship.*

Here is a list of words with this meaning:

| | | |
|---|---|---|
| acquaintanceship | friendship | relationship |
| companionship | kinship | |
| comradeship | partnership | |

## 4 Boats and other vehicles

**-ship** combines with nouns to form new nouns that refer to types of boats or other vehicles. For example, a 'battleship' is a large boat or ship intended for use in military combat; a 'spaceship' is a vehicle which can travel in space.

*...the remains of a sunken battleship.*
*He set sail on the troopship Cameronia from Glasgow to South Africa.*
*...watching Earth's first spaceship setting off for the moon.*
*...an overaged, obsolete steamship.*

Here is a list of words with this meaning:

| | | | |
|---|---|---|---|
| airship | flagship | spaceship | troopship |
| battleship | gunship | steamship | warship |

# -ship

## Words with other meanings

censorship
championship
courtship

dictatorship
hardship
ladyship

lordship
readership
scholarship

sponsorship
township

# -side

## 1 The edge of something

PRODUCTIVE USE: **-side** combines with nouns that refer to a place or object in order to form words which refer to the edge of the place or object mentioned. For example, the 'riverside' is an area on or near the bank of a river; a 'fireside' chair is a chair next to a fire.

*...the relative cool of the riverside vegetation.*
*...sobbing bitterly at the graveside.*
*A bus took us to a lakeside hotel in Queenstown.*
*We stopped for lunch by the roadside.*
*She drank a tumbler of Perrier from the bedside cabinet.*

Here are some examples of words with this meaning:

bedside
deskside
dockside
fireside
graveside

hearthside
hillside
kerbside
lakeside
mountainside

oceanside
parkside
poolside
quayside
ringside

riverside
roadside
seaside
trackside
waterside

## 2 Part of something

PRODUCTIVE USE: **-side** combines with nouns and adjectives to form new nouns. Nouns formed in this way refer to that part of something that involves or is described by the original nouns and adjectives. For example, the 'passenger-side' of a car is the opposite side to where the driver sits; the 'hinge-side' of a door is the edge to which the hinges are attached.

**Spelling:** Words formed in this way are usually written with a hyphen, but some of the more common ones are written as one word.

*...leaning over, she opened the door of the passenger-side.*
*He stood in the corner by the door and the left-side wall.*
*...digging top quality meadow turves and stacking them, grass-side down.*
*He mashed out the butt of his cigar against the underside of the table.*

*The palm-side of his clenched fist beat down on the opponent.*

Here are some examples of words with this meaning:

| | | | |
|---|---|---|---|
| earthside | hingeside | openside | southside |
| farside | innerside | palm-side | underside |
| grass-side | lee-side | passenger-side | upperside |
| greenside | left-side | right-side | weather-side |
| headside | northside | sand-side | |

## Words with other meanings

| | | | |
|---|---|---|---|
| alongside | blind-side | legside | outside | subside |
| aside | broadside | nearside | preside | upside |
| backside | countryside | offside | reside | wayside |
| beside | inside | onside | stateside | |

# Sino-

**Sino-** occurs in words which have 'Chinese' or 'China' as part of their meaning. For example, the 'Sino-Soviet' border is the border between China and Russia.

# -sion

See **-ion.**

# -size, -sized

## 1 The same size as something else

PRODUCTIVE USE: **-size** and **-sized** combine with nouns to form adjectives that describe one thing as being approximately the same size as another. For example, if a house is 'mansion-size', it is almost as big as a mansion; if a photograph is 'postcard-sized', it is approximately the same size as a postcard. **-size** and **-sized** have exactly the same meaning when they are used in this way but **-sized** is slightly more common. Many nouns can be used with either **-size** or **-sized.**

Note that the adjectives formed with the noun 'man' are an exception to this general rule. For example, if something is described as 'man-sized', it is roughly the same size as a man; if something is described as 'man-size', it is suitable for use by a man. See also paragraph 2.

*...a mansion-size rectory.*
*...horrifying photographs in poster-sized enlargements.*

# -size, -sized

*There was a heavy splash as a man-sized alligator left the bank.*
*...a teaspoon-size mound of peas.*
*The lemur is cat-sized, with soft grey fur.*

Here are some examples of words with this meaning:

| | | | |
|---|---|---|---|
| apple-sized | cottage-size | mansion-size | postcard-sized |
| button-sized | doll-size | man-sized | poster-sized |
| cat-sized | envelope-sized | mouse-sized | room-size |
| child-sized | farm-size | page-size | stamp-size |
| city-size | finger-size | pea-sized | teaspoon-size |
| coin-sized | fist-sized | pin-size | wall-size |

## 2 Suitability for a particular purpose

PRODUCTIVE USE: **-size** also combines with nouns to form adjectives
that describe something as being a suitable size for a particular
purpose. For example, if a packet of soup is described as 'family-
size', it is meant to be big enough to feed a whole family; if a
photograph is 'passport-size', it is the right size to stick in your
passport.

Note that **-sized** is not usually used with this meaning.

*.... two large family-size packets of soup.*
*We are trying to get child-size brooms.*
*The size and clarity of a pocket-size screen is usually unsatisfactory.*

Here are some examples of words with this meaning:

| | | | |
|---|---|---|---|
| adult-size | family-size | passport-size | snack-size |
| child-size | man-size | pocket-size | |

## 3 Describing the size of something

PRODUCTIVE USE: **-size** and **-sized** combine with adjectives that
indicate size in order to form new adjectives. Adjectives formed in
this way give more specific information about the size of a
particular object. For example, if something is 'jumbo-size', it is
extremely large; if a model is 'full-sized', it is the same size as the
thing it represents.

*...jumbo-size fountain pens.*
*...an average-sized family of six.*
*The peeling door opened into a fair-sized room.*
*...a medium-size city.*
*...giant-size tins of soup.*

Here are some examples of words with this meaning formed with **size**; most of them can also be formed with **sized**:

| | | | |
|---|---|---|---|
| average-size | good-size | middle-size | ordinary-size |
| fair-size | jumbo-size | mid-size | single-size |
| full-size | large-size | moderate-size | small-size |
| giant-size | medium-size | normal-size | standard-size |

**Words with other meanings**

| | |
|---|---|
| king-size | outsize |
| life-size | pint-size |

# socio-

**socio-** occurs in words which have 'social' or 'society' as part of their meaning. For example, 'sociology' is the study of human societies and of the relationships between groups in these societies; 'socio-economic' questions involve both social and economic factors.

Here is a list of words with this meaning:

| | | |
|---|---|---|
| sociobiology | socio-industrial | socio-political |
| socio-economic | sociolinguistic | socio-psychological |
| socio-historical | sociological | |

# -some

## 1 Attributes and characteristics

**-some** combines with nouns and verbs to form adjectives. The adjectives formed describe the characteristics and attributes of people and occasionally things. For example, if someone is 'quarrelsome', they are always quarrelling with people; if someone or something is 'bothersome', they are annoying or irritating.

*...he becomes impossibly quarrelsome and abusive, even violent.*
*... a loathsome, dark, evil thing.*

Here is a list of words with this meaning:

| | | |
|---|---|---|
| adventuresome | flavoursome | meddlesome |
| bothersome | loathsome | quarrelsome |
| burdensome | lonesome | venturesome |

## 2 Causing an emotion

**-some** combines with nouns, verbs, and adjectives to form new adjectives. Adjectives formed in this way describe a person or thing that causes someone to feel a particular emotion, usually an

# -some

unpleasant one. For example, if something is 'worrisome', it makes people worry; if a person or thing is 'troublesome', they cause annoying problems or difficulties.

*The destruction of your radio is a serious and worrisome affair.*
*To Kunta, lions were fearsome, slinking animals that would tear apart a goat.*

Here is a list of words with this meaning:

| | | | |
|---|---|---|---|
| awesome | irksome | troublesome | worrisome |
| fearsome | tiresome | wearisome | |

## 3 Groups

**-some** combines with small numbers such as 'two', 'three', or 'four' to form nouns that refer to a group containing that number of people, usually when they are doing something together.

*We decided to make the attempt as a threesome.*
*I was glad to see him on the beach when our foursome wandered onto it.*

### Words with other meanings

| | | |
|---|---|---|
| chromosome | noisome | wholesome |
| handsome | toothsome | winsome |

# -speak

PRODUCTIVE USE: **-speak** combines with nouns, and especially people's names, to form new nouns. Nouns formed in this way refer to the language in which a particular subject is discussed or to the way that someone characteristically speaks. For example, 'lawyer-speak' is the obscure legal language often used by lawyers; 'Woolf-speak' refers to the way Virginia Woolf typically uses language.

*...anyone wanting advice, and who didn't understand lawyer-speak.*
*...that unique language known as computer-speak.*
*Students soon learn to recognise teacher-speak.*
*The novel contains many examples of Woolf-speak.*

Here are some examples of words with this meaning:

| | |
|---|---|
| computer-speak | marketing-speak |
| consumer-speak | media-speak |
| lawyer-speak | teacher-speak |

# step-

**step-** combines with nouns such as 'brother', 'parent', and 'child' to form new nouns. Nouns formed in this way refer to the members of a family in which one or more of the adults has been married more than once. For example, a woman's 'stepdaughter' is the daughter of her husband by a previous marriage; someone's 'stepfather' is the man who has married their mother after the death or divorce of their natural father.

**Spelling:** Words formed in this way are usually written as one word, but some of the less common ones can be written with a hyphen.

*She was never out of the company of her stepdaughters.*
*The children were staying with Betty's stepmother in Glasgow.*
*...Margaret Burnham's stepbrother Bob.*

Here is a list of words with this meaning:

| | | | |
|---|---|---|---|
| stepbrother | stepdaughter | stepmother | stepsister |
| step-children | stepfather | step-parent | stepson |

# -stricken

PRODUCTIVE USE: **-stricken** combines with nouns that refer to an unpleasant emotion or experience in order to form adjectives. Adjectives formed in this way describe people or things that are very badly affected by such emotions or experiences. For example, if you are 'panic-stricken', your panic is so great that you are unable to control it; if a country is 'famine-stricken', it is affected by a very bad shortage of food.

*The slightest suspicion of danger and they freeze, panic-stricken.*
*The great majority of poverty-stricken people live in rural areas.*
*When Roosevelt died Hearst was grief-stricken.*
*The quiet of the store was suddenly pervaded by a subdued but fear-stricken tension.*
*He was immediately horror-stricken at what he'd done and shot himself.*

Here are some examples of words with this meaning:

| | | | |
|---|---|---|---|
| awe-stricken | grief-stricken | panic-stricken | terror-stricken |
| famine-stricken | guilt-stricken | plague-stricken | |
| fear-stricken | horror-stricken | poverty-stricken | |

# -style

PRODUCTIVE USE: **-style** combines with nouns and adjectives to form words which describe something that resembles or is characteristic of the thing referred to or described by the original noun or

## -style

adjective. For example, a 'Victorian-style' dress is similar to those worn by Victorian women; if food is cooked 'American-style', it is made in the same way as American food and is supposed to look and taste like it.

*She was dressed in a long, Victorian-style dress.*
*Greece is a big producer of oriental-style tobaccos.*
*He still wore his old-style suits.*
*She was sitting Indian-style on the floor.*

Here are some examples of words with this meaning:

| | | | |
|---|---|---|---|
| African-style | bungalow-style | Hollywood-style | old-style |
| American-style | commando-style | Indian-style | Russian-style |
| antique-style | English-style | military-style | Tokyo-style |
| baroque-style | European-style | modern-style | Tudor-style |
| British-style | French-style | Moscow-style | US-style |
| buffet-style | German-style | new-style | Victorian-style |

### Words with other meanings

| | | |
|---|---|---|
| freestyle | hairstyle | life-style |

# sub-

## 1 Gradation

PRODUCTIVE USE: **sub-** combines with nouns to form new nouns. Nouns formed in this way refer to things that are secondary or less important examples of whatever is referred to by the original nouns. For example, a 'sub-committee' is a small committee whose members come from a larger and more influential committee; a 'sub-contractor' is a person or firm that has a contract to do a small part of a job which another firm is responsible for.

**Spelling:** Words formed in this way are usually written with a hyphen, but some of the more common ones are written as one word.

*...the Parliamentary defence committee's sub-committee on low flying aircraft noise.*
*Supporters succeeded in forming a sub-party within the party.*
*The police said that crime had fallen in the subdivision covering the city centre.*

*In the Indian subcontinent the monsoon is awaited with hope and trepidation.*

Here are some examples of words with this meaning:

| | | | |
|---|---|---|---|
| sub-agent | sub-contractor | sub-paragraph | substructure |
| sub-branch | subculture | sub-party | sub-system |
| sub-centre | subdepartment | sub-plot | subtenant |
| sub-chief | subdivision | subsection | sub-text |
| sub-class | sub-editor | subset | sub-total |
| sub-committee | sub-group | sub-species | subtype |
| subcontinent | sub-heading | sub-station | subvariety |

Note that **sub-** occasionally combines in this way with verbs. For example, if you 'subdivide' something, you divide again something that has already been divided.

*The group may then be divided and subdivided.*
*I lived for three years nearly rent-free by subletting rooms to friends.*
*Mintech increasingly subcontracted its civil programme to the private sector.*

## 2 Beneath

**sub-** combines with nouns, adjectives, and occasionally verbs to form new nouns, adjectives, and verbs. Words formed in this way refer to or describe things that are beneath or lower down than something else. For example, a 'submarine' is a ship that can travel under the sea, as well as on its surface; a 'subterranean' river flows underground.

*A submarine lying still on the seabed stands a good chance of not being noticed.*
*...mermaid princesses reclining on rocks in sub-aquatic settings.*
*The boat was sinking. The stern was completely submerged, and the bow was rising.*

Here is a list of words with this meaning:

| | | | |
|---|---|---|---|
| sub-aquatic | submarine | subsea | subterranean |
| sub-basement | submerge | subsoil | subtitle |
| subcurrent | suboceanic | sub-surface | subway |

## 3 Lesser

**sub-** combines with nouns and adjectives to form new nouns and adjectives. Words formed in this way refer to or describe people or things that are inferior, smaller, or less powerful than whatever is referred to or described by the original nouns and adjectives. For example, if goods are 'substandard', they fail to meet a required standard and are therefore unacceptable; if a plane flies at a 'subsonic' speed, it travels slower than the speed of sound.

# sub-

*Substandard civil engineering costs more in lives than it saves in materials.*
*...a woman who was clearly educationally subnormal.*
*...the subhuman conditions of the jails.*

Here is a list of words with this meaning:

| | | | |
|---|---|---|---|
| subfertile | sub-humid | subsonic | sub-zero |
| sub-freezing | sub-literacy | substandard | |
| subhuman | subnormal | subteenage | |

Note that **sub-** occasionally combines with adjectives and nouns to form new adjectives. Adjectives formed in this way describe things that unsuccessfully imitate a particular style or way of doing something. For example, a 'sub-Tennysonian' style of writing resembles Tennyson's poetry, but is not as good.

*The ideas they sought to embody were far too highbrow for my sub-Tennysonian style.*
*He spoke in a generalized sub-Cockney whine.*

## 4 Power and control

**sub-** also occurs in nouns, adjectives, and verbs which express the idea that one person or thing exerts power over or controls another. For example, if soldiers 'subdue' a group of people, they gain control over them, usually by force; if someone is 'submissive', they do whatever other people want them to.

*The troops were sent to subdue the tribesmen.*
*The trade union movement is not prepared to be subservient to any movement.*
*...the subjugation of the interests of the working class.*

Here is a list of words with this meaning:

| | | | |
|---|---|---|---|
| subdue | subjugation | submissive | subordinate |
| subject | sublimate | submit | subservient |

Note that 'subject' can also be a noun with another meaning and is in the list below.

## Words with other meanings

| | | | |
|---|---|---|---|
| subconscious | subscribe | subsidize | subterfuge |
| subject | subscription | substance | subtract |
| subjective | subsequent | substantial | suburb |
| subjunctive | subside | substitute | subversive |
| sublime | subsidiary | subsume | subvert |

162

# super-

## 1 Degree

PRODUCTIVE USE: **super-** combines with adjectives to form new adjectives. Adjectives formed in this way express the idea that the quality described is present in an unusually large degree. For example, if something is 'superabundant', it is present in extremely large quantities; if someone is 'super-intelligent', they are extremely intelligent.

**super-** also combines with the adverbs and nouns that are related to the original adjectives.

**Spelling:** Words formed in this way can be written with a hyphen or as one word.

*I would choose this plant for its superabundant flowers and fruits.*
*Haemoglobin is super-efficient at the task of carrying oxygen.*
*...a miniaturized, super-cheap, highly reliable computer.*

Here are some examples of words with this meaning:

| | | |
|---|---|---|
| superabundant | superfine | super-precious |
| super-active | super-fluidity | super-quick |
| supercharged | super-friendly | super-rich |
| super-cheap | superheated | supersaturated |
| super-clever | super-heavy | super-secure |
| superconductor | super-hygienic | super-sensitive |
| super-conscious | super-intelligent | super-simplification |
| super-dominant | superintense | supersophisticated |
| super-efficient | supermodern | super-speed |

## 2 Size, power, and ability

PRODUCTIVE USE: **super-** combines with nouns to form new nouns that refer to a bigger, more powerful, or more important version of a particular thing. For example, a 'supermarket' is a very big shop selling many different goods; a 'supertanker' is a very large ship able to carry a large amount of cargo; a 'superpower' is a country whose military forces are very strong.

**Spelling:** Words formed in this way can be written with a hyphen or as one word.

*...the Vatican supermarket, brim-full of food at subsidized prices.*
*...the rise of Japan as an economic, financial and technological superstate.*
*...the application of the power of the super-computers towards advancing medical science.*

# super-

*...a super-union with more than two million members.*

Here are some examples of words with this meaning:

| | | | |
|---|---|---|---|
| super-athlete | super-hero | super-ministry | superstate |
| superbrain | superhighway | super-organism | superstore |
| super-computer | super-leader | superpower | supertanker |
| supercontinent | superman | super-species | super-union |
| super-genius | supermarket | superstar | superwoman |

## 3 Beyond

**super-** combines with adjectives to form new adjectives. Adjectives formed in this way describe things that go beyond the limits of what the original adjectives usually describe. For example, a 'supersonic' aircraft is one which travels faster than the speed of sound; if something is 'superhuman', it is beyond the powers or experiences of a normal person. **super-** also combines with the adverbs, nouns, and verbs that are related to the original adjectives.

*...the hazards of flying such aircraft at supersonic speeds.*
*Pep pills produce supernormal alertness.*
*...the supernatural contrivance of an angel descending from heaven.*

Here is a list of words with this meaning:

| | | |
|---|---|---|
| superhuman | supernatural | supersonic |
| supernational | supernormal | |

### Words with other meanings

| | | | |
|---|---|---|---|
| superannuated | superfluous | supernumerary | supertax |
| supercilious | superimpose | supersede | supervise |
| superego | superintend | superstition | |
| superficial | superlative | superstructure | |

# sur-

**sur-** occurs in words which have 'over', 'above', or 'excess' as part of their meaning. For example, a 'surcharge' is a charge which is made as well as the usual amount, often as a tax or penalty; a 'surplus' of something is more of it than you need.

Here is a list of words with this meaning:

| | | |
|---|---|---|
| surcharge | surmount | surplus |
| surfeit | surpass | surreal |

# sym-, syn-

**sym-** and **syn-** occur in words which have 'with', 'together', or 'similar' as part of their meaning. For example, if something is 'symmetrical', its two halves are mirror images of each other; a 'synthesis' of different ideas is a mixture of these ideas in which they blend together; if you 'synchronize' two actions, you do them at the same time.

Here is a list of words with this meaning:

| | | | |
|---|---|---|---|
| symbiosis | sympathy | synchronize | synonym |
| symmetrical | symphony | syndicate | synthesis |

# techn-

**techn-** occurs in words which have 'skill', 'craft', or 'art' as part of their meaning. For example, a 'technician' is someone whose job involves skilled practical work with scientific equipment; 'technology' is the study or use of scientific knowledge for practical purposes in industry.

Here is a list of words with this meaning:

| | | | |
|---|---|---|---|
| technical | technician | technique | technology |

Note that **techno-** is also used as an abbreviation of 'technology' and it occurs in words which have technology as part of their meaning. For example, a 'technocentric' society is one that depends on technology and uses it a great deal.

Here is a list of words with this meaning:

| | | | |
|---|---|---|---|
| technocentric | technocracy | technomania | technosociety |
| technochemical | technocrat | technophobe | technostructure |

# tele-

**tele-** occurs in words which express the idea that something is distant or that something happens over a distance. For example, a 'telephone' is an electrical device which transmits speech so that you can talk to someone who is in a different place; 'telecommunications' is the technology of sending signals and messages over long distances using electrical equipment.

Here is a list of words with this meaning:

| | | |
|---|---|---|
| telecommunications | telepathy | telescope |
| telecommuter | telephone | televise |
| telegram | telephoto | television |
| telegraph | teleprinter | |

Note that **tele-** is also sometimes used as an abbreviation of either

## tele-

'telephone' or 'television'. For example, 'telesales' is a method of selling goods by telephone; a 'telecast' is a television broadcast.

Here is a list of words with this meaning:

telecast          telesales          teletext

## theo-

**theo-** occurs in words which have 'god' as part of their meaning. For example, a 'theocracy' is a society which is ruled by priests who represent a god; a 'theologian' is someone who studies the nature of God and the relationship between God and human beings.

Here is a list of words with this meaning:

theocracy       theological       theology       theosophy

## thermo-

**thermo-** occurs in words which have 'heat' as part of their meaning. For example, a 'thermometer' is an instrument for measuring temperature; a 'thermostat' is a control which automatically keeps a heating system at a constant temperature.

Here is a list of words with this meaning:

| | | | |
|---|---|---|---|
| thermochemical | thermoelectric | thermonuclear | thermostat |
| thermodynamic | thermometer | thermopollution | thermotherapy |

## -tion

See **-ion**.

## -to-be

**-to-be** combines with nouns to form new nouns. Nouns formed in this way refer to things or people that will become whatever the original nouns describe. For example, a 'mother-to-be' is a woman who is pregnant and about to become a mother; a 'husband-to-be' is a man who has decided to get married but hasn't yet done so.

*The mother-to-be arrives for her regular obstetrical check-ups.*
*...the brilliant emperor-to-be Justinian, who subsequently reigned from 527 to 565 AD.*
*'I don't know when I'll meet him,' Miss Yoo Ok Soon said of her husband-to-be.*

Here is a list of words with this meaning:

| | | |
|---|---|---|
| bride-to-be | husband-to-be | parents-to-be |
| emperor-to-be | mother-to-be | wife-to-be |

PRODUCTIVE USE: This is not a particularly common use but new words can be formed by adding **-to-be** to nouns.

*...the roofbeams of the house-to-be.*
*...the technological arrangements of the society-to-be.*

Note that **-to-be** also combines with 'soon' and 'never' to form adjectives.

*The soon-to-be widow did not comprehend that her husband would die.*
*...the never-to-be astronauts.*

# too-

PRODUCTIVE USE: **too-** combines with adjectives to form new adjectives. Adjectives formed in this way refer to things that have more of the quality described than is useful or desirable.

*The too-easy availability of credit has a moral impact.*
*To drill his seed on too-cold ground was to have it rot, or the birds get it.*
*...the too-familiar list of economic difficulties.*
*...the shock of his too-blond hair.*

Here are some examples of words with this meaning:

| | | | |
|---|---|---|---|
| too-blond | too-easy | too-late | too-much |
| too-clean | too-familiar | too-literal | too-placid |
| too-close | too-high | too-long | too-rapid |
| too-cold | too-intimate | too-loud | too-rigid |
| too-desperate | too-large | too-massive | too-tight |

# trans-

## 1 Moving from one side of something to the other

PRODUCTIVE USE: **trans-** combines with nouns and adjectives that refer to or describe a place in order to form words which describe something that goes across the place mentioned. For example, the 'trans-Siberian' railway is a railway that crosses Siberia; a 'transatlantic' flight is a flight that goes from one side of the Atlantic to the other.

**Spelling:** Words formed in this way can be written with a hyphen or as one word.

*...then to Vladivostok and via the Trans-Siberian railway to Moscow.*
*...a relentless attempt to delay the Trans-Alaska Pipeline.*

## trans-

*...last year's Carlsberg singlehanded transatlantic race.*

Here are some examples of words with this meaning:

| | | |
|---|---|---|
| trans-Alaska | transatlantic | trans-Siberian |
| trans-Amazonian | transcontinental | trans-world |
| transAmerica | transoceanic | |

There are two other groups of words which are similar in meaning to those explained above but in which **trans-** combines with stems which are not current words in English.

The first group contains nouns and verbs that refer to or describe the process by which something goes from one place to another. For example, if you 'transport' something, you take or send it from one place to another.

Here is a list of words with this meaning:

| | | | |
|---|---|---|---|
| transceiver | transit | transmit | transpose |
| transfer | transmigration | transplant | |
| transfusion | transmission | transport | |

The second group of words contains nouns and adjectives that refer to or describe the process by which one thing crosses or goes through another. For example, if something is 'transparent', it allows light to pass through it and you can see through it.

Here is a list of words with this meaning:

| | | |
|---|---|---|
| transept | transparency | transpiration |
| translucent | transparent | transverse |

## 2 Totally changing

**trans-** also occurs in words which refer to or describe the process by which something completely changes its shape or form. In this meaning, **trans-** often combines with stems that are not current words in English. For example, if you 'translate' something, you change it from one language into another; if you 'transform' something you totally change its appearance.

*Translation and simultaneous interpretation will be done by machines.*
*The transition to a war footing had gone very smoothly.*
*The transcript of grand jury hearings is sealed.*
*...Shakespeare with his obsession with transsexual heroines.*

Here is a list of words with this meaning:

| | | |
|---|---|---|
| transcribe | transition | transmute |
| transcript | translate | transsexual |
| transcription | translation | transubstantial |
| transform | transliteration | transubstantiation |
| transformation | transmogrify | transvestite |

## Words with other meanings

| | | | |
|---|---|---|---|
| transaction | transfix | transient | transitory |
| transcend | transgression | transistor | transnational |
| transcendent | transhipment | transitivity | transpire |

# tri-

**tri-** occurs in words which indicate that something has three parts. For example, a 'trilogy' is a series of three related books by the same author which have the same subject or characters; a 'triplet' is one of three babies born at the same time to the same mother.

Here is a list of words with this meaning:

| | | | |
|---|---|---|---|
| triangle | tricycle | tripartite | tripod |
| tricentennial | trilateral | triple | triptych |
| tricolour | tri-level | triplet | trisyllabic |
| tri-continental | trilogy | triplicate | triumvirate |

# -type

PRODUCTIVE USE: **-type** combines with nouns and adjectives to form words which describe something that is similar to or typical of the thing referred to by the original noun or adjective. For example, a 'Swedish-type' house is a house similar to those built in Sweden; 'academic-type' work is work you do on academic subjects at school or university, as opposed to other kinds of work.

*It was a long wooden Swedish-type house which looked almost black.*
*Traces of the hormone-type weedkillers can wreak havoc on sensitive crops.*
*...a typical five-seat, executive-type car.*
*...the plain lenses of his schoolboy-type glasses.*
*Day nurseries are often run by a hospital-type matron.*

Here are some examples of words with this meaning:

| | | | |
|---|---|---|---|
| academic-type | executive-type | military-type | snack-type |
| Burmese-type | gothic-type | police-type | Swedish-type |
| church-type | hormone-type | rail-type | war-type |
| European-type | hospital-type | schoolboy-type | Western-type |

# -ular

**-ular** combines with nouns to form adjectives. Adjectives formed in this way describe things that involve or are characterized by whatever the nouns refer to. For example, if someone is 'muscular',

## -ular

they have well-developed muscles; if something such as sugar is 'granular', it is made up of lots of granules. Words formed in this way are fairly formal and are used more commonly in written English than in spoken English.

*His shoulders were broad and muscular.*
*...a Nobel Prize winner in the field of molecular biology.*
*Most of the roads were still impassable to vehicular movements.*

Here is a list of words with this meaning:

| | | | |
|---|---|---|---|
| cellular | curricular | modular | valvular |
| consular | glandular | molecular | vehicular |
| corpuscular | granular | muscular | ventricular |

**-ular** also combines with nouns that refer to shapes in order to form adjectives that describe things with that shape. For example, if something is 'circular', it is shaped like a circle; if something is 'rectangular', it is in the shape of a rectangle.

*...a large circular pool of very clear water.*
*I found him at an angular desk in a room full of busy-looking journalists.*
*Bear Island is triangular in shape, with its apex to the south.*
*...special tubular tyres.*

Here is a list of words with this meaning:

| | | | |
|---|---|---|---|
| angular | globular | rectangular | triangular |
| circular | quadrangular | tabular | tubular |

### Words with other meanings

| | | | |
|---|---|---|---|
| avuncular | jocular | perpendicular | singular |
| binocular | jugular | popular | spectacular |
| insular | particular | regular | vernacular |
| irregular | peninsular | secular | |

# ultra-

PRODUCTIVE USE: **ultra-** combines with adjectives to form new adjectives. Adjectives formed in this way express the idea that the qualities described are true or present to a very large degree. For example, if someone is 'ultra-intelligent', they are extremely intelligent; if something is 'ultra-modern', it is very modern or up-to-date.

*... the intellectual power of computers and Ultra-Intelligent Machines.*
*...an ultra-light plastic pot containing tablets.*
*They delight in her exuberant, ultra-feminine wit.*
*The family plods on generation after generation, ultra-conservative.*
*27 organizations signed a warning of the 'enormous damage' ultra-orthodox legislation would have.*

Here are some examples of words with this meaning:

| | | |
|---|---|---|
| ultra-cautious | ultra-intelligent | ultra-rich |
| ultra-civilized | ultra-left | ultra-secret |
| ultra-clean | ultra-light | ultra-sensitive |
| ultra-conservative | ultra-low | ultra-sharp |
| ultra-English | ultra-modern | ultra-smart |
| ultra-fast | ultra-orthodox | ultra-smooth |
| ultra-feminine | ultra-pious | ultra-sophisticated |
| ultra-high | ultra-powerful | ultra-tiny |

**ultra-** also sometimes combines with nouns to form other nouns that refer to an extreme version of something.

*Shintoism gave a religious basis for Japanese ultra-nationalism and ultra-militarism.*
*Women excel in the ultra-distance events where they sometimes beat many of the men.*

### Words with other meanings

| | | |
|---|---|---|
| ultramarine | ultrasound | ultraviolet |
| ultrasonic | ultrastructure | |

# un-

## 1 With adjectives, adverbs, and nouns

**un-** combines with adjectives and their related nouns and adverbs to form new adjectives, nouns, and adverbs. Words formed in this way describe or refer to things that are the opposite of whatever the original adjectives, adverbs, and nouns describe or refer to. For example, if someone finds something 'unacceptable', they think it is not acceptable; if someone is 'unfortunate', they have bad luck and unpleasant experiences as opposed to good fortune.

*What they have to tell us may be intellectually shocking or emotionally unacceptable.*

*...an uneven or rough surface.*
*He detested and, if he could, avoided personal unpleasantness.*
*Hargreaves, unwillingly, felt drawn to Melmotte in his isolation.*

Here is a list of adjectives with this meaning:

| | | | |
|---|---|---|---|
| unable | unconscious | unhappy | unpleasant |
| unacceptable | uncooperative | unharmonious | unpredictable |
| unalive | undemocratic | unhelpful | unrealistic |
| unalterable | uneatable | unintelligent | unremarkable |
| unaware | unemotional | unkind | unsafe |
| unbelievable | unemployed | unlucky | unsuccessful |
| unbiased | unfair | unmusical | untidy |
| uncertain | unfaithful | unnatural | unusual |
| unclean | unfortunate | unnecessary | unwell |
| uncomfortable | ungentlemanly | unofficial | unwilling |

Here is a list of nouns and adverbs with this meaning:

| | | |
|---|---|---|
| unacceptability | unfairly | unpleasantness |
| unacceptably | unfairness | unpredictability |
| unalterability | unfortunately | unpredictably |
| unalterably | unhappily | unrealistically |
| unbelievability | unhappiness | unsuccessfully |
| unbelievably | unhelpfully | untidily |
| uncertainly | unhelpfulness | untidiness |
| uncertainty | unluckily | unusually |
| uncomfortably | unnaturally | unwillingly |
| unconsciously | unofficially | unwillingness |
| undemocratically | unpleasantly | |

PRODUCTIVE USE: **un-** can combine with almost any adjective or noun but the words formed are often unusual and are used for emphasis or contrast. They should be used with extreme care.

*...your shocked and horrified unbelief.*
*...an act of the greatest uncharity, the very negation of the spirit of kindness.*
*The other girl had suddenly gone un-brave and confessed all.*

## 2 With participles

**un-** combines with participles to form adjectives which express the idea that something has not happened or is not true. For example, if someone is 'unbeaten' at something, no-one has beaten them yet; if someone is described as 'unsmiling', they are not smiling.

*...Lennox Lewis, the unbeaten young heavyweight who is looking for a British title bout.*
*The passage contains my unrehearsed and largely unprepared remarks.*

*...their peaceful, undemanding co-existence.*

Here is a list of words with this meaning:

| | | | |
|---|---|---|---|
| unaltered | unexamined | unloving | unsmiling |
| unbeaten | unexcavated | unneeded | unstamped |
| unbuilt | unexpected | unoffending | unswallowed |
| uncaring | unfinished | unorganized | untaught |
| uncarpeted | unflattering | unpainted | untested |
| unchanging | unharmed | unprecedented | untrusting |
| uncivilized | unhesitating | unprepared | unuttered |
| undamaged | uninterrupted | unprinted | unventilated |
| undemanding | uninviting | unread | unwritten |
| undisturbed | unloved | unrehearsed | unyellowing |

Adjectives formed in this way can be used to form **-ly** adverbs.

For more information on **-ly** adverbs, see **-ly**.

*Captain Imrie accepted the judgement as unhesitatingly as if an oracle had spoken.*
*He stared at me unblinkingly.*

# 3 With verbs

**un-** combines with verbs to form new verbs. Verbs formed in this way express the idea that the process or state referred to by the original verb is reversed. For example, if you 'undress', you take off the clothes you are dressed in; if you 'uncover' something, you remove whatever was covering or hiding it.

*Let him help to dress and undress himself.*
*Whatever is now covered up will be uncovered.*
*I unlocked the padlock and opened the lid.*
*He reached into the lunch bag and took out the second sandwich and unwrapped it.*

Here is a list of words with this meaning:

| | | | | |
|---|---|---|---|---|
| unbend | uncrease | unleash | unplug | untether |
| unclasp | undo | unlock | unroll | untie |
| unclip | undress | unmake | unscrew | untwist |
| uncover | unlearn | unpack | unseal | unwrap |

For more information on prefixes with a negative meaning, see **de-**, **dis-**, **il-**, and **non-**.

## Words with other meanings

| | | | | |
|---|---|---|---|---|
| undue | unless | unnerve | until | unto |

# under-

## 1 Insufficient

PRODUCTIVE USE: **under-** combines with verbs, nouns, and past participles to form new verbs, nouns, and adjectives. Words formed in this way express the idea that there is not enough of something or that something has not been done as much or as well as is needed. For example, if you describe something as 'underdeveloped', you think it has not been developed enough; if you 'underestimate' someone or something, you think they are smaller, less powerful, or less capable than they really are.

**Spelling:** Words formed in this way are usually written as one word, but some of the less common ones can be written with a hyphen.

*The problems of the underdeveloped world will remain intractable.*
*The hospitals were seriously under-financed.*
*While over-indulging in eating, they also under-indulge in exercise.*
*He was an undergrown boy, thin, with a long pale face.*
*...the measured understatement of true professional geographers.*

Here are some examples of words with this meaning:

| | | |
|---|---|---|
| under-capacity | under-indulge | undersize |
| underdeveloped | under-manned | understaffed |
| underemployed | undernourished | understatement |
| under-equipped | underpay | undersubscribed |
| underestimate | underprepared | under-trained |
| under-exercised | underpriced | under-use |
| under-financed | under-production | undervalue |
| undergrown | under-rehearsed | underweight |

## 2 Beneath

PRODUCTIVE USE: **under-** also combines with nouns and verbs to form words which refer to or describe things that are beneath something else or that happen below something else. For example, if something is 'underground', it is below the surface of the ground; if you 'underline' a piece of writing, you draw a line beneath it; your 'underclothes' are the clothes you wear next to your skin under your other clothes.

*It was a long way down, for Alex's office was one floor underground.*
*A propagator is an enclosed glass box with soil in it and under-soil electric heating.*
*I put on the clothes but not the underwear.*
*...under-glass cultivation.*

174

*He underlined his signature with a little flourish.*

Here are some examples of words with this meaning:

| | | | |
|---|---|---|---|
| underarm | underfoot | underlit | under-soil |
| underbelly | under-glass | underpass | undersurface |
| underblanket | underground | underscore | underwater |
| undercarriage | undergrowth | undersea | underwear |
| underclothes | underline | underside | |
| underfloor | underlip | undersigned | |

## 3 Numbers

PRODUCTIVE USE: **under-** combines with numbers to form nouns and adjectives. Nouns formed in this way are always used in the plural form and refer to people who are younger than the age mentioned. For example 'under-fives' are children who are younger than five years old. Adjectives formed in this way describe people or things that are younger or smaller than the age or size that those numbers refer to. For example, if you are playing in an 'under-twenty-one' sports team, you are aged twenty or less.

*They offer educational day care for two hundred under-fives.*
*The under-twenty-ones have their sights on the under-twenty-one World Cup.*

## 4 Rank

**under-** combines with nouns that refer to people's jobs in order to form new nouns. Nouns formed in this way refer to people who have a lower rank or status than someone else. For example, an 'undergraduate' is a student who has not yet graduated and who is studying for his or her first degree; an 'under-gardener' is a gardener who is supervised by a head gardener.

*The age range of undergraduate college students is eighteen to twenty-two.*
*Who's Who invites civil servants of the rank of under-secretary or above to submit biographies.*
*He returned as assistant under-librarian at the University Library.*

Here is a list of words with this meaning:

| | | |
|---|---|---|
| under-butler | under-gardener | under-secretary |
| under-class | undergraduate | underservant |
| under-dairymaid | under-librarian | undersheriff |
| under-footman | under-manager | |

### Words with other meanings

| | | | |
|---|---|---|---|
| undercover | undergo | underpin | undertaker |
| undercurrent | underhand | understand | undertone |
| undercut | underlie | understudy | underworld |
| underdog | undermine | undertake | underwrite |

# uni-

**uni-** occurs in words which have 'one' or 'single' as part of their meaning. For example, if something is 'unique', it is the only one of its type; a 'unisex' hairdresser is a single shop that is used by both men and women.

Here is a list of words with this meaning:

| | | | |
|---|---|---|---|
| uniform | unilateral | unique | unite |
| unify | union | unisex | unity |

# up-

## 1 Direction or position

**up-** combines with nouns and verbs to form words which describe or refer to a person or thing that is moving towards, or is situated in, a higher or more remote place or position. For example, if you go 'uphill', you climb a slope or hill; 'upland' places are situated on high hills, plateaus, or mountains; you describe a place as 'up-country' when it is farther north, farther inland, or more remote than the place you are in.

*...a side-street that led uphill quite steeply.*
*There were plenty of side roads leading away into the hills and the upland villages.*
*He advised that torpedo boats be brought upriver.*
*He plans to straighten the upstairs, clean the downstairs, and scrub the kitchen floor.*

Here is a list of words with this meaning:

| | | | |
|---|---|---|---|
| up-country | uphill | upside | upstretched |
| up-current | upland | upstage | upthrust |
| updraught | upriver | upstairs | upwards |
| upfield | uprush | upstream | upwind |

## 2 Increase or improvement

**up-** combines with verbs and occasionally nouns to form new verbs and nouns. Words formed in this way describe or refer to the process by which something increases or changes and improves. For example, if you 'upgrade' something, you change it so that it becomes more important and better in quality; if you 'update' something, you improve it by making it more modern.

*The district manager had wanted to upgrade staff who worked unsupervised.*

*Computers can update their own software and acquire new
programs for themselves.
...a sudden upsurge of fatherly compassion.*

Here is a list of words with this meaning:

| | | | |
|---|---|---|---|
| update | uprate | upsurge | upturn |
| upgrade | upscale | uptrend | |

## 3 Disturbance

**up-** also combines with verbs and nouns to form new verbs, nouns,
and adjectives. Words formed in this way describe or refer to some
sort of disturbance, trouble, or confusion. For example, if you 'upset'
something, you knock it over, if you 'upset' a person, you make
them unhappy, and if you 'upset' a process or procedure, you cause
it to go wrong; an 'uprising' is a revolt or rebellion.

*He almost upset the canoe in his struggle to leap overboard.
Belinda was looking hurt and upset.
Davis's death has upset our routine.
The forest near them burst into uproar.*

Here is a list of words with this meaning:

| | | | |
|---|---|---|---|
| upended | uprising | uproar | uproot | upset |

### Words with other meanings

| | | | |
|---|---|---|---|
| upbeat | upfront | upkeep | upshot |
| upbraid | upheaval | uplift | upstanding |
| upbringing | uphold | upmarket | uptake |
| upcoming | upholstery | upright | uptight |

# -ure

**-ure** combines with verbs to form nouns that refer to the action or
state described by the verb. For example, 'departure' is the act of
going away or departing from somewhere; 'composure' is the state
of being calm, unworried, and composed.

*Just before the departure from Aden, fierce fighting broke out.
The meeting was a failure.
Helen was struggling hard to keep her composure.
...the closure of the Suez Canal.
...an illegal seizure of property.*

Here is a list of words with this meaning:

| | | | |
|---|---|---|---|
| closure | disclosure | failure | portraiture |
| composure | enclosure | forfeiture | procedure |
| curvature | expenditure | mixture | sculpture |
| departure | exposure | pleasure | seizure |

## -ure

### Words with other meanings

| | | | |
|---|---|---|---|
| adventure | figure | leisure | picture |
| architecture | fixture | legislature | pressure |
| creature | furniture | literature | signature |
| culture | future | moisture | structure |
| feature | gesture | nature | temperature |

# vice-

**vice-** combines with nouns describing ranks or titles to form new nouns that describe ranks or titles that are less important than the first. For example, a 'vice-president' holds a position second only to the president; the 'vice-captain' of a sports team is next in importance to the captain.

*George Washington and John Adams were president and vice-president.*
*Captain Illingworth and vice-captain Cowdrey were at a loss.*
*...the positions of chairman, vice-chairman and secretary.*

Here is a list of words with this meaning:

| | | |
|---|---|---|
| vice-admiral | vice-consul | vice-presidency |
| vice-captain | vice-governor | vice-president |
| vice-chairman | vice-minister | vice-principal |
| vice-chairwoman | vice-premier | vice-provost |

# video-

**video-** occurs in words whose meaning includes 'televised pictures'. For example, a 'video-recorder' is a machine that records television programmes onto a 'video-tape' so that people can watch these programmes at some later time on a television set.

Here is a list of words with this meaning:

| | |
|---|---|
| video-cassette | video-recorder |
| video-coach | video-tape |

# -ward, -wards

PRODUCTIVE USE: **-ward** and **-wards** combine with nouns and adverbs of direction to form words which describe the direction in which something is moving or facing. For example, if someone faces 'westward', they face the west; if something moves 'downwards', it moves from a higher position to a lower one.

Note that words formed with **-ward** can usually be used as either adverbs or adjectives; words formed with **-wards** are mainly used as adverbs.

*He was shading his eyes, looking westward.*
*The ship sank off St Helena in 1612 on its homeward journey.*
*The child screwed up his eyes, and looked intently skywards.*
*He reached for the accelerator lever and pushed it upwards.*
*He sometimes made a downward beat with his raised right fist.*
*Sweet-smelling smoke swirled ceiling-ward.*

Here are some examples of words with this meaning:

| | | | |
|---|---|---|---|
| backward | eastwards | onward | skywards |
| backwards | floorward | onwards | southward |
| ceiling-ward | floorwards | outward | southwards |
| ceiling-wards | homeward | outwards | upward |
| downward | homewards | seaward | upwards |
| downwards | inward | seawards | westward |
| earthward | inwards | shoreward | westwards |
| earthwards | northward | shorewards | |
| eastward | northwards | skyward | |

Note that 'inward' and 'outward' also have meanings which are not connected with moving or facing in a particular direction. They are used to describe the inside or the outside of something, especially someone's thoughts and feelings or their appearance and expressions.

*...an expression of pain and inward concentration.*
*'Yes, of course I'll stay,' I said with outward calm.*

### Words with other meanings

| | | | |
|---|---|---|---|
| afterward | forward | steward | untoward |
| afterwards | leeward | toward | wayward |
| coward | reward | towards | windward |

# -ware

**-ware** combines with nouns, adjectives, and occasionally verbs to form nouns. Nouns formed in this way refer to things that are made of a particular substance, have particular qualities, or are intended for a particular use. For example, 'brassware' refers to objects made of brass; 'kitchenware' refers to objects such as pans and cooking utensils which are intended for use in the kitchen.

*...the beauty of the Kashmiri carpets and old brassware.*
*Huge chinaware pots overflowed with pink camellias.*

## -ware

*...Bullers, the fine arts and giftware group.*

Here is a list of words with this meaning:

| | | | |
|---|---|---|---|
| brassware | copperware | giftware | kitchenware |
| chinaware | dinnerware | glassware | silverware |
| coarseware | earthenware | houseware | stoneware |
| cookware | fineware | iron-ware | tableware |

Note that 'hardware' and 'software' are computer terms; 'hardware' refers to the machinery of the computer and 'software' refers to the programs that are written for it. 'Hardware' can also refer to the tools and equipment used in the home and garden.

# well-

## 1 Describing something good

PRODUCTIVE USE: **well-** combines with past participles to form adjectives. Adjectives formed in this way express the idea that the things or people they describe have attributes which are pleasing or useful or that something has been done successfully. For example, if you describe someone as 'well-behaved', they behave in a way you approve of; if a house is 'well-built', it has been built to a high standard; if a person is 'well-built', they are strong, physically fit, and healthy.

*You always seemed so neat and clean and well-behaved.*
*...a well-balanced, good-looking upright position.*
*A well-designed office is a place where people are comfortable and work well.*
*Biko was tall and well-built, with pleasant features.*
*...a series that was well-written, finely directed, and well-acted.*
*The four of them were highly intelligent, well-trained, and qualified women.*

Here are some examples of words with this meaning:

| | | | |
|---|---|---|---|
| well-acted | well-built | well-furnished | well-preserved |
| well-adjusted | well-chosen | well-kept | well-qualified |
| well-arranged | well-cut | well-made | well-timed |
| well-balanced | well-designed | well-nourished | well-trained |
| well-behaved | well-dressed | well-organized | well-understood |
| well-bred | well-educated | well-prepared | well-written |

**well-** is also used with this meaning to form the noun 'well-being' which refers to good health, pleasure, and a sense of worth in someone's life.

## 2 Amount or degree

PRODUCTIVE USE: **well-** also combines with past participles to form adjectives which express the idea that there is a large amount of something or that something has been done a great deal. **well-** can also be used to show that the qualities the adjectives describe are particularly intense or extreme. For example, if a person or fact is 'well-known', it is known by a lot of people; if something is 'well-chewed', it has been chewed many times.

...anyone who is rich and well-known.
...a cloth-capped miner in his well-worn corduroy trousers.
They worked like a well-oiled machine.
...the well-established principle of family life.

Here are some examples of words with this meaning:

| | | | |
|---|---|---|---|
| well-attended | well-deserved | well-known | well-respected |
| well-beaten | well-drained | well-lit | well-scrubbed |
| well-buttered | well-earned | well-loved | well-travelled |
| well-chewed | well-established | well-matured | well-tried |
| well-corseted | well-hidden | well-oiled | well-ventilated |
| well-covered | well-impressed | well-populated | well-worn |

The explanations given in paragraphs 1 and 2 are connected. In some words the meaning they have depends on the context in which they are used; for example, if you talk about a 'well-cooked' meal, you mean it has been cooked skilfully and that it tastes nice, but if you describe cabbage as 'well-cooked' you mean it has been cooked for a long time and perhaps cooked for too long. In certain other words the two meanings overlap; for example, if an event has been 'well-publicized', it has been publicized successfully but it has also been widely publicized and a lot of people know about it.

Here is a list of words with both meanings:

| | | |
|---|---|---|
| well-armed | well-fed | well-paid |
| well-charted | well-financed | well-publicized |
| well-cooked | well-grown | well-read |
| well-defined | well-guarded | well-rehearsed |
| well-developed | well-informed | well-stocked |
| well-documented | well-insulated | well-watered |
| well-equipped | well-marked | |

## 3 Friendliness or sympathy

**well-** combines with participles to form adjectives. Adjectives formed in this way express the idea that someone feels friendly or sympathetic to someone else. For example, if you do something which is 'well-intentioned', or are described as 'well-meaning', you wish to be useful, helpful or kind. **well-** also sometimes combines with this meaning with nouns to form new nouns. For example, a

# well-

'well-wisher' is someone who feels favourably towards another person or thing and wishes them success.

*Well-disposed people are amused by it. Others can be offended.*
*...the possibility of doing harm by well-intentioned efforts.*
*Many of the tasks performed by well-meaning officials could be much better done by self-reliant local communities.*
*The fine eighteenth-century iron gates were given by an American well-wisher.*

Here is a list of words with this meaning:

| | | | |
|---|---|---|---|
| well-disposed | well-meaning | well-received | well-wisher |
| well-intentioned | well-meant | well-regarded | |

## Words with other meanings

| | | | |
|---|---|---|---|
| well-heeled | well-off | well-spring | well-versed |
| well-nigh | well-sinkers | well-to-do | |

# -wide

## 1 Extent

PRODUCTIVE USE: **-wide** combines with nouns that refer to a place, area, or organization. Words formed in this way express the idea that something exists or happens throughout the whole of that place, area, or organization. For example, a 'worldwide' problem affects everybody in the world; a 'company-wide' pay rise applies to everybody who works for a particular company.

**Spelling:** Words formed in this way are usually written with a hyphen, but some of the more common ones are written as one word.

*The demonstration attracted worldwide media coverage.*
*...offering nationwide a 24 hour weather channel.*
*...the 1976 EEC-wide survey on people's attitudes to poverty.*
*A campus-wide rally was being organized.*
*A community-wide law would prove difficult to enforce.*

Here are some examples of words with this meaning:

| | | | |
|---|---|---|---|
| area-wide | continent-wide | nationwide | society-wide |
| campus-wide | countrywide | planet-wide | state-wide |
| city-wide | EEC-wide | population-wide | system-wide |
| company-wide | industry-wide | religion-wide | worldwide |

## 2 Measurement

PRODUCTIVE USE: **-wide** combines with any unit of distance to form adjectives that describe the width of something.

*I used to lie on the foot-wide parapet that ran round the top of the house.*
*...two-metre-wide lengths of silk.*
*...a three-inch-wide strip of flexible formica.*

# -wise

## 1 Similarity

PRODUCTIVE USE: **-wise** combines with nouns to form words which describe actions or states that are similar to those of the people or things referred to by the nouns. For example, if something moves 'clockwise', it moves in a circle and in the same direction as the hands of a clock.

**Spelling:** Words formed in this way are usually written with a hyphen, but some of the more common ones are written as one word.

*The wheel periodically spun clockwise as if of its own accord.*
*He came striding past swaying sailor-wise in his walk.*
*Face your crisis and don't hide your head in the sand, ostrich-wise.*
*He clenched his fist and beat hammer-wise on the wall at his right.*

Here are some examples of words with this meaning:

| | | |
|---|---|---|
| clockwise | monkey-wise | slantwise |
| crab-wise | ostrich-wise | sleepwalker-wise |
| hammer-wise | sack-wise | star-wise |
| machine-wise | sailor-wise | step-wise |

## 2 With regard to something

PRODUCTIVE USE: **-wise** combines with nouns, and occasionally adjectives and adverbs. Words formed in this way express the idea that something is true with regard to, or in connection with, the specific thing or quality originally referred to. For example, if you describe yourself as socialist 'vote-wise', you vote socialist but are not actively involved in politics; if an athlete's performance in a race is bad 'time-wise', he or she may have come high up in the finishing order but in a slower time than they hoped for.

**Spelling:** Words formed in this way can be written with a hyphen or as one word.

*We are mostly Socialists, vote-wise, and that's about all.*
*'It's not good, caloriewise, to have a high starch intake,' she said.*
*Tuesdays and Wednesdays are a bit restricted, menu-wise.*

# -wise

*Time-wise, I was about eight hours behind England.*

Here are some examples of words with this meaning:

| | | | |
|---|---|---|---|
| caloriewise | drinkwise | percentage-wise | status-wise |
| colour-wise | menu-wise | picture-wise | time-wise |
| comfort-wise | newswise | socially-wise | vote-wise |

Note that words formed in this way are informal and some speakers consider that they are not good English.

### Words with other meanings

| | | | |
|---|---|---|---|
| crosswise | likewise | penny-wise | worldly-wise |
| lengthwise | otherwise | streetwise | |

# -woman

**-woman** combines with nouns to form new nouns. Nouns formed in this way refer to women who do a particular job or who come from a particular place. You use **-woman** when you want to refer specifically to women rather than to men or people in general. For example, an 'Irishwoman' is a woman who comes from Ireland; a 'barwoman' is a woman who works in a pub or bar serving drinks.

*It is a political statement, which does not lose its force when the Irishman or Irishwoman travels or lives abroad.*
*Clare Francis is a novelist and former yachtswoman.*
*Sylvia was a clever needlewoman and made all her own clothes.*
*As a true countrywoman, she bottles and preserves all the things that grow in her garden.*

Here is a list of words with this meaning:

| | | | |
|---|---|---|---|
| barwoman | countrywoman | helmswoman | saleswoman |
| businesswoman | craftswoman | horsewoman | Scotswoman |
| careerwoman | Dutchwoman | Irishwoman | spokeswoman |
| chairwoman | Englishwoman | needlewoman | sportswoman |
| cleaning-woman | Frenchwoman | policewoman | yachtswoman |

For more information on words referring specifically to women, see **-ess**. For more information about words referring to people in general, see **-folk, -kind, -man, -people,** and **-person.**

# -work

## 1 Showing what something is made of

**-work** combines with nouns that refer to a substance or material in order to form new nouns. Nouns formed in this way refer to things made of that substance or material. For example, 'ironwork' refers to things such as gates or balconies made from iron in a decorative and skilful way; a 'wickerwork' chair is made of wicker.

**Spelling:** Words formed in this way are usually written as one word, but some of the less common ones can be written with a hyphen.

*I am always on the look-out for ornamental ironwork.*
*...fat wickerwork armchairs with feathery cushions.*
*Some new brickwork showed where two extra rooms had been added.*
*...jobs such as washing down paintwork, and cleaning ceilings.*

Here is a list of words with this meaning:

| | | | |
|---|---|---|---|
| brasswork | lacework | pipework | stonework |
| brickwork | leatherwork | plasterwork | threadwork |
| cement-work | metalwork | scrollwork | tilework |
| crochet-work | paintwork | silverwork | wickerwork |
| ironwork | pastrywork | steelwork | woodwork |

Note that **-work** can also be used in this way to show the form of something. For example, 'latticework' is any structure that is made in the form of a lattice; 'basketwork' refers to baskets and other objects woven from wicker and cane.

*They went to a table far down the room, behind a latticework screen.*
*...little basket-work tables with tops of ice-green glass.*
*...two-storey stone dwellings, all displaying iron grillwork on their balconies.*

## 2 Activities

**-work** also combines with nouns to form new nouns that refer to what you do with the things indicated by the original noun. For example, 'footwork' is the way in which you move your feet, especially in sport or dancing; 'paperwork' is the part of a job which involves dealing with papers, such as accounts, bills, or letters.

*Anticipation and nimble footwork enabled her to keep rallies going.*
*He must do some paperwork before going to bed.*
*The camerawork wasn't bad for students.*

Here is a list of words with this meaning:

| | | | |
|---|---|---|---|
| bookwork | camerawork | legwork | paperwork |
| brainwork | footwork | metalwork | video-work |
| brushwork | lathe-work | needlework | woodwork |

## 3 Tasks

PRODUCTIVE USE: **-work** also combines with nouns to form new nouns that refer to tasks which are related to the thing named. For

# -work

example, 'schoolwork' is the work that a child does at or for school; 'housework' is work done in the house such as cleaning and washing.

*She does well in her schoolwork, and works extremely hard.*
*The men shared all housework, including washing and ironing.*
*The examiners will take account of the course-work done by candidates.*

Here are some examples of words with this meaning:

| | | |
|---|---|---|
| casework | homework | schoolwork |
| classwork | housework | speech-work |
| course-work | management-work | wage-work |
| groupwork | model-work | |

## 4 A type of job

PRODUCTIVE USE: **-work** also combines with nouns that refer to a place of work, a time, or a particular system in order to form new nouns. Nouns formed in this way refer to the kind of job someone does. For example, 'shop-work' is work done in a shop; 'shiftwork' is the system by which different people work different shifts.

**Spelling:** Words formed in this way can be written with a hyphen or as one word.

*He had become less and less satisfied with shop-work.*
*In Sweden the unions have tried to have shiftwork banned.*
*Many families have been ruined through nightwork.*
*They look upon farmwork as something inferior.*

Here are some examples of words with this meaning:

| | | | |
|---|---|---|---|
| day-work | nightwork | practical-work | show-work |
| desk-work | office-work | saleswork | store-work |
| dockwork | pitwork | shiftwork | |
| farmwork | police-work | shop-work | |

## Words with other meanings

| | | | | |
|---|---|---|---|---|
| artwork | fieldwork | handiwork | part-work | teamwork |
| bodywork | firework | masterwork | patchwork | waxwork |
| clockwork | framework | network | piece-work | |
| craftwork | groundwork | openwork | spadework | |
| earthwork | guesswork | overwork | speedwork | |

# -worthy

## 1 Assessment of worth

PRODUCTIVE USE: **-worthy** combines with nouns to form adjectives. Adjectives formed in this way describe people or things that

186

deserve or merit whatever the nouns refer to. For example, if someone is 'trustworthy', they are reliable and responsible and can be trusted completely; if something is 'newsworthy', it is interesting or important enough to be reported on news programmes or in newspapers.

**Spelling:** Words formed in this way are usually written as one word, but some of the less common words can be written with a hyphen.

*She is well-balanced, hard working and trustworthy.*
*I can hardly remember one right decision, one praiseworthy action.*
*He hadn't done anything applause-worthy yet.*
*We will, if we think you are creditworthy, give you a loan.*

Here are some examples of words with this meaning:

| | | |
|---|---|---|
| applause-worthy | newsworthy | stageworthy |
| award-worthy | noteworthy | trustworthy |
| creditworthy | praiseworthy | |
| headline-worthy | respect-worthy | |

## 2 Vehicles

**-worthy** also combines with nouns to form adjectives that describe vehicles which are in a good condition and are safe for travelling.

*Once their craft was seaworthy again it was escorted out of the protection zone.*
*They then certified N-731-TA as completely airworthy.*
*...a car that he had lovingly re-painted and tinkered with to make it road-worthy.*

Here is a list of words with this meaning:

| | | | |
|---|---|---|---|
| airworthy | roadworthy | seaworthy | trackworthy |

# -wright

**-wright** occurs in nouns that refer to people who create, build or repair something. For example, a 'playwright' is a person who writes plays; a 'cartwright' is someone who makes and repairs carts.

Here is a list of words with this meaning:

| | | |
|---|---|---|
| cartwright | playwright | wainwright |
| millwright | shipwright | wheelwright |

# -y

## 1 Characteristics

PRODUCTIVE USE: **-y** combines with nouns to form adjectives. Adjectives formed in this way express the idea that something or someone is similar to or is characterized by the thing the noun refers to. For example, if something is 'dirty', it is covered with dirt; a 'smoky' room is one that is full of smoke.

**Spelling:** A final 'e' is replaced by '**-y**'. If a word of one syllable ends in a 'b', 'd', 'g', 'n', or 't' preceded by a single vowel, the 'b', 'd', 'g', 'n', or 't' is doubled before adding '**-y**'.

*Castle saw a stack of dirty dishes in the sink.*
*Horse-drawn sleds slithered across the snowy streets.*
*The back of the cab was dusty with cigarette ashes.*
*...feathery trees on pink stone hills.*

Here are some examples of words with this meaning:

| | | | | |
|---|---|---|---|---|
| bloody | dusty | hairy | sexy | stringy |
| blotchy | fatty | itchy | sketchy | stumpy |
| bulky | feathery | leafy | smoky | sunny |
| bushy | flowery | mighty | sneaky | thirsty |
| cloudy | foggy | muddy | snowy | tinny |
| dirty | grassy | rainy | stoney | worthy |

## 2 Colour

PRODUCTIVE USE: **-y** combines with colour adjectives to form new adjectives. Adjectives formed in this way describe something which is approximately that colour, or that has that colour in it. When words formed in this way are followed by another colour, they indicate the particular shade of that second colour. For example, if a flower is 'pinky' purple, it is a shade of purple that is quite similar to pink.

Note that **-y** is not used with 'white' or 'black'.

*...borders of pinky purple tulips.*
*...shortish, yellowy black hairs.*
*The peaks were already turning plummy maroon.*
*He turned a funny colour, a kind of greeny purple.*

## 3 Affectionate names

PRODUCTIVE USE: **-y** also combines with almost any noun or name in order to give it a more affectionate or familiar form. These words are often used by children, by adults when they are talking to children, or when someone wants to express affection. Words formed in this way are very informal.

*'I'll find out for you, Janey.'*
*'Where is your father, Danny? Can I speak to him?'*
*Sam wanted me to take him to see the birdies in the park.*
*'Give the ball to the doggy, John.'*

## Words with other meanings

| | | | | |
|---|---|---|---|---|
| cagey | handy | lofty | savoury | tiny |
| cheeky | hardy | murky | scanty | touchy |
| corny | heady | musty | seedy | wary |
| crafty | hearty | naughty | shifty | weary |
| dreamy | horny | phoney | steady | |
| dumpy | husky | puny | stocky | |
| earthy | jaunty | roomy | stuffy | |

Note that not all words ending in **-y** are adjectives; **-y** also occurs in some common nouns.

# Exercises

## 1 Forming nouns

**A** The suffixes in the following list combine with nouns and verbs to form new nouns that refer to people or professions. Look at the list of nouns. Write down the noun or verb from which they have been formed in the space provided. The first one has been done for you.

| SUFFIX | VERB/NOUN | NOUN FORMED |
|--------|-----------|-------------|
| -ant | *defend* | defendant |
|  | ................... | assistant |
| -ee | ................... | trainee |
|  | ................... | addressee |
| -ess | ................... | actress |
|  | ................... | princess |
| -er | ................... | driver |
|  | ................... | painter |
| -ian | ................... | historian |
|  | ................... | musician |
| -ist | ................... | novelist |
|  | ................... | scientist |
| -or | ................... | supervisor |
|  | ................... | visitor |

**B** Each of the sentences below contains a word printed in bold. Complete each sentence by using this word to form a noun which refers to a person who does a particular thing. Write down the answer in the space provided. The first one has been done for you.

1  If you are **employed** by a company, you are one of its
   ......*employee*...... s

2  A ................................. is someone whose job is **politics**.

3  A woman who works as a ................................. does the same job as a **waiter**.

4  The ................................. s in a discussion are the people who **participate** in it.

5  The person who **conducts** an orchestra or choir is called the
   .................................

191

6 Your ........................................ is the person who **teaches** you.

7 A ........................................ is someone who earns their living by

playing the **piano**.

8 If someone **examines** you, you are the ........................................ and he

or she is the ........................................

**C** The suffixes in the following list are used to form nouns that refer to
an activity, a process, or a state or condition. Look at the list of nouns
formed from them. Write down the noun, verb, or adjective from which
they have been formed in the space provided. The first one has been
done for you.

| SUFFIX | VERB/NOUN/ ADJECTIVE | NOUN FORMED |
|---|---|---|
| -al | *arrive* | arrival |
| -ance | ........................ | abundance |
| -cy | ........................ | constancy |
| -dom | ........................ | kingdom |
| -ence | ........................ | independence |
| -ful | ........................ | mouthful |
| -hood | ........................ | boyhood |
| -ing | ........................ | dancing |
| -ion | ........................ | invention |
| -ism | ........................ | criticism |
| -ity | ........................ | sensitivity |
| -ment | ........................ | agreement |
| -ness | ........................ | happiness |
| -ship | ........................ | ownership |

**D** Read the following short story. Write down the correct noun in the
space provided beneath the story using the words in **bold** to help you.
The first one has been done for you.

*Whilst at college, I remember listening to a lecture given by a rather
pompous (1) who was discussing the values of strong (2) in politics.
Firstly he presented his (3) of (4), then continued by arguing that (5) by a
political leader was a positive attribute as resolute decisions could be
made but that the basic (6) in society could still be maintained. He felt
strongly that schools did not provide the kind of (7) needed for the
development of good leadership qualities which should be instilled from*

*early* (8). *He felt also that modern society encouraged qualities such as* (9) *and* (10) *and gave no positive* (11) *to the young. However, when an earnest young student explained that he would like to become a* (12) *or a* (13) *in industry, and asked about courses to follow, the politician said, with a curt* (14), *"That's a silly question to ask me! I am a politician not a careers adviser!"*

| | | | |
|---|---|---|---|
| 1 **politics** | *politician* | 8 **child** | .................. |
| 2 **leader** | .................. | 9 **lazy** | .................. |
| 3 **define** | .................. | 10 **cynic** | .................. |
| 4 **leader** | .................. | 11 **guide** | .................. |
| 5 **dominate** | .................. | 12 **politics** | .................. |
| 6 **free** | .................. | 13 **manage** | .................. |
| 7 **encourage** | .................. | 14 **dismiss** | .................. |

# 2 Forming verbs

**A** **-en**, **-ify**, and **-ize** combine with nouns and adjectives to form verbs. Look at the following lists of adjectives and nouns. Put the corresponding verb in the space provided. The first one in each list has been done for you.

| ADJECTIVE → VERB | | NOUN → VERB | |
|---|---|---|---|
| hard | *harden* | horror | *horrify* |
| modern | .................. | memory | .................. |
| deep | .................. | beauty | .................. |
| intense | .................. | sympathy | .................. |
| false | .................. | apology | .................. |
| fat | .................. | glory | .................. |
| sterile | .................. | length | .................. |

**B** Now look at the following sentences. Complete them by writing down the correct form of one of the verbs in the lists above. Write the correct form in the space provided. The first one has been done for you.

1 He *apologized* .................. for interrupting her.

2 She tried to .................. her room with posters and plants.

3 A study has been ordered into the feasibility of

.................. the airport's main runway by two hundred

metres.

4 However much they .................................... , they all felt it was her fault.

5 Soya is excellent food for ..................................... cattle.

6 She laughed and that seemed to ..................................... her voice.

7 £40,000 had been spent on ..................................... the station.

8 ..................................... the bottles by immersing them in boiling water for fifteen minutes.


# 3 Forming adjectives

**A** The following suffixes combine with verbs to form adjectives.

| -able | -ible | -ed | -ful | -ive | -ing |
|-------|-------|-----|------|------|------|

Look at the verb printed in **bold** and write down the appropriate adjective in the space provided. The first one has been done for you.

1 Mr Quickwater has a great many ...*admirable*... qualities. **admire**

2 There was an .................................... story in the paper this morning. **amuse**

3 I have extra French lessons with a .................................... schoolmaster. **retire**

4 He made himself .................................... by handing round the coffee cups. **use**

5 Deaths caused by reckless driving are .................................... **avoid**

6 He felt very .................................... towards her and loved her dearly. **protect**

7 The coat was .................................... in shades of blue and green. **pattern**

8 She slept on a .................................... bed with rough, prickly sheets. **collapse**

9 .................................... paper tissues are more hygienic than handkerchiefs. **dispose**

10 The photos made him look quite .................................... **attract**

**B** The following suffixes combine with nouns and adjectives to form other adjectives.

| -able | -al   | -ary | -ful  | -ic | -ish |
|-------|-------|------|-------|-----|------|
| -ive  | -like | -ly  | -ous  | -y  |      |

Look at the noun or adjective printed in bold and write down the appropriate adjective in the space provided. The first one has been done for you.

1 The time seemed to stretch out in a
  *dreamlike* .................... manner.     **dream**

2 There is the danger of an ........................................
  explosion that could be caused by a gas leak.     **accident**

3 She thought how ........................................ he'd been
  and was not angry any more.     **fool**

4 The newspapers printed a shocking and
  ........................................ story.     **shame**

5 The sky was ........................................ and light rain
  was falling.     **cloud**

6 The hotel was large and ........................................     **comfort**

7 Judy was very ........................................ about my
  work.     **compliment**

8 Most tinned fruits contain ........................................
  amounts of sugar.     **excess**

9 She is such a ........................................ sweet-
  tempered child that everyone just naturally loves
  her.     **friend**

10 There were two letters from Michael, warm,
  ........................................ , and full of information.     **humour**

# 4 Forming negatives

A large number of prefixes are used to form words with negative meanings. Some of the most common ones are listed below.

| dis- | il-  | im-  | in- |
|------|------|------|-----|
| ir-  | non- | un-  |     |

Now look at the words listed below. Write down their negative forms next to the appropriate prefix. The first one has been done for you.

| | | | | |
|---|---|---|---|---|
| legal | smoker | capable | practical | athletic |
| security | relevant | possible | obey | officially |
| agreement | loyal | happy | rational | willingness |
| logical | mature | responsible | ability | convenient |

dis- ..................................................................................

il- *illegal* .....................................................................

im- ..................................................................................

in- ..................................................................................

ir- ..................................................................................

non- ...............................................................................

un- ..................................................................................

## 5 -able and -ible

**-able** and **-ible** combine with verbs to form adjectives. Look at the following list of verbs. Write down the corresponding adjective in the space provided. You will need to compare the entries for **-able** and **-ible** to see which ending is used. The first one has been done for you.

| VERB | ADJECTIVE | VERB | ADJECTIVE |
|---|---|---|---|
| accept | *acceptable* | value | .......................... |
| divide | .......................... | comprehend | .......................... |
| notice | .......................... | irritate | .......................... |
| enjoy | .......................... | depend | .......................... |
| convert | .......................... | permit | .......................... |

## 6 anti-

**anti-** can be used with two different meanings. Write 'A' in the space provided if it means that one thing opposes another. Write 'B' if it means that one thing prevents another from happening.

1 Following the appalling behaviour of the English football fans in Italy many people were anti-English.

   ...........

2 Anti-seasickness tablets should be taken two hours before starting a journey.

   ...........

196

3 After fitting the anti-theft device to her car, she hoped it would not be stolen again.

...........

4 The anti-apartheid movement in South Africa gained a lot of publicity when Nelson Mandela was released.

...........

5 Although it is more than two years since his wife died, he is still taking anti-depressants.

...........

6 Put anti-freeze in your radiator to prevent the water from freezing overnight.

...........

7 It was the first serious anti-war demonstration for fifteen years.

...........

8 Toothpastes containing fluoride and anti-bacterial properties should be able to virtually eradicate tooth-decay.

...........

9 The General took control of the army at the height of the anti-Ceausescu protests.

...........

10 The Church is managing to survive in the face of a great deal of anti-religious propaganda.

...........

# 7 -bound

**A** **-bound** can be used with three different meanings. Write 'A' in the space provided if it means that someone or something is restricted in some way. Write 'B' if it means that someone or something is travelling in a particular direction. Write 'C' if it indicates the sort of covering that something has.

1 He removed a small, rectangular cloth-bound package from the bottom of his bag.

...........

2 No one seemed to have any idea what had happened to the luggage belonging to the four London-bound passengers.

...........

3 Britain is still considered by many to be a class-bound society.

...........

4 Morris Zapp slouched in the seat of the eastbound aircraft.

..........

5 Many young mothers become depressed because they are
housebound.

..........

**B** Write one sentence for each of the words listed below to show that
you understand what they mean.

class-bound    duty-bound    homeward-bound
leather-bound snowbound

# 8 cross-

Look at the statements below. Are they true or false? Write 'true' in the
space provided if you think they are true. Write 'false' if you think they
are false.

1 A cross-party agreement involves two or more political parties.

..........

2 A cross-channel ferry sails across more than one channel.

..........

3 A cross-border dispute occurs across the frontiers of different
countries.

..........

4 A cross-cultural organization involves or deals with more than one
culture.

..........

5 A cross-country race is a race in which two or more countries are
involved.

..........

# 9 extra-

Choose a word from the box to complete the sentences on the next page.
Write down the answer in the space provided. The first one has been
done for you.

| extra-bright | extra-hot | extra-sensory | extra-terrestrial |
|---|---|---|---|
| extra-curricular | extra-long | extra-special | |
| extra-hard | extra-mild | extra-strong | |

1 I'm going to buy you an *extra special* .............. present as a reward for all your hard work this year at school.

2 Many students benefit greatly from involvement in ........................................... activities.

3 Everyone agreed that this summer's exams were ........................................... , which probably accounted for the high failure rate.

4 Because this house is going to be 3 storeys high, the foundations have to be ...........................................

5 There has been a concentrated search for ........................................... life on Mars.

6 Woollen clothes should be washed with an ........................................... detergent.

7 I don't believe in ........................................... perception, or flying saucers either.

8 ........................................... children often get bored at school because the work is too easy.


# 10  -ful

**-ful** can be used with two different meanings. Write 'A' in the space provided if it refers to a quantity. Write 'B' if it describes a quality.

1 He drank a mouthful of cold black coffee.

..........

2 My legs and back are stiff but not painful.

..........

3 He is one of the most powerful men in the country.

..........

4 He ate a bowl of natural yoghurt served up with a spoonful of honey.

..........

5 She had a whole houseful of furniture.

..........

6 The park lay quiet and peaceful in the early morning.

..........

7 He had nice sad eyes with beautiful lashes.

   ...........

8 Roger gathered a handful of stones and began to throw them.

   ...........

9 Pour a bucketful of cold water on top of the ash.

   ...........

10 He was full of youthful curiosity and idealism.

   ...........

# 11 hyper-

Choose a word from the box to complete the sentences below. Write down the answer in the space provided. The first one has been done for you.

| | | | |
|---|---|---|---|
| hyperactive | hypercreative | hyperinflation | hypersensitive |
| hyper-alert | hyper-critical | hypermarket | |
| hyper-cautious | hyperdevoted | hyper-modern | |

1 The man became  *hypersensitive* ..................... to the slightest
  movement around him.

2 Boulogne and its ....................................... are a popular destination for
  shoppers.

3 He had a small, vicious, ....................................... dog, always on the
  look-out for intruders.

4 Teenagers tend to be ....................................... of their own parents.

5 Councillors outlined plans for a ....................................... shopping
  precinct in the city centre.

6 I found him to be much more lively than I expected, almost

   .......................................

7 The Chancellor took steps to stabilize the economy and cut

   .......................................

8 Many parents are ....................................... and do not allow their
  children enough freedom.

## 12  -ion

**-ion** combines with verbs to form nouns. Look at the following list of verbs. Write down the corresponding noun in the space provided. The first one has been done for you.

| VERB | NOUN | VERB | NOUN |
|------|------|------|------|
| situate | *situation* | possess | .................... |
| act | .................... | realize | .................... |
| explain | .................... | connect | .................... |
| decide | .................... | create | .................... |
| produce | .................... | reduce | .................... |

## 13  -ism and -ist

Choose a word from the box to complete the sentences below. Write down the answer in the space provided. The first one has been done for you.

| | | | |
|------|------|------|------|
| baptism | hooliganism | pessimist | typist |
| criticism | hypnotist | sexist | vegetarianism |
| feminism | optimist | terrorist | vandalism |

1  Many people still take their children to church for
   *baptism* ....................

2  Because I was such a ............................. I had assumed I
   would fail my exams.

3  The popular image of ............................. unfortunately tends
   to repel many women.

4  The Government is planning a crackdown on football violence and
   .............................

5  ............................. is becoming increasingly popular because
   of the unhealthy image of meat.

6  ............................. advertising in women's magazines
   frequently infuriates me.

7  She was a ............................. in the office of The Inspector of
   Taxes.

8  The President warned troops of the increased danger of
   ............................. attacks.

9 Some severe public ............................................. of the ban had been voiced.

10 I am an ............................................. and I still believe the situation can only get better.

# 14 -less

Look at the statements below. Are they true or false? Write 'true' in the space provided if you think they are true. Write 'false' if you think they are false.

1 A person who is careless is unable to love or care for others.

...........

2 If you are expressionless, it is difficult for people to see how you are feeling.

...........

3 It is possible to become breathless when you are feverish.

...........

4 A tuneless piece of music has not been tuned to a particular radio station.

...........

5 If someone is spineless, they do not have a spine.

...........

# 15 off-

Look at the statements below. Are they true or false? Write 'true' in the space provided if you think they are true. Write 'false' if you think they are false.

1 If you buy an off-peak rail ticket, you are paying the highest price for it.

...........

2 An off-court argument between two tennis players happens away from the tennis court.

...........

3 An offshore oilrig is situated in the sea, away from the shore.

...........

4 If a soldier is off-guard, he has moved away from the place where he usually does his guard duty.

...........

5 If something is off-centre, it is not exactly in the middle of a space or surface.

..........

# 16 -over

**A** Put the words in the box into the following lists according to their meaning. The first one has been done for you.

| over-anxious | overdo | overhang |
| overawe | over-eighteen | overhead |
| overcharge | over-emphasize | over-forty |

| EXCESS | AGE | POSITION |
|--------|-----|----------|
| .................................... | .................................... | *overhang* |
| .................................... | .................................... | .................................... |
| .................................... | .................................... | .................................... |
| .................................... | .................................... | .................................... |
| .................................... | .................................... | .................................... |

**B** Write one sentence for each of the words listed below to show that you understand what they mean.

overdo    overhang    over-eighteen    overcharge    over-anxious

# 17 pre-

pre- can be used with two different meanings. Write 'A' in the space provided if it means that one thing happens before another. Write 'B' if it means that something has already been done.

1 I hate the pre-Christmas panic that seems to hit my family in the middle of December.

..........

2 Eventually the pre-paid envelopes were sent from the mail order company.

..........

3 His preconceived ideas made it impossible for anyone to get him to listen to their side of the argument.

..........

4 There were many pre-fourteenth century portraits in the exhibition.

..........

5 The jury unanimously reached the decision that the killing was premeditated.

...........

6 He married late and his wife predeceased him.

...........

7 Bake the cake in a pre-heated oven for twenty minutes.

...........

8 Zoe had invited us round early for a pre-dinner drink.

...........

9 Some football players develop a special routine to cope with pre-match nerves.

...........

10 We had been given tickets to a preview of the film.

...........

# 18  -ship

Make sure you understand the different meanings of **-ship**. Underline the odd word out in each list and write a sentence to say in what way it is different.

1 workmanship, citizenship, musicianship, horsemanship.

2 chairmanship, ambassadorship, partnership, professorship.

3 spaceship, steamship, gunship, warship, cadetship.

4 membership, comradeship, friendship, relationship, kinship.

# 19  -size and -sized

What is the meaning of the suffixes **-size** and **-sized** in the following sentences? Write 'A' in the space provided if it means that one thing is the same size as another. Write 'B' if it means that something is a suitable size for a particular purpose. Write 'C' if it describes how big something is.

1 She bought a child-size bike for his 8th birthday.

...........

2 A new button-sized coin has just been issued by the Bank of England.

...........

3 Our new car? It's just an average-size family car.

...........

4 Although he detested eating liver, his aunt always insisted on putting a finger-size slice on his plate.

...........

5 Could you buy me a medium-size tin of peas and a jumbo-size packet of cornflakes?

...........

6 They always take a pocket-size calculator with them when they do the shopping.

...........

7 The racing car had a man-size space for the driver but no more.

...........


# 20 super-

The following sentences all contain words beginning with **super-**. The sentences have been divided in two and mixed up. Read both parts of all the sentences and decide which halves go together. Write the appropriate letter next to the numbers at the bottom.

| | |
|---|---|
| 1 The vast supertankers we have nowadays | A must have been a superhuman feat. |
| 2 Jumping over that wall | B especially the super-heavyweights. |
| 3 A new superstore has just opened, | C super-modern design. |
| 4 My aunt loves watching wrestling and boxing, | D are a danger to the environment. |
| 5 The new office blocks were built to a | E and you can get almost anything you need there. |

1 ...........  2 ...........  3 ...........  4 ...........  5 ...........

# 21 under-

**A** Put the words in the box into the following lists according to their meaning. The first one has been done for you.

| | | |
|---|---|---|
| under-boiled | undergraduate | underpass |
| underclothes | underline | underpriced |
| under-equipped | under-manager | undersize |
| underestimate | undernourished | under-tens |

| BENEATH | INSUFFICIENT | NUMBER | RANK |
|---|---|---|---|
| .................... | *under-equipped* | .................... | .................... |
| .................... | .................... | .................... | .................... |
| .................... | .................... | .................... | .................... |
| .................... | .................... | .................... | .................... |
| .................... | .................... | .................... | .................... |

**B** Write one sentence for each of the words listed below to show that you understand what they mean.

underestimate    undergraduate    underline    undernourished
under-tens

# 22 well-

Look at the statements below. Are they true or false? Write 'true' in the space provided if you think they are true. Write 'false' if you think they are false.

1 If someone is well-nourished, they generally eat a lot of food.

..........

2 A well-dressed man always wears smart or elegant clothes.

..........

3 A well-cut suit is a suit that has been cut into many pieces.

..........

4 If you have a pair of well-worn shoes, your shoes have been used so often that they look rather old.

..........

5 If a theatre critic writes about a well-acted play, she means that there were a lot of people acting in the play and its duration was much longer than usual.

..........

6 If someone is well-balanced, they are balancing correctly so that they do not fall over.

..........

7 A well-known fact is known by a lot of people.

..........

8 If you refer to someone's well-being, you are referring to whether they are healthy and happy and enjoy their life.

..........

9 A well-read person has read a lot of books.

..........

10 Someone who is well-meaning uses words very precisely.

..........

# Answer key

## 1 Nouns

### A
-ant  defend; assist
-ee   train; address
-ess  act, actor; prince
-er   drive; paint
-ian  history; music
-ist  novel; science
-or   supervise; visit

### B
1 employee
2 politician
3 waitress
4 participant
5 conductor
6 teacher
7 pianist
8 examinee; examiner

### C
-al    arrive
-ance abundant
-cy    constant
-dom  king
-ence independent
-ful   mouth
-hood  boy
-ing   dance
-ion   invent
-ism  criticize
-ity   sensitive
-ment agree
-ness happy
-ship owner

### D
1 politician
2 leadership
3 definition
4 leadership
5 domination
6 freedom
7 encouragement
8 childhood
9 laziness
10 cynicism
11 guidance
12 politician
13 manager
14 dismissal

## 2 Verbs

### A
ADJECTIVE → VERB
harden
modernize
deepen
intensify
falsify
fatten
sterilize

NOUN → VERB
horrify
memorize
beautify
sympathize
apologize
glorify
lengthen

### B
1 apologized
2 beautify
3 lengthening
4 sympathized
5 fattening
6 deepen
7 modernizing
8 sterilize

## 3 Adjectives

### A
1 admirable
2 amusing
3 retired
4 useful
5 avoidable
6 protective
7 patterned
8 collapsible
9 disposable
10 attractive

### B
1 dreamlike
2 accidental
3 foolish
4 shameful
5 cloudy
6 comfortable
7 complimentary
8 excessive
9 friendly
10 humorous

## 4 Negatives

dis-  disability,
      disagreement, disloyal,
      disobey.
il-   illegal, illogical.
im-  immature, impossible,
      impractical.
in-   inability, incapable,
      inconvenient,
      insecurity.
ir-   irrational, irrelevant,
      irresponsible.
non- non-athletic, non-
      smoker
un-  unhappy, unofficially,
      unwillingness.

## 5 -able and -ible

acceptable
divisible
noticeable
enjoyable
convertible
valuable
comprehensible
irritable
dependable
permissible

## 6 anti-

1 A
2 B
3 B
4 A
5 B
6 B
7 A
8 B
9 A
10 A

## 7 -bound

1 C
2 B
3 A
4 B
5 A

## 8 cross-

1 true
2 false. *A cross-channel ferry
sails across the English
Channel.*
3 true
4 true
5 false. *A cross-country race
takes place across fields
and the open countryside
instead of along roads or a
running track.*

## 9 extra-

1 extra-special
2 extra-curricular
3 extra-hard
4 extra-strong
5 extra-terrestrial
6 extra-mild
7 extra-sensory
8 extra-bright

## 10 -ful

1 A
2 B
3 B
4 A
5 A
6 B
7 B
8 A
9 A
10 B

## 11 hyper-

1 hypersensitive
2 hypermarket
3 hyper-alert
4 hyper-critical
5 hyper-modern
6 hyperactive
7 hyperinflation
8 hyper-cautious

## 12 -ion

1 situation
2 action
3 explanation
4 decision
5 production
6 possession
7 realization
8 connection
9 creation
10 reduction

## 13 -ism and -ist

1 baptism
2 pessimist
3 feminism
4 hooliganism
5 vegetarianism
6 sexist
7 typist
8 terrorist
9 criticism
10 optimist

## 14 -less

1 false. *A careless person is someone who does not pay enough attention to what they are doing, with the result that they make mistakes.*
2 true
3 true
4 false. *It is a piece of music that has the notes arranged in a random way or sounds unpleasant.*
5 false. *If someone is spineless they are weak and cowardly.*

## 15 off-

1 false. *An off-peak rail ticket would be cheaper than usual because you would use it at a time when there is less demand than usual.*
2 true
3 true
4 false. *If someone is off-guard, they are not expecting a surprise or danger that suddenly occurs.*
5 true

## 16 over-

EXCESS: overawe, overcharge, overdo, over-emphasize, over-anxious
AGE: over-forty, over-eighteen
POSITION: overhead, overhang

## 17 pre-

| | |
|---|---|
| 1 A | 6 A |
| 2 B | 7 B |
| 3 B | 8 A |
| 4 A | 9 A |
| 5 B | 10 A |

## 18 -ship

1 Citizenship is the state of being a citizen. The other words all refer to a skill or ability.
2 A partnership is a relationship between two or more people. The other words all refer to positions or occupations.
3 Cadetship is the position or state of being a cadet. The other words all refer to types of boat or crafts.
4 Membership is the state of being a member. The other words all refer to a relationship or connection between two or more people or things.

## 19 -size and -sized

1 B
2 A
3 C
4 A
5 C
6 B
7 B

## 20 super-

1 D
2 A
3 E
4 B
5 C

## 21 under-

BENEATH: underclothes, underline, underpass
INSUFFICIENT: under-boiled, under-equipped, underestimate, undernourished, underpriced, undersize
NUMBER: under-tens
RANK: undergraduate, under-manager

## 22 well-

1 false. *Someone who is well-nourished eats food that is good for them and keeps them healthy.*
2 true
3 false. *A well-cut suit has been designed and made to a high standard, and looks smart.*
4 true
5 false. *If someone describes a play as well-acted, they mean it has been performed to a high standard by the actors taking part in it.*
6 false. *If someone is well-balanced, they are sensible and do not have many emotional problems.*
7 true
8 true
9 true
10 false. *Someone who is well-meaning tries to be useful, helpful, or kind.*